THEOLOGIANS OF OUR TIME

THEOLOGIANS

EDITOR
LEONHARD REINISCH

FOREWORD BY
CHARLES H. HENKEY

Karl Barth

Rudolf Bultmann

Emil Brunner

Paul Althaus

Paul Tillich

OF OUR TIME

Reinhold Niebuhr

Karl Adam

Romano Guardini

Heinrich Schlier

Hans Urs von Balthasar

Yves Congar

Karl Rahner

THE UNIVERSITY OF NOTRE DAME PRESS

*The original version
of this work was
published by C. H.
Beck'sche Verlagsbuchhandlung
in 1960 in Munich
under the title of*
THEOLOGEN UNSERER ZEIT

2nd Printing, September 1966

Foreword

The appearance of great theological thinkers and the renewal of interest in theology are not just accidental and peripheral phenomena of our age. Neither can they be explained by existential anxiety or fear in the face of the terrible possibilities of an atomic destruction, or by the utter forlornness that penetrates down to the personal roots of modern man. It is true that modern development has brought humanity close to the brink of collapse into total chaos. However, on the other hand, we must also consider the positive aspects of this new situation. I will mention only two things: First, there is the ecumenical broadness of human existence, which now for the first time in human history truly envelops the whole globe —no country, no people can isolate itself from this common human destiny.[1] And secondly, there are the fantastic perspectives opened up for human existence by the achievements of modern science. Since it would be entirely false and one-sided to see in modern life

[1] Cf. E. Benz, *Kirchengeschichte in Oekumenischer Sicht* (Leiden-Köln: E. J. Brill, 1961), pp. 1-12.

only the decay of former values and of human stability, we must admit that this new horizon of human existence should also become theologically meaningful—and meaningful in a positive sense.[2] The current upsurge of theological interest—to mention only the intensification of theological studies on the secular campuses here in this country—plus the emergence of great, zealous theologians are facts not caused by fear; nor can it all be considered an off-beat phenomenon, a sort of escapism of the few from the hopelessly drab and empty modern world into a metaphysical transcendental realm. Theologians of our time, like the prophets of the Old Testament, are the beacon lights in the darkness that is enveloping human existence today. They manifest and express the vital reaction of faith in a faithless, secularistic world—a vital reaction characteristic of the ever-living, ever-conquering spirit of Christian self-consciousness—and not a reaction in the apologetic sense of defending the traditional values.[3]

The roots of modern theological development go back to the beginning of the nineteenth century. Since the great French revolution in 1790, marking the entry of the new age, Christianity generally began to identify itself with the outgoing world view and became vulnerable to one stunning blow after the other. Thus Christianity sought its escape into the conservative, defensive line and hence the apologetic nature of its ensuing theology. Although the very early part of that century marked the sporadic beginnings of a theological revival, it was not until the Oxford movement in England (1833-1845)—especially Newman with his essay on the development of Christian doctrine (1845)—that the revival really took hold. In Germany, the Tuebingen School founded by F. C. Baur produced a J. A. Moehler. In Denmark, Kierkegaard became the herald of a positive Christian reawakening and laid the basis for a dialectical theology which much later succeeded in overthrow-

[2] Cf. Suhard, *The Church Today, Growth or Decline*; also K. Rahner, "The Prospect for Christianity" in his *Free Speech in the Church* (New York: Sheed & Ward, 1960).

[3] The apologetic attitude which dominated the theological literature changed completely into positive and creative thinking.

ing the increasingly unchristian, liberal trend in Protestant think-ing. In the second half of the century with the proclamation of the dogma of the Immaculate Conception (1854) began a strong Catholic theological initiative which ended in the First Vatican Council (1869-70)—featuring such great names in theology as Passaglia, Schrader, Franzelin, and Scheeben and which triggered a scholastic renaissance under Leo XIII. On the Protestant side, the largely historical, critical struggles of Ritschl, Harnack and Troeltsch have also paved the way for this much-needed advance in Christian theology.[4]

All these positive theological initiatives nevertheless did not find a strong echo in the practical Christian life. The real breakthrough came after the First, and more so after the Second, World War. It seems humanity needed that horrible catalyst, in order to become human again in the sense of the transcendental openness of man towards God. Theology ceased to be a matter for professionals only, exclusively for clerics, and advanced more and more into the focus of public interest. Not only was the Western hemisphere affected—nor was it just the Christian sphere, for even the non-Christian world experienced the turning of the tide. *God, religion, faith*—no longer stored away like the toys of human childhood—once again reappear on the horizon as truly existential and most vital to the needs in human life.

Today's theologians are not mere star-gazers working in the seclusion of their observatories: rather modern theology is anthro-pocentric (Rahner), Christocentric (Barth), and also ecumenical—thus comprehending and penetrating the total human dimension. If in the Incarnation the Son of God became man in the full and true sense of the word, and became the ultimate norm for human destiny, it is through the human self-realization in Christ "the man" that we must reach the divine. The *old* theology, living in a limited homogenously Christian world, had confronted the non-Christian sphere only through its missionaries, and expanded mostly by colonization. The non-Christian sphere has always been

[4] Cf. R. Aubert, *La théologie catholique au milieu du XXè siecle*, 1954; Hocedez, *Histoire de la Théologie au XIXè siecle*, 1949-1950.

considered as necessarily backward and inferior, but the non-Christian world has risen in our midst like a giant among dwarfs. Is this new age perhaps emerging as a faith in its own self, contrary to its Creator? Or, is it just the usual challenge to the *ecclesia militans?* Somewhere in his writings, Karl Rahner gives a wonderful analysis of the apparent atheism of modern man. In the primitive worldview, God and heaven were very close to man's daily life. There was almost a kind of continuity between natural and supernatural. However, the modern scientific picture of the world has opened up infinite distances. In fact, for the modern man, it is much harder to find God, and he therefore needs more theology than philosophy. In primitive days theology was very strongly philosophical and it outgrew its role as the handmaid of philosophy. Today, philosophy turns more and more to theology, at least in the sense of natural theology, and at times even pretends to replace theology. Today in this apparently profane and anti-Christian drive of man towards a better humanity, his human unrest is easily recognized by its adventurous, groping insecurity—no doubt motivated by that radical, authentic unrest of the human heart towards God.

New daring insights, not yet thoroughly tested and not yet smoothed by the wisdom of the ages, are always disturbing. However, it is not so much the original theological thinkers, but their enthusiastic followers, who become at times both imprudent and impudent in their expressions. This is certainly not very helpful towards the building of a new theological synthesis in our modern age. For the present, the new theology is full of unsolved problems; the terminological tools are not yet completely developed and it is far from being settled and clear. Nevertheless its representatives—the towering personalities, some of whom are presented in this little volume—with their broad learning, thorough scholarship, creative genius, deep faith and their honest struggle for the truth, must convince us that there is more at stake than just purely scholarly, theoretical discussion, a mere rewording of old affirmations and beliefs, a mere change in the pattern of thought. The conquest for Christ of the newly discovered human dimension, of the new age in human historical existence, is the center of the new initiative.

We readily acknowledge that not everything the "new theology" has produced is pure gold.[5] But, we wish to point out two really positive achievements: First, Catholic theologians have become deeply influenced by problems which were originally raised by Protestant theologians, without deviating from Catholic truth, while Protestant theologians are borne more and more by the weight of their own honest thinking towards an affirmation of the Catholic point of view. Secondly, there is also a growing rapprochement between theology and the natural sciences: theologians no longer regard suspiciously the new discoveries as being potential enemies of the old faith. Scientists, on the other hand, no longer identify the theologians with dark-garbed inquisitors, ready to obliterate innovations without even questioning the merits involved.

We admit, also, that there is a danger in going too fast and too far, because such a course can easily lead to chaos. Therefore, the new theology, at least on the Catholic side, listens in respectful obedience to the current warnings in this regard from the Holy See in its encyclical *Humani Generis*. But we must remember that such negative warnings do not necessarily represent the full and lucid manifestations of the mind of the Church. Proportionately, there have been official encouragements from the Holy See to move forward and not lag behind in the conquest of the modern age for Christ.

It is consequently in keeping with the true Catholic spirit to take up the challenge of the modern times, to aim not only at a staunch resistance and defense, but even more at conquest. And it can be done, especially if one takes seriously the wise words of Karl Rahner in the introduction to his brilliant essay on Inspiration:

It is permissible to consider that, in the realm of theology as in the realm of sciences, it is legitimate to experiment, to work with hypotheses, remembering that, even in their originator's opinion, they may

---

[5] A. H. Maltha, *Die neue Theologie* (München: Manz Verlag, 1960).

turn out to be barren when tested by the criticism of his colleagues and confrères working in sacred theology. Theology is certainly anything but a mummified structure of thought. It can create openings for adventures of the mind and of the heart, if we have but the courage to embark upon them, and both the courage and humility to retrace our steps as soon as we become aware of having erred. This qualification is made in all seriousness. If we are convinced that in theology, as elsewhere, there are real problems which still require better, clearer, more comprehensive and possibly even simpler solutions, we shall certainly not begrudge having to face such problems. Nor shall we be likely to confuse brotherly criticism with official censorship if a proposed hypothesis is proved to be inadequate or even false.

To ask questions about a doctrine which, in its basic dogmatic contents is beyond discussion, is not tantamount to doubting or contesting a doctrine of the Faith. . . . He, who believes that, even in the most intimate circles, only final and absolute solutions should be discussed, shows his incapacity for seeing any new answer or problem in theology.[6]

It is hoped that our truly existential struggle towards Christian conquest now and in the future, as presented by the great minds in this volume—and also by those not mentioned here like Otto Karrer, Henri de Lubac, Oscar Cullmann, Hans Asmussen, and others—will positively contribute to the Christian formation of human existence in this modern age, at the threshold of which, it seems to us, we have just arrived.

CHARLES H. HENKEY

[6] K. Rahner, *Inspiration in the Bible* (New York: Herder and Herder, 1961), pp. 7-8.

Contents

KARL BARTH

BY

Ernst Wolf

It is no easy task to draw the portrait of a genius in the main outlines of his work and action, especially while we are still fortunate
enough to have him with us. The task is harder still when these
outlines are blurred, on the one hand by personal obligation and
admiration (even though tempered, perhaps, by critical judgment),
and on the other hand by misunderstandings and even stubborn
and malicious prejudice, as well as the misjudgments to which they
give rise.

It has been rightly said that Karl Barth is "the most important
and most influential Protestant theologian of our generation"
(Hans Lilje). It has also been said, and again truly, that it was
Barth who summoned the Church and its servants to get back to
the real issue—back to God. This statement leads us to the very
core of Karl Barth's work, to which we shall return later.

At the same time, Karl Barth has also been seen as the great opponent—though a loving, understanding opponent—of nineteenth-
century Protestant theology and its immediate antecedents, a theol-

ogy, that is, which in the end surrendered the cause of God to the pride and self-assertion of spiritual-religious man raising himself against God.

These remarks serve to suggest the position which Karl Barth occupies in the historical development of theology and church and the life of the intellect. Others have assessed him differently: some have rashly identified him with the so-called dialectical theology that followed upon the First World War, and thereby would consign him to past history; still others, invincibly ignorant, keep talking of a Barthian school of thought, conceived as the counterpart to an equally ill-defined Lutheranism and opposing such catchphrases as "Christomonism" on one side to a "two-kingdom-doctrine" on the other. But on inspection these assessments turn out to be nothing more than facile—and false—ways to avoid the strict demands made by Barth's work.

From every fresh line that Karl Barth writes there may spring into startling and at times even shocking life the burning actuality of his thought, its high orginality that stems from listening to the word of God. Dialectical theology as such did, of course, have its season, but it is not a thing of the past. For in Barth's work the whole force of the impulse that gave rise to dialectical theology "has been preserved in secret at white heat, to break forth in its time with the same fire" (Siering). And then, there seems to be a hidden law governing the work of great men: pushed aside, more or less violently, by the immediately following generations, as if in an instinctive effort to free themselves from what they have outgrown, the work of great men stands revealed soon after in all its grandeur and lasting validity. More's the pity, and the loss, for those who closed their eyes to it.

The core of Barth's work and his historical position, and, through these two, the man himself cannot be understood unless one senses something of his deep, intense, joyous devotion to theology as the most enthralling and most living of all sciences (as he himself often called it), and this notwithstanding both his painstaking labor on detail and his enormous productivity. Nor can we fail to sense that devotion once we expose ourselves to his gigantic work, unmatched

2

in modern Protestant theology: a veritable cathedral of Christian thought, richly structured, cohesive, dynamically alive, concrete and full of humanity. A bibliography compiled in 1956, when he was seventy, gives an idea of the size of his output. It lists more than four hundred works, among them both large volumes and tightly packed essays, besides over one hundred translations including some into Japanese and Korean. The decisive thing, however, which foils all attempts to discern significant shifts in his thinking, is the inner unity of his entire opus. Thus it is meaningful to ask for the ultimate basic principle of Barth's position.

"There can be no doubt," the Catholic theologian Hans Urs von Balthasar said in his keen anaylsis of Barth's work, "that Barth's latest thought is in a very obscure yet also very active sense identical with his earliest thought, and that the tremendous scope of his *Church Dogmatics* (his principal work, so far twelve volumes of 7,500 pages) represents after all the explosion of a force which, though compressed, has been present from the very outset—a spiritual rather than a vital force."

The explosion, which took place in Barth's two commentaries on the Letter to the Romans (1919 and 1922) started with this discovery: "God is God and altogether different from all things human, even from human religion and human culture."

Barth himself, then a young professor in Goettingen, realized the explosive nature of this discovery, and that it was something which could not be used as a plaything, as could other theological slogans:

"Never break away! Never be content with just 'God is God'! Never preach!" (it is in preaching that explosions occur) "Nor ever simply give word to those platitudes that fill your mind if you will not do the other!" he writes to friends in 1922. Rather: "Learn to state 'God is God' with theological precision—that means, with all the joyousness it now reveals: 'Jesus Christ!'"

"Jesus Christ," Barth said in his first Barmen thesis of 1934, "such as scripture bears witness of Him for us, is the one word of God that we must hear, that we must trust, and that we must obey in life and death." This is nothing other than the "rediscovery of heaven" (in Siering's charming phrase) which had been lost to all abstruse Christian philosophy and religion: a heaven not staked out by speculation as the abode of the spirits, nor somehow ideologically contrived as a fatal "beyond," but the heaven witnessed and thrown open by the word of scripture, which is above the earth in that it holds and contains both the power, the exceeding might of God's love, and the reality of only this earthly existence within history. A rediscovery of heaven, then, expressly for the world of the modern technologized mind, to serve as a sobering and also consoling reminder of the source and even more the goal of man's deeply entangled life.

Jesus Christ is the *one* word of God that calls man, as man, to life, by placing him within the realm of life and freedom in common humanity before God and in God. The task of theology, then, is to speak of God truly by speaking of Jesus Christ as God's creative, redeeming, revelatory word, by speaking at last of "God's humanity"—God's great affirmation of man chosen in Christ.

The development of Barth's idea "God is God" takes this turn: "Recognition of God's divinity: the very ground and source of the recognition of His humanity." And again: "God's humanity—rightly understood that must mean God's relation to, God's bending toward man, God who talks to man in promise and command, God existing, laboring, acting for man, the communion God holds with man, God's freely given grace in which He is and wants to be none other than the God of man."

Barth himself described it as a turn, not as a turning back, of his thinking: "A turn in the thinking of Protestant theology in which we are today (1956) engaged, not in opposition and yet in contrast to a turn taken earlier. . . . What began to press in upon us with such intensity some forty years ago was not so much the humanity as the divinity of God: that which in God's relation to man is absolutely His alone—His awful majesty and distance, strangeness, His being altogether other than man; the judgment man must undergo because of God's grace and in God's grace, because God wants to be and is man's God." And: "It was the sheer invention of baffled or angry minds when we taught that God is All, man nothing," and "there can be no doubt that in those days the idea of God's humanity threw us off-center, from the main proposition into a subordinate clause."

That earlier turn had been a critical and polemical necessity in coping with liberal and positive theology of the nineteenth century. For nineteenth-century theology, grown religionist, anthropocentric and, by that token, humanistic, had elevated human piety into the central concern of its doctrine, and had accordingly attempted to find man's way to God by means of historical criticism and the phenomenology and psychology of religion. The first violent clash did not yield any final answers.

"It could not. Even the turn in which we are engaged today will not be a last word. But that concerns a future generation."

What is at stake, and what is at the center of Barth's theology, is that "the divinity of the living God has its meaning and its strength only in the context of His history and His dialogue with man, hence in His companionship with man, and that is the point which cannot ever again be surrendered: at stake is God's companionship with man, founded in His sole sovereign authority, set and defined and ordered by Himself alone. Who God is, and what He is in His divinity, He does not establish and reveal in a void of divine self-sufficiency—He makes it manifest precisely by being, speaking, and acting as man's partner (though an absolutely superior partner). It is the living God who acts that way. The freedom in which He acts that way is His divinity—the divinity which as such also bears the character of humanity. . . . God's divinity, rightly understood, includes His humanity."

Has it been sufficiently understood that here Barth has also given the decisive answer to man's question "What am I?" The science specifically concerned here, psychology, is every day finding out more and more that man cannot understand the ever-new enigma of his own self by studying animals but must reach out for an "unknown" that lies beyond self-observation. Or has it been noticed that Barth's definition of the subject matter of theology states exactly what Luther once said: "The real subject of theology should be man who is corrupt and guilty of sin *and* God who is the justifier and savior of sinful man." That little word "and," here employed in its one and only legitimate theological use, recurs in Barth's formulation of God's partnership with man. We shall come to it later.

And how do we know of this partnership? The answer is: by the testimony of God's word.

"The Jesus Christ given to us in scripture is surely not man in the abstract, man self-satisfied with a touch of religion and a touch of religious morality, man without God and hence his own God. But neither is He God in the abstract—God in His divinity separated from man, strange and distant and un-human if not inhuman. Jesus Christ is not shut off against man below, nor against God above. Rather, Christ is the history, the dialogue in which God and man meet and exist together. He is the reality of the covenant concluded, kept and fulfilled by both sides. In His person Jesus Christ is as much the true God of man as He is God's true man and faithful partner, as much the Lord lowered into community with man as He is the servant raised into community with God.... He is both, neither mixed nor distinct, but all one and all the other." In this oneness Christ the mediator and conciliator "stands before man in God's name, demanding and arousing faith, love, and hope; and before God, in the name of mankind, atoning, interceding. In this He witnesses and warrants God's free grace to man, but also man's free gratitude to God. Thus in His person He establishes God's right in man, but no less man's right before God. His person is the covenant in all its fullness, the kingdom at hand in which God speaks and man listens, God gives and man receives, God commands and man obeys."

As mediator and conciliator, Christ reveals both God and man:
"Who and what God truly is, who and what man truly is, cannot be found out or contrived just any which way, but must be seen in that in which the truth of both does in fact dwell: in the fullness of their communion, their covenant which is revealed in Christ." God's divinity is "primary and basic." God is in Christ "the subject speaking and acting with sovereign authority.... It is He who

is free, He in whom all freedom has its ground, its meaning, and its origin."

Therefore, "Man's freedom"—a freedom freely given—"is completely contained within God's freedom in Jesus Christ. If God did not come down, man could not rise. . . . This sequence cannot be reversed. . . . Something even more concrete may here be seen: In Jesus Christ, God's freedom is His freedom to love."

Thus God's divinity includes rather than excludes His humanity, His love of mankind.

"It would be a false God's divinity that did not bring us face to face with His humanity as well. Such false divinities are once for all laughed to scorn in Jesus Christ. In Christ it is decided once for all that God is not without man." This is the "mystery in which God meets us in Jesus Christ's existence: God in His freedom does not want to be without man but with man, regardless of man's merits. God wants in fact to be man's partner, his almighty consoler and savior—and in this sovereign decision God is human. God's free affirmation of man, His free sharing and ranging Himself with man—that is God's humanity."

Here God is father to the prodigal son, king to the steward in debt, and Samaritan to the man fallen among robbers. But this is no longer the "fatherly love" of a nineteenth-century Protestantism which has shriveled to the tenuous belief in a Providence made up of all the sentimentality, shakiness, and inconstancy of human loving; this is the love of a Father who is Lord of the world and of judgment, and who therefore has the power of true compassion.

This understanding of the principle that "God is God" has certain consequences. First, it stresses that man has been "singled out." Not that Barth looks at man with much optimism; on the contrary, the illusionless judgment of scripture on man's self-seeking, self-assertive nature prompts him to hold a very different view. But man is singled out "because he is the being whom God has willed to raise up as His partner in the covenant." No view of man, however pessimistic, may deny him that distinction. Rather, "we must look upon and deal with every human being—even the quaintest, foulest, most miserable—from the assumption that by the everlasting decision of God's will Jesus Christ is his brother too, God Himself his Father. Once we have understood the humanity of God, no other attitude toward any fellow human being whatsoever is any longer possible. This attitude is identical with the practical —yes, practical—acknowledgment of his human rights and human dignity. If we were to refuse him these rights, this dignity, we ourselves would in the same breath renounce having Jesus Christ as our brother, God our Father."

Here are the roots of Barth's flat rejection of every kind of anti-Semitism, racial discrimination, political segregation—there can be no other theological grounds for that rejection.

From the gift of humanity to man there follows further the task of human culture. "What else is human culture but man's attempt to be a man and thus do honor to his human endowment, to put it to work?"

The great battle against so-called Kultur-Protestantism was, after all, directed only against the spurious league between Christianity and culture which looked on Western civilization as a convenient tool put at our disposal to seek moral advancement in the general direction of God's kingdom—a league which in the end cheated culture out of its true task, the attempt to obey God by living man's life on this earth. Barth expressed all this as early as 1926 in his lecture on *The Church and Culture*:

"Seen in the context of creation, culture is the original promise made to man of what he is to become." In itself, seen as nothing more than human activity, culture "is a mad pouring of water into the bottomless barrel of the Danaidae," because when man forgot the divine law he forfeited his share in the original promise. But in Christ, creation was renewed "with its great affirmation of man, its reasonableness of reason. It restores to man the vision of a meaning to his work, and in this gift, in this God's deed to man, that is, in Christ, man's task and problem become to him a joyous promise —a promise not apart but implied and included in the forgiveness of sin. And this now is the reason why the Church cannot refuse to be concerned with the task and the problem with which man as man is faced. Only in practice, never in principle, may the Church leave man's task and problem to society and its experts. Only in practice, never in principle, may it agree to such separations as that between Church and State."

At this juncture ethics emerges—as a consequence drawn from dogmatics or, more precisely, as included in dogmatics. It seems difficult to understand that there are still men who maintain that Barth's approach would never allow him to develop an ethics. Barth's ethics is in hand, solid, concrete, in the form of a volume in the *Dogmatics* dealing with *The Ethics of Creation*. We encounter it throughout Barth's writings. In the volumes of the mighty *Dogmatics* that remain to be written, ethics significantly includes the doctrine of the so-called sacraments, since the ethics of Christian action within this world and among one's fellows may be subsumed under what Barth calls "the divine service in politics." All of Barth's personal activity in certain political and church situations —the "political" Barth who is so often frowned upon—is nothing else than his attempt to carry out, from day to day, the mission of Christian existence within human civilization, in the most concrete fashion: concrete, hence unprogrammatical, and far more level-headed than the presumably "realistic" thinking of those who here accuse him of illusionism simply because he will not fit into their ideologies and political programs.

To Barth, theology is in a very special way a part of culture. Theology must prove its pertinence by trying to see, understand, and lend voice to God's dealings with man which in their turn give rise to man's dealings with God: God's words and deeds of grace; man's words and deeds of gratitude, demanded, awakened, and nourished by them.

"The fundamental form of theology, in keeping with its subject matter, is prayer and preaching. Theology can be none other than a dialogue. Christian speech is both a prayer to God and a talking to man. It is kerygma, the herald's summons, the message that invites and urges upon us not free-wheeling speculation but that very special thoughtfulness of faith and obedience, in which man from being an interested onlooker advances into that true involvement where he recognizes his own God in the divinity of Jesus Christ and recognizes in his own humanity himself as the subject of God's judgment and God's grace, the recipient of God's promise and God's command—where man with his own reason, will and mind joins in the active dealings between God and man."

What is proclaimed here is first of all God's affirmation of man, God's freely given grace. He must "set the Gospel aglow," for surely "God does not turn His face toward man without a sharp and unconditional rejection of man's transgression." Theology, too, must deal with this rejection, "but now as nothing other than the negation which Jesus Christ took upon Himself for our sakes." The much-contested reversal of Luther's scheme of Law and Gospel into "Gospel and Law" corresponds to the thoroughly scriptural priority of affirmation over negation. The Gospel here stands for the first time revealed for what it is: "the truly glad tidings for truly sinful man."

And finally: "It is the recognition of God's humanity by which Christianity, by which the Church lay claim to our attention, our affirmation, and our grateful allegiance—each of us in his place sharing the life of the Church and joining in its service." That claim is only strengthened by the much needed criticism of an institutional Church which in "the century of the Church" (to use Dibelius' phrase) had grown clerical and self-seeking instead of serving God. Barth had voiced such criticism, at times sharply, since his essay *Quousque Tandem* of 1930. For the Church is essentially "the communion of saints" fit "to represent, for the time, the sanctification of all humankind that took place in Christ."

"God's humanity is meant for the old and for the new Israel, for every individual as he exists in his own life, not in a void. Jesus Christ is the head of His body, and in that way alone also head of His members." And again: "We believe in the Church as the place in which the crown of humanity, that is, man's fellow humanity, may become visible in Christocratic brotherhood. Even more: we believe in the Church as the place in which God's honor wills to dwell on earth, in which the humanity, the humanness of God wills to take tangible form here in time and here on earth."

Accordingly, Barth changes his outline of a "Christian Dogmatics" of 1927 into the *Church Dogmatics* of 1932, which elaborates fully, and in constant dialogue with the theological and intellectual history of the past century, all that we have suggested above from earlier writings. Now that the dogma of the Church is the theme, even such "scandalous" subjects as Nestorianism and the doctrine of the Trinity find their place. For the problems with which they deal are still alive today, such as, for example, when Barth interprets the Trinity as "the problem of God's irremovable subjectivity in His revelation," and undertakes to explain it in new terms. As the work progresses, we follow its growing concentration upon Christology, and the growing shift in dogmatic method, which from a stress upon the diastasis between affirmation and negation moves to a stress upon the complementary analogy of faith as an epistemological principle though not an available epistemological tool. It is the *analogia fidei* or *relationis*, that of similarity of God and creature, the creature being captured by God. If dialectics emphasizes the barrier, the impossibility of putting God into adequate words, analogy stresses instead the gift of God's grace, and that God Himself will relate our words to His truth if only we will listen to His word. Both have in common that they demand act and decision; that dogmatic thought, in keeping with its matter, must be existential and responsible thought. Existence resides in the confrontation of the "I' and the "thou"; it is constitutive in the eternal confrontation of the three divine persons, and also for God-created man, since "to be man means fundamentally and all-embracingly to be with God."

Not for a long time has there been a dogmatics as close to preaching as that of Barth. Part by part, it is far more sensational than our sluggish contemporaries are ready to admit. It does indeed grow out of preaching, out of the preacher's need and distress.

"I have been twelve years a pastor—I had my theology, or rather not mine but that of Wilhelm Hermann, my unforgettable teacher. But many circumstances combined to drive me more and more up against the specific pastor's problem of preaching. . . . I tried to pick my way between the problems of man's life on one side, and the contents of the Bible on the other. What else can theology be if not the expression of this escapeless situation and problem of the preacher, the truthful description, so far as possible, of this pressure that crowds in upon the man who tackles such a task? Is it true? Man wants to hear, to understand, to know, and that is why, knowing not what he does, he reaches out and seizes that unheard-of possibility to pray, to open up his Bible, to speak, to listen, and to sing of God."

At first, Barth looks upon this "theology of the word of God," which at that point he adopts in his exegesis of the Reformation writers, as no more than a "marginal note," a corrective needed by all theology. But then his great conversation with that vast theological heritage gets fully underway in its attempt to master a gigantic mass of substance. Perhaps for the first time since Reformation days his conversation becomes urgently engaged with Roman theology as well, even to a point where Barth now often receives livelier attention from that quarter than from Protestantism. But although Barth rethinks theologically the Credo of the Church and retests every tradition, he himself does not turn traditionalist. He reaches out to the beginnings of the reformers to make their heritage critically his own—and here, again, he keeps his freedom from all confessionalism. It is much harder to pin down exactly the reform character of Barth's theology than to brush it aside with that label of the "reformed Swiss." His criticism of Calvin is no less stringent than his criticism of Luther, and he is right both times. His theology is universal, ecumenical—a church theology in that it is committed exclusively to the testimony of scripture.

Thus Barth is always on his guard against slipping into human theologoumena. His unconditional "No" is part and parcel of his positive acquisition of the Reform heritage. What is ultimately involved are the countless misunderstandings and misreadings of that problematical word *and* between God and man which Barth tries to develop positively in his formulation of partnership and of the covenant.

The resounding "No!" is directed only against that use of the word *and* which, under the guise of a natural theology, would join revelation and faith on one side, and nature, reason and history on the other, into one single unity—that use, which under the guise of the Roman *analogia entis* of various similar attempts of recent Protestant theology, would lay down an unbroken road leading from nature to grace, from reason to faith; or which in the manner of the "German Christians" of the Third Reich would even attempt, under the password "Germany for Christ," to incorporate national-socialist ideology, "Germany's Hour," yes, and even Hitler himself, into its message of a new revelation.

Barth's "No" is addressed equally to a Church that would conform to the day-to-day political-historical situation, let alone to one political party. Precisely in this sense Barth has called out his "No" repeatedly with some vigor; for it is only in this attempt from below that the notion of man's divinity takes control, missing completely true God no less than true man. In his rejection of such anthropocentric theology (which can be found also in today's existentialism), with its doctrine of "points of contact" or a "primal revelation" before and besides Christ, Barth takes up once again the decisive critical impulse of the Reformation. Here is the turn in the history of Protestant theology which is irreversible—the attempt to resolve the problem which Barth, too, perceived: to recapture in critical examination the moments of truth present even yet in neo-Protestantism, such as, for example, the achievements of historical biblical criticism.

Coupled with these rejections is Barth's resumption of Reformation thought from that point where, so to speak, it got bogged down. It appears in his treatment of certain theological problems such as the problem of predestination, of Law and Gospel, or in the area of what he has called "divine service in politics."

His work *Justification and Justice (Rechtfertigung und Recht,* 1938), for example, forms the basis for the rethinking of a Protestant theory of law. The much discussed *Christian Community and Civic Community (Christengemeinde und Bürgergemeinde,* 1946) begins a gradual discarding of neo-Protestant and Hegelian theories of state. The exciting lecture *The Teaching of the Church regarding Baptism* (1943) raises for the first time the question of baptism as a dogmatic problem, against the traditionalism of the Reformation.

And finally the Church itself. In Barth's thought, the Church is engaged in a perennial reformation, forever on the road from confessional rigor to a genuine confession of faith. But as the Church of Jesus Christ it remains altogether unbuttressed, open, involved in the world as the world's servant, at one with the world's needs—and yet, forever under the temptation to withdraw behind the wall of confessionalism, and, in spite of all its claims of being public, to leave the world and man to their own devices.

The great theological turn was soon to prove its strength in the battle among the German churches. It was Karl Barth who handed to the young Confessional Church its theological arsenal, he who inspired it with his call to *Theological Existence Today* (1933), he who guided it in moments of confusion, and he who called his warnings—not always heeded—when the young Church threatened to lose its way and fall from obedience. The Barmen Declaration, confession of the self-renewing Church whose tenets were affirmed by both Lutherans and Reformed, represents something like Barth's *summa theologiae*. And the resistance that the Church in Germany and neighboring countries offered to the totalitarianisms of the time can be historically understood only in the light of Barth's work (even though much of the ground then conquered at great pains has since been surrendered). The absolute need of a genuine theology for the survival of the Church has here become apparent as conclusively as it did in the early days of the Reformation—and, by the way, so has the inevitable later retrenchment and distortion.

The ministry of preaching joins hands with theology in the Church's struggle to survive when it comes to the "Church in the world," the service that the word of God must render to the world. Thus, the theologian Barth is joined by Barth "the politician"—legitimately, just like the prophets of the Old Testament. That is why Barth opened his mind early to the religious socialism of men like Ragaz and Kutter until their socialism, from a simple service to the world, turned into a program. That is why Barth, to the horror of bourgeois Christendom, joined the Socialist Party for a time: to him it seemed the party in whose hands the fight for social justice was relatively safest. And that is why he has again and again—though never without compelling reason—taken a stand on political issues, at the price of giving scandal to many. But it would be a grave mistake to hold the "political theologian" (as he has rashly been called) against his theology, or to attempt confuting Barth the theologian with Barth the politician. Only a true, profound understanding of Barth's theology will enable us to understand rightly his political judgments which in the end did often turn out to be right, and which have their roots deep in his theology. Let the problem of East and West serve as an example:

"It is not that I could ever work up the slightest sympathy for Eastern Communism as it has presented itself so far," Barth writes in the most recent sketch of his development since 1948. "But I do not see that politically or as Christians we are compelled, or even permitted, to draw from that aversion and rejection the consequences that the West has drawn increasingly through the last fifteen years. Anticommunism as a matter of principle seems to me a still greater evil than Communism itself. Have we forgotten that only the "Hitler in Ourselves" can be an anticommunist in principle? And what are we to think of a Western philosophy, political ethics and, alas, even theology whose wisdom has nothing better to offer than the fiction of Eastern collective man as the angel of darkness, Western "organization man" as the angel of light, and which then uses this sort of metaphysics and mythology to perform the required blessing of arms in the absurd race called the Cold War? Were we so little sure of the justice of the Western cause, the inner resistance of Western man, that we could come up with nothing better than this senseless alternative—freedom and human dignity, or else mutual atomic annihilation—and that we even dared to pass such annihilation off as, from the first, a deed of true Christian love of neighbor? I would think that the West should know better, should seek and find better ways to come to grips critically—and come to grips it must—with the power and the ideology of the Communist East. And I think above all that it should have been the mission of the Christian churches to come to the aid of the responsible political authorities, and of public opinion, by offering its greater witness of the peace and the hope of the Kingdom of God...."

Barth knows full well that such remarks (whose solid foundations we lack the space to discuss here) have left him exposed more than once; that he has "now completely lost what modest goodwill among my opponents I had achieved during the Hitler era"; and yet all through this last decade such "temptations" have dogged his steps.

"The older I get, the more I am confirmed in the realization that, if only you have a good conscience when you give in to such temptations, it is wise not to defend and justify yourself too zealously, or better still, not to defend and justify yourself at all. Sooner or later, matters as a rule become clear all by themselves, and appear in their proper light and proportion." This, too, is a part of Barth's ministry of the word, of which he said: "The servant of the word is a concretely involved man—involved in the Word become flesh, and in the witness of His prophets and apostles."

Such are the sources of Karl Barth's authority as teacher of the Church, and of that deep joyousness with which he bends all his thinking to God's victory, bringing the great tidings that "God triumphs, God will triumph, as He has long since triumphed in Jesus Christ: not over us but for us."

RUDOLF BULTMANN

BY

Ernst Wolf

Rudolf Bultmann was born on August 20, 1884, in Oldenburg, a province of northern Germany bordered by the sea. One might be tempted to trace to that origin certain traits of his personality and his work: the stubborn relentlessness of his critical inquiry and of his loyalty to his own truth, as well as a sly humor and tempered bluntness in his dealings with his fellows. But while these native traits may have prepared him for what he was to become they did not shape him; what formed him was his spiritual struggle with those scholarly problems of theology which he encountered and those which he made his own.

Even now it can be stated with assurance that Bultmann's scholarly work has left a deep mark on Protestant theology of the last forty years, and is not without its importance for Catholic and even Jewish theology. It represents a massive attempt to assimilate the heritage of the age of historicism and theological liberalism—its history and philosophy of religions—to the new departure of so-called dialectical theology and to the recovery of basic insights of the Reformation and their meaning for theology and Church today. In 1950, to celebrate the fiftieth anniversary of their first appearance, Bultmann significantly reissued Harnack's controversial lectures on *What Is Christianity?* His introduction, based in part on Karl Barth, stated that the so-called liberal interpretation of Christianity, which even today still largely dominates popular interpretation, "is in no wise a lifeless residue of a vanished era which no longer needs to be taken seriously. On the contrary this 'liberal' understanding, at the very least, contains active impulses which, though obscured, nonetheless preserve their legitimacy and will recover their validity.... This, of course, is tantamount to saying that Harnack's *What is Christianity?* is to be read not only as a historic document, but also as a contribution to contemporary theological discussion.... And in view of the present danger of a new orthodoxy, and of the restoration of a narrow denominationalism, it is necessary that his voice not die out...."

However, Harnack must be read critically, for, says Bultmann:

"True loyalty is never an 'archaizing repetition,' but only a critical appropriation which makes the legitimate impulses of tradition its very own and endows these emphases with validity in a new form."

The decisive criticism here is this:

"Despite the fact that Harnack undertook the task of describing the 'essence of Christianity' in the spirit of a historian primarily, he nonetheless never portrayed the *essence itself* as a historical phenomenon."

Bultmann here raises the one great problem that has become his own main concern. At the same time, and applying his method of textual analysis to Harnack's work, he attempts to trace Harnack's legitimate motives:

"Harnack's polemic against the traditional Church Christology is to this extent fully justified. The latter indeed commits the decisive error of developing Christianity as a 'doctrine.' Only Christ can give the kerygmatic character to everything which is 'taught' as Christian. It is only Christ who transfigures the doctrine into kerygma. Therefore, Christ is correctly preached not where something is said *about* Him, but only where He Himself becomes the proclaimer. Harnack should have, at least, made an effort to conceive of Christ from this standpoint.... Despite the incompleteness of the formulation, Harnack's aim is to express the unworldliness of Christian existence."

Harnack's weakness was not to have recognized the significance of the historical school of religious inquiry. Here is the point where the New Testament scholar Bultmann picks up the thread. In his first major work, *The History of the Synoptic Tradition,* he energetically advances the "morphological method"—form criticism—that others have developed, influenced also by his recent interest in dialectical theology which caused him to set substantive criticism ahead of literary criticism. The book shows throughout how well Bultmann combines within himself the philologist with the philosopher, whose clarity of conceptualization owes much to his close contact with Martin Heidegger at Marburg, and how he combines exegesis with systematic thought, the historical with the dogmatic approach. Philology, exegesis, and the historical approach account for his striving after the strictest possible method of historical interpretation; systematic thought, dogma, and philosophy produce the remorselessness of his search for truth—while both combined lead to his strong emphasis on subjective truthfulness. The problem under discussion is that of *faith and knowledge.* Henceforth, Bultmann will again and again concern himself with the problems of hermeneutics, including the special problem of the "demythologization" of the New Testament.

The same complex of problems is treated still more comprehensively in *History and Eschatology,* his Gifford Lectures of 1955. His delightful inquiry into *Primitive Christianity in Its Contemporary Setting* (1949) lays greater stress upon presentation and analysis of the historical material; and his great commentary on the Gospel of John (1941) shows the strictness of his historical and critical exegesis as well as his endeavor to bring out the kerygma, the message of salvation, in an interpretation addressed to our day. Finally, his *Theology of the New Testament* (2 vols., 1955) is the ripe fruit of a fusion of exegesis with dogmatic insight.

Basically, Bultmann, like Harnack, searches for the essence of

Christianity. But he lays more stress upon history than the historian Harnack, and more stress on dogma than the dogmatists of Harnack's day, who had in fact become philosophers of religion. A few passages from Bultmann's essay on "Christianity as a Religion of East and West" will serve to show his deepest concern and his deepest insight:

"If Christianity—originally an oriental religion—became a religion of the West and, indeed, far more than that, a world religion, is the reason not that basic possibilities for the understanding of human existence are revealed in it, which we find everywhere and in every age the same, and so also in the West?"

His question is inspired by his answer. What is decisive to Bultmann is not that Christianity, like other oriental religions, has been "hellenized" in the Graeco-Roman West. (That was the overriding theme of Harnack, historian of dogma.) Bultmann's concern is "what spiritual gift, and what 'historical' force the Orient, and Christianity as an oriental religion, brought to the West with messianism and the Christ-cult, and what new possibilities for the understanding of human existence were thereby made accessible to the West." Bultmann's answer:

"The first thing is *a new sense of history and the historically significant existence of man*" (*Essays,* p. 220) looking no longer to the past but to the future. "The decisive thing is that *world history was conceived of as a meaningful coherent whole,* that reflection on the meaning of history was awakened, and a philosophy of history was given free play, which the ancient world had not yet known." Part of this understanding of history is Christian individualism as "a conception of human existence as such ... which consists in the knowledge and perception of this basic isolation of the ego." Further: "Man as he exists in history, as one who has become conscious of his isolation in the presence of God, stands *over against the world in a peculiar way which* is also foreign to Greek antiquity." This is the discovery of "*the non-mundane nature of man's being....* Man's self stands over against the world as a fundamentally transcendent entity, radically different from everything belonging to the world outside the human sphere; and this idea is held so consistently that the self is still reckoned to stand beyond all that is contained in the soul which may be experience and is something concrete."

This radical detachment of man from the world is accompanied by a new understanding of suffering:

"In suffering, man is brought to himself, while everything foreign, everything of the world in him, in which he mistakenly seeks his essential being, is removed from him, and the chains that bind him to the here and now are torn asunder; there takes place in him that process of withdrawal from the world, in the form of which the life of the believer should take its course. But in being brought to himself in this way, he does not become aware of his own strength, but becomes clearly aware of himself as the man who is not in control of himself—as the man of no account. In this way, however, abandoning all illusions of self-mastery, he is to recognize himself before God as the man who exists purely and simply in dependence of God's grace. And in this very way he is pleasing to God, and so he is open to receive the grace of God, whose 'strength is made perfect in weakness': for—as Paul says— 'when I am weak, then am I strong' (II Cor. 12:9 f.). Out of suffering there develops for man an inner strength in which he is superior to every trick of fate: suffering to him is a source of strength. But in that rests the very inmost nature of the Christian religion: God is manifest in the crucified One, whom He has made Lord as the risen One. 'Though he was crucified through weakness, yet he liveth by the power of God" (II Cor. 13:4). As the Gospel of John says, His crucifixion is His exaltation, His glorification. The *cross* then is the sign under which Christianity has set out on its victorious career into the Western World, and in the figure of the crucified One an embodiment of the deity was brought to the West, which contradicted all the views of the ancient world in the Occident: the passion as the manifestation of divine strength and grace!"

It is typical that Bultmann goes one step further here, to ask whether the specifically occidental sense of humor might not have been formed under the influence of Christianity. His answer:

"Humour is clearly Christian, when serene detachment from the world is not mere resignation, but the consciousness of freedom, which has arisen out of the experience of failure, out of the experience that the seriousness and anxious care, with which man wishes to realize his own plans for his life, are senseless; and that in such a failure man is really brought to himself for the first time, and is free for love, in which all his doings take on a real seriousness."

The new understanding of human life as historical leads to a closer definition of the peculiarity of the Christian faith:

"Christian faith seems to discern that man lacks the freedom which is a presupposition of historical decisions. If I at any time in a concrete situation am to accept responsibility for the future ...I obviously must be able to take up a position outside that situation: I must be free. But I do not in fact have such freedom. In fact, my decisions are always determined by my own past—not in the sense of causal determination, but because I am determined by my own will. For every man is ruled by his will to hold on to his own self.... True, every man can be aware of his responsibility, and at the moment of decision he has a relative freedom. But the question is whether he knows that his freedom is only relative, in other words, that it is limited by his own self because he has been shaped by his own past. Radical freedom would mean freedom from one's own self. A man who sees his historicity as radical, that is, who sees himself radically as belonging to the future, must know that his true self can come only as a gift brought to him by the future. But, in fact, there is in man the desire to control the future. ...As long as he is caught in that illusion, man remains unchanged ...he fails to understand that only a free man can truly shoulder responsibility, and that he must look for no guarantee, not even for that of a moral law.... But man cannot by his own will and his own power free himself of himself.... He can receive freedom only as a gift. And that is what the Christian faith confesses to receive: the gift of freedom by which man frees himself of himself, and so receives himself anew as a gift. 'He that findeth his life shall lose it; and he that shall lose his life for me shall find it'

(Matt. 10:39). This is not a general truth such as man could tell himself; it is a truth that man has to be told. And this precisely is the meaning of the Christian message—not that it proclaims the general idea of God's grace, but that it is the address, the talking-to-me which gives to me the grace of God that is for me, which frees man of himself. This proclamation is legitimized by the revelation of God's grace in Jesus Christ. The New Testament proclaims Jesus Christ as the eschatological event, the act of God by which He has put an end to the old world. In the proclamation, the eschatological event strives from instant to instant to become present, and in faith it turns from instant to instant into the event. For him who believes, the old world is at an end; he is 'a new man in Christ.' The old world is for him at an end just because there has been an end to his old self; he is a new, a free man. . . ."

The proclamation addressed to man calls for decision, "the decision of faith: I here make a decision not for a responsible act, but for a new understanding of myself as a man who by God's grace is freed of himself and has received himself anew as a gift. I decide for a life by the grace of God . . . so that all my decisions, all my responsible actions are grounded in love. Such a life, the life purely for others, is possible only to him who is free of himself. . . . The paradox of Christian existence is that he who believes is detached from the world—in a way lives an unworldly existence, and yet remains within the world, within his own historicity. Historical existence is existence from the future. The believer, too, exists from the future. First, because his faith and freedom can never be possessions; being eschatological events, they can never become facts that belong to the past, but have reality always as events only. Second, because the believer remains within history. In principle, the future always holds out to man the gift of his freedom. Christian faith means the power to accept that gift from instant to instant. Man's freedom of himself, the gift of divine grace, always becomes reality in the freedom of the historical decision."

Bultmann's concern is with this "paradox of Christ as the historical Jesus and the ever-present Lord," and therewith "the paradox of Christian existence as at the same time both eschatological and historical." That paradox means for him the same thing as that crucial proposition of Luther's, "both just and at the same time sinner," with which the great reformer defines the life of the Christian in the world.

His view of the eschatological mode of existence as man's detachment from the world, no less than the reform doctrine of justification by faith alone, without the works of the commandment, led Bultmann to his deep concern with the problems of theological hermeneutics—the art of understanding the biblical texts—which he describes as "the consistent application of that view in the area of knowledge." His position is set forth in *New Testament and Mythology* (1942), a work in some sense programmatic which deals with the problem of the demythologization of the New Testament message. An extensive and violent debate among scholars and churchmen followed its publication, rising at moments to the accusation of near-heresy. In part, the debate hinged on the key term "demythologization," especially since it was generally overlooked that Bultmann's criticism was not meant to segregate the myths from the biblical texts; rather what he meant to do was to interpret rightly the truths they were intended to convey—to give them the "existential interpretation" that draws out their meaning for man's understanding of being and existence. Myth, to Bultmann, is "that manner of thinking and speaking which turns the unworldly into a worldly object" and so attempts to make it manageable—especially when it relates the content of the proclamation to man's inner life. But any such attempt sidesteps the true decision which puts one's own self in question.

"The proclamation can call for the decision of faith only when it has shown that the confession of my sinfulness and the confession to God's grace in Christ are *possibilities* for my existence, which to reject is guilty unbelief. That, now, is exactly what existential interpretation does achieve, or to put it more humbly: that is what existential interpretation achieves in my opinion, to which I hold until somebody shows me a better hermeneutic method."

The statement throws light upon the great importance that

"prior understanding" concerning the possibilities and limitations of human existence has, for a true and faithful understanding of the Gospel message, the kerygma. Bultmann's method caused a stir especially when he applied it to certain statements of the Gospel, and in particular when he described the resurrection of Christ as "an expression of the importance of the cross." The Gospel message of the resurrection, he said, must be interpreted, not as "a miraculous certificate . . . on the strength of which the inquirer could now be sure of his faith in Christ," but as "the eschatological fact . . . by which Christ conquered death and brought to light life and eternity."

"In this way the resurrection is not a mythological event adduced in order to prove the saving efficacy of the cross, but an article of faith just as much as the meaning of the cross itself. Indeed, *faith in the resurrection is really the same thing as faith in the saving efficacy of the cross,* faith in the cross as the cross of Christ. Hence you cannot first believe in Christ and then in the strength of that faith believe in the cross. To believe in Christ means to believe in the cross as the cross of Christ. The saving efficacy of the cross is not derived from the fact that it is the cross of Christ: it is the cross of Christ because it has this saving efficacy. Without that efficacy it is the tragic end of a great man.

"We are back again at the old question. How do we come to believe in the cross as the cross of Christ and as the eschatological event *par excellence*? How do we come to believe in the saving efficacy of the cross?

"There is only one answer. This is the way in which the cross is proclaimed. It is always proclaimed together with the resurrection. Christ meets us in the preaching as one crucified and risen. He meets us in the world of preaching and nowhere else. The faith of Easter is just this—faith in the word of preaching.

"It would be wrong at this point to raise again the problem of how this preaching arose historically, as though that could vindicate its truth. That would be to tie our faith in the word of God to the results of historical research. The word of preaching confronts us as the word of God. It is not for us to question its credentials. It is we who are questioned, we who are asked whether we will believe the word or reject it. But in answering this question, in accepting the word of preaching as the word of God and the death and resurrection of Christ as the eschatological event, we are given an opportunity of understanding ourselves. Faith and unbelief are never blind, arbitrary decisions. They offer us the alternative between accepting or rejecting that which alone can illuminate our understanding of ourselves.

"The real Easter faith is faith in the word of preaching which brings illumination. If the event of Easter Day is in any sense an historical event additional to the event of the cross, it is nothing else than the rise of faith in the risen Lord, since it was this faith which led to the apostolic preaching. The resurrection itself is not an event of past history. All that historical criticism can establish is the fact that the first disciples came to believe in the resurrection. The historian can perhaps to some extent account for that faith. But the historical problem is not of interest to Christian belief in the resurrection. For the historical event of the rise of the Easter faith means for us what it meant for the first disciples—namely, the self-attestation of the risen Lord, the act of God in which the redemptive event of the cross is completed.

"We cannot buttress our own faith in the resurrection by that of the first disciples and so eliminate the element of risk which faith in the resurrection always involves. For the first disciples' faith in the resurrection is itself part and parcel of the eschatological event which is the article of faith."

And so we find ourselves in fact in the same spot with the first disciples, "in the paradoxical situation of the first Christians 'between the ages,' that is, between the 'old' and 'new' eon which is the Christian situation as such."

From Bultmann, the systematizer, we have come to Bultmann, the New Testament scholar. In the process it has become clear how much the two are one in true theology. Bultmann's great *Theology of the New Testament* confirms that intimate connection, as page by page it keeps a firm hold on the relation between theology and Gospel message.

"The task of New Testament theology is to present the theological ideas of the New Testament scriptures—both those explicitly developed (such as Paul's doctrine of the law) and those that work implicitly by means of story, admonition, polemic, or words of comfort."

Bultmann, however, presents them not as "a systematically structured unity," but rather "in their differences according to the various writings or groups of writings." He does this to make clear that "there can be no such thing as a normal dogmatic of the Christian faith. In other words, it is not possible to give a final solution to the problem of theology: the problem of conveying that understanding of God, and hence of world and man, which comes with faith." Again, "the statements of theology, being explications of the understanding that comes with faith, may be more or less to the point."

We have arrived at the task of New Testament scriptural criticism, a subject which played a decisive part in his *The Study of the Synoptic Gospels* of 1932, where he advanced the morphological method, form criticism, in an endeavor to form "a picture of the various components of tradition" in the first three Gospels.

"The most important single step is the basic realization that the theological ideas of the New Testament represent the unfolding of the faith itself as it grows out of the new faith-given understanding of God, world, and man—or, as it grows out of the new self-understanding. The new self-understanding does not mean an understanding in the sense of an anthropology which objectifies man as a phenomenon of the world. It means an existential understanding of my self, fusing with my understanding of God and world. For I am myself not as a worldly phenomenon that can be isolated and objectified; I am myself in my existence forever inseparable from God and world." New Testament theology does not "present the subject matter of faith, it presents faith itself in its self-interpretation," though "it does not lose sight of the subject matter. For faith is seen in the New Testament not as a self-understanding which arises self-empowered out of human existence, but as God-empowered, opened by God's act. Faith is not a choice among the possibilities of self-understanding that exist for man generally: it is the response to God's word that comes to man in the Gospel of Jesus Christ. It is faith in the kerygma that speaks of the act of God in the man Jesus of Nazareth." Theological ideas, if they are to avoid the danger of turning into general verities divorced from life, must always be interpreted as "an explication of the self-understanding awakened by the kerygma." And conversely: "The kerygma can be understood as kerygma only if the self-understanding it awakens is understood as a possibility of human self-understanding, and so turned into a challenge, a decision."

Bultmann dealt with the kerygma in the Gospel of Jesus (not in the personality of Jesus), in his book *Jesus and the Word* (1926). We can speak of the person of Jesus only, he writes, by speaking of the "bearer of the word," the word by which God calls for the decision:

"He who understands the word, and takes it to heart, knows: there is no other possibility of God's forgiveness becoming a reality for man except the word. In the word, and in no other way, Jesus brings forgiveness. Is His word the truth, is He sent by God?— that is the decision His hearer must face, and Jesus' word stands: blessed is he who does not take scandal in me!"

In the New Testament, faith is promised that it shall know the truth; it may at times speak of doing the truth, or of being in the truth. "This means, for one thing," Bultmann writes in his commentary on the Gospel of John, "that knowledge of the truth is not a contemplation in the sense of the Greek *theorein,* which comes from distance and gives distance—it is the acceptance of truth that comes from an obedient submission to the revelation, from man's decision to live not by the *pseudos* (lie) in arrogated self-sufficiency, but in self-surrender as God's creature. But it also means at the same time that faith will be filled with understanding as soon as it opens itself to its object, and that faith is not the blind acceptance of a dogma."

Over and over, Bultmann urges the seamless oneness of life and doctrine, being and knowing. This holds true also for his personal life. When the Nazi government in 1935 forbade the theological faculties to take a stand in the church controversy, Bultmann replied in a letter: "It is completely impossible for the teacher of theology not to take a stand in the present concerns of the Church, if he is not to abandon that connection of scholarship with life in the concrete from which alone scholarship derives its legitimacy." He was one of the very few who acted accordingly: with his remarkable expert opinions on matters of the controversy and also, for example, by pitching in during the war when religious instruction in the schools of Marburg was to be stopped for lack of teachers. And to round out his portrait, let us not forget the picture of the professor preaching from the pulpit, or standing by the church door, collection box in hand, and humbly doing service with the elders. And all this in that freedom which for him had come to be a central problem of his theology.

EMIL BRUNNER

BY

Wenzel Lohff

Nearly forty years ago, the religious and academic world witnessed
the extraordinary spectacle of a group of young pastors declaring
war upon the whole tradition of theological thought in the name
of the Gospel, and of winning over within a few short years the
large majority of theologically-minded youth. The conflict between
the new movement and earlier theological ideas found its sharpest
expression in a book published in 1924, under the title *Mysticism
and the Word* (*Die Mystik und das Wort,* der Gegensatz zwischen
moderner Religionsauffassung und christlichem Glauben, dar-
gestellt an der Theologie Schleiermachers). Its author, then the
thirty-four-year-old lecturer at Zurich, Emil Brunner, with this
work took his place in the front rank of theological reformers, side
by side with Eduard Thurneysen and Karl Barth, whose famed
commentary on the Letter to the Romans had appeared a few
years before. But while in Barth's work the new insights of faith
burst into words in an original and almost violent manner, Brunner supplied the cool head whose rigorous and detached intellectual

labor gave a reckoning of the old and the new ways of teaching the truths of faith. The judgment he pronounced upon all neo-Protestant theology, exemplified in Friedrich Schleiermacher, was that it had abandoned and so lost the truth of faith no less than the reality of God's word.

Brunner's judgement is concentrated in the key word "mysticism." Only a decade earlier various religious-aesthetic attempts—attempts of a literary cast—had exalted "mysticism" as the acme of religious culture: now it was seen as the most blatant opposite of faith. To Brunner, mysticism was the attempt to bypass the clear fact of the word of God, and to base faith upon experiences of a metaphysical sort.

"Where the word is, there is a clarity clear as day. 'God said: Let there be light! The word that was in the beginning was the light of man.' Mysticism seeks half-light and silence. Faith finds the light of day in the word. If it is true that mysticism is a pseudo-spirituality, and if to seek salvation in mysticism is indeed the most total aberration, this will come out in its relation to the word. Here is the storm center. Either/or: either mysticism, or the word."

For Brunner, there can be only this mutually exclusive either/or between faith founded upon devout experience—even if it were all Christian experience throughout the history of the Church—on the one hand, and on the other hand the listening to God's word. But he must not be understood to assert that theology had secured firm possession of God's word, to the point where she could now oppose it to devout experience as one tangible reality against another. Far from it!

"In so far as we fancy to 'possess' the word and think of knowledge as our property, and as theology takes up a position in the place of God—in so far what we practice is anything but theology. ... Which of the two might be the greater evil, the intellectualism of orthodoxy or the psychologism of the romantic school, is a pointless question. Both come from the same muddy source, irreverence. Both want to possess rather than to believe."

A theology, then, which intends faith to be real faith, has to begin with a merely negative task:

31

"When God speaks, the job of all theology is to clear away everything that stands in the way of this speaking and this listening—including theology itself. Theology then is not construction but a clearing-away. It is not for nothing that the imperatives of the Bible are negative so much more often than they are positive, that in the writings of the prophets the 'No' rings so much clearer than the 'Yes,' and that God's highest revelation is the cross. God gets His right only where man gets his wrong."

Here echoes the same "No!" with which Karl Barth, brilliant and powerful exponent of the new movement, first of all had opposed all those neo-Protestant theologians who attempted to present a plausible truth of faith resting upon the ever narrowing basis of rational experience. This "No" is not an end in itself; it is a first word, not the last. Once the first word is spoken, Brunner goes on, when we have made the great reservation by which God's Word is wholly distinct from the word of man, we must under this reservation bear concrete witness to the reality of God and to the reality of man in faith. As early as 1927, Brunner published under the title *The Mediator* the first, and for a long time the only, substantial work of theological rethinking that unfolds the belief in Christ. Other works followed. In 1932 appeared a theological ethic entitled *The Divine Imperative*; in 1937 a theological anthropology called *Man in Revolt—a Christian Anthropology*. In these books Brunner succeeds in unfolding the Christian life in the Church and the self-knowledge of faith, in ways so real, rich, and varied that he again and again gives the lie to the opponents of the new theology, who charge it with having torn God and world apart, of having condemned faith to be no more than the never-ending abstract criticism of culture.

Still, these works on the doctrine of the Church do not express Brunner's own deepest concern. He had sounded his own unmistakable note, even in those early polemics, against Schleiermacher which had proved him a spokesman of the theological renewal. We mentioned earlier the difference in idiom: Barth's passionately rhetorical and at times baroque diction, against

Brunner's language with its great rational lucidity and simplicity. What holds for Brunner's language is confirmed in the manner and direction of his thought. It is a thought that chooses clear alternatives and seeks to illuminate intellectual structure. "Mysticism—and the word": they are mutually exclusive opposites in method and thought structure as well. Brunner's inaugural speech at Zurich University is significantly entitled "Philosophy and Revelation." Not much later he contributed to a philosophical handbook an article on the philosophy of religion of Protestant theology that, at first glance, is bound to amaze those who knew his rejection of nineteenth-century philosophical theology. Could this be a return to the abandoned position of an apologetic flirting with a religion based on reason? Let Brunner speak for himself:

"A philosophy of religion in the true sense cannot exist within Christian theology, for the simple reason that theology deals not with religion but with revelation. Religion, whatever else it may be, is a form of human life, while revelation is God revealing Himself. The substance of faith is that which to man's reason is absurd, the paradox—and all genuine statements of faith bear the hallmark of logical impossibility, contradiction."

No, there can be no question here of an old-style apologetic. A faith whose mark it is to be paradoxical to the mind, a revelation which asks reason to give up its self-assertion—these cannot be made palatable to reason with reason's own arguments.

Yet the existence of philosophy, and of philosophizing reason, presents faith with a problem that faith must solve. Man's philosophizing attitude toward the world is a hard fact; can faith just simply turn its back upon it? Rational understanding of reality is a necessity of human life; can the witness of the revelation of God the Creator just simply pass it by? Or ask that it be abandoned? Is it that faith has its being in two realities: rationally in the godless reality of this world, faithfully in a reality that has nothing to do with this world? Does not a faith that is so separated from all reason turn once again into something mystical, an uncontrollable experience? And would it not then be all too easy for unbelief to reject the claim of revelation by simply pointing out:

I do not have such experiences, and therefore this faith is nothing to me? These are the questions to which Brunner turns in *Revelation and Reason* (1941):

"In many conversations with people outside the Church, I have constantly found that they confuse the faith which the Church proclaims with all kinds of irrational ideas for which they, quite rightly, as conscientious members of a civilized community, do not care to be held responsible. It is, of course, true that the Church has a message to proclaim which, so long as man remains in his self-chosen isolation, will be 'folly' and an 'offense.' All the more urgent, therefore, is the obligation of the Church to see to it that this 'offense' is not confused with accidental elements with a repelling effect, derived from misunderstanding and 'short circuits.' In a genuinely theological activity, alongside of the *one* thing which cannot be *proved*—or, rather, which such a 'proof' would destroy—there is much that can and should be proved, namely, that the Christian faith is not, and does not intend to be, saddled with errors and weaknesses that exist only in the mind of the ignorant outsider."

To give a description of the relation between faith and the rational knowledge of reality is the new, the "other task of theology" to which Brunner now turns his energies. Theology cannot rest satisfied in drawing afresh upon the sources in order to show revelation's testimony to the teachings of the Church. It must also supply human reason with evidence that the fundamental questions of human existence find their answers in the teachings of the Church.

"To show that faith does not ignore or suppress any legitimate concern of the reason—that I need not ignore any scientific or other knowledge in order to be a believer but that, on the contrary, the true interest of reason is only rightly preserved and maintained in faith—is not, it is true, the primary task of the Church, but it is a necessary task; a Church that thinks it can neglect this task with impunity will find that this neglect will wreak a bitter revenge. Contempt for this task does not arise, as is generally thought, from a particular zeal for religion, from a special intensity of faith, but from a certain theological arrogance, to which the questions which stir the minds of thoughtful lay people mean nothing at all, because a theologian of this kind is moved to serious thought only by his own affairs."

There would be no harm, according to Brunner, in again calling the task he here describes by the old name "apologetic." It remains true, of course, that the concept of apologetic has fallen into disrepute through the unacceptable procedures of neo-Protestant theology. Besides, revelation replies to man's vital questions precisely by first stripping him of rational self-assertion and forcing him to the confession: "I am a lost sinner." Thus it is perhaps better to speak, not of an apologetic, but rather of an eristic theology, a fighting, aggressive theology. Such an eristic theology, then, does on the level of theoretical discussion exactly what the preacher does in the pulpit when he calls for repentance. Brunner remarks:

"The true preacher tries to drive the thinking hearts of his audience into a corner where they are left with only one alternative: either the empty, desperate, defiant 'No!' of reason forced against the wall; or else, to enter through the narrow gates of faith. Therefore the real task of theological eristics is to teach man to understand his quest for God. What matters is to bring him face to face with the duality of his existence, with the contradiction whose true name is Sin, in such a manner that he cannot sneak out of the contradiction by turning it into an object of his reasoning."

"Such a theology, ever alive and changing and adapting itself to the situation, always 'at grips with the enemy,' which preaches by calling man to his senses—a theology which to begin with offers the Gospel to man only indirectly by destroying his illusions; which shows him that at bottom he is searching for something quite different from what he had in mind; which seizes man by his pet ideas and questions him about them in the Socratic manner until those ideas have been questioned to pieces: this Christian Socratic method, far more Socratic than its inventor, in that it does not try to draw truth out of man but is content to draw from him the confession of untruth—such an eristic theology is surely no small matter. It is the 'grain of salt' without which every dogmatic, however correct, must turn rotten."

With statements such as these Brunner means to make clear the duty of theology to so present God's word that it will touch man's rational self-understanding. But he offers still another essential consideration: the growing de-Christianization of life today, and with it the ever-growing confusion and disorientation of men's minds. These compel theology to concern itself with man's existential problems as a service of love:

"The problems of the 'world' have grown too tragic for us to stand by any longer and leave their 'solution' to a way of thinking that has lost touch with the Christian message. The events of our own day have at last compelled us to see that there must be a Christian foundation to all culture."

"A Christian foundation to all culture"—how far removed this seems from the starting point of the movement of theological renewal, with its rejection of Kultur-Protestantism. Yet the new formulation is consistent. For what was rejected was the neo-Protestant attempt to rise from rational experience toward an understanding of revelation—not the reverse approach used here which starts from revelation to seize upon man's reason. In Brunner's words:

"Revelation, in the act of faith, lays hold upon man's reason, but never does reason lay hold upon revelation." The problem of reason and revelation "finds its general solution in the fact that revelation can never find a place in reason, but reason finds a place in revelation."

This postulate places Brunner in the tradition of the great Christian thinkers of the modern age: Pascal, Hamann, above all Kierkegaard. They are the Christian philosophers who gave exemplary expression to the importance of faith for man's way in the reality of this world:

"Christian philosophy is, therefore, both possible and necessary, because as Christians we neither can nor should cease to think. It is not reason, but rationalism, that makes Christian philosophy appear impossible. The thinker must reckon seriously with the fact that the material of thought does not come first from the reason.... Christian philosophy is possible because faith does not ignore or coerce the thinking reason, but leads it back to its original purpose and sets it free. From this point of view faith consists simply in this, that the illusion of the autonomous reason, which is the basis of all philosophical dogmatism, has been dissolved, and the thinking self has once more been set where it belongs, at the place where it is no longer that which comprehends everything but where it is the subject which is itself comprehended. ... Where 'knowing' the world is concerned, faith means the regaining of a truly critical, and therefore realistic, way of thought."

Christian philosophy, then, cannot mean for Brunner the attempt to guide man's thought back into the dogmatic shell of a Christian world view—not after the old shell was cracked precisely by critical thought. But then, in what way is such thinking Christian?

Obviously, Brunner is aware that there is factual knowledge whose truth is not dependent upon faith. There is no such thing as a Christian mathematics. But in proportion as thought moves further beyond the area of objective data, the area of strict science, there is a growing influence of the insights of faith upon the rational understanding of reality. That holds true in particular for intellectual activities that deal with man himself—that is, for the study of political, legal, ethical, and moral relations. There is no such thing as a Christian doctrine of military tactics, but there is a Christian doctrine of war; no such thing as a Christian doctrine of chronometry, but a Christian doctrine of time. Brunner, in fact, sets down a law that governs the importance of faith for rational thought: the law of "closeness of relation to the center of existence." The closer a problem to the realities of personal existence, the more important faith becomes for its solution. Thus, the personalistic formulation of Christian thinking is in direct opposition to the objective form within which bygone ages tried to confine man's world view by means of church doctrine.

"But if faith is the most intimate personal experience—experience of God through His word—then there is as little reason to object to the validity of this experience in philosophical thinking as there is to object to the validity of any other experience. But the fact that this experience, in contrast to all others, is the fundamental experience of man, namely, that in which there is not only shown, but *given* to him, the meaning of and the reason for his existence, cannot, from the standpoint of thought, be any reason for denying its validity. No human being can think from a purely negative point of view. Everyone who philosophizes does so from a definite starting point, upon which he, as this particular man, stands. The Christian philosophizes from the point at which God's revelation sets him."

Brunner devoted a good part of his energies to offering words of Christian guidance on the spiritual problems of the times. His great works on ethics and anthropology assign to the judgments of faith a place among and above the established world-views. Faith, he says in his anthropology, overcomes the one-sidedness of the image of man presented by idealism and naturalism, by understanding man as a creature facing all other creatures and yet one of them. Faith, he shows in his ethic, overcomes the one-sidedness of individualism and collectivism by understanding man as an individual face to face with God, and yet one among his neighbors. Faith overcomes the one-sidedness of capitalism and of socialism by teaching us to understand that free creaturehood implies the power to dispose of one's own property, and yet calls upon the creature to give human and social service to his fellows.

Nor is this all. The questions of the Christian way in the world arise anew and in new form from day to day; therefore, the guidance of the Christian conscience must from day to day assume new forms. Accordingly, Brunner, the publicist of the Church whose words must answer to the present situation, steps up to take his place by the side of Brunner, the scholarly theologian. His voice is heard in publications of all kinds, religious journals, intellectual magazines, as well as in the *Neue Zürcher Zeitung,* showing that he practices what he preaches: theology must stay "at grips with the enemy." To his students, he likens the task of the systematic theologian to that of the front-line officer who must take his post wherever there is danger.

One problem has concerned Brunner above all others: how to establish a just order in the life with one's fellows, the problem of justice. In the book he devoted to the subject, *Justice and the Social Order* (1943), he writes:

"The crisis in law and order which bears the name of the totalitarian state is the outward manifestation of the crisis in the conception of law. Humanity today is faced with the necessity of finding an issue from that crisis both in its inward and its outward aspects. One way, popular up to the present, is barred; we can no longer appeal to history. The totalitarian state has squandered the heritage of history.... On what basis can reconstruction begin? Where is the idea of justice which alone renders such reconstruction possible? This question is not only *one* of those confronting us today. It is *the* question of the day. One thing is obvious. No reconstruction can be based on the maxim that justice is a relative thing. As surely as no house can be built on a swamp, as surely no just society can be erected on the thesis that justice is relative."

The arbitrary use of power in the totalitarian state appears to Brunner as the final consequence of the decay of all binding spiritual order. It turns into the fundamental problem of the Christian faith: is the Christian faith still able to endow the life of men with strength and direction as it did in the past?

"For nearly two thousand years the classical and Christian idea of justice, the 'Christian law of nature,' sustained and directed occidental jurisprudence, and was conceived to provide an adequate expression in philosophic terms for man's innate, underived sense of right. What would be simpler, therefore, than to return to it?"

But such a return is not a simple matter. The spiritual assumptions which allowed us to speak naively of natural law exist no longer. The fact that the old concept of natural law could lose its binding force plainly shows that it was inadequate. But the problem that natural law was intended to resolve remains inescapable:

"The idea of justice, man realizes, assigns to him a place within an order. He is part of a structure in which he occupies a specific position, a structure which orders his whole life, the association of each man with all his fellows, and with the natural conditions of life. . . . Therefore in any human encounter governed by justice—and by nothing else—I see the other man as the occupant of his specific place within the structure, as one for whom it has already been decided that this or that is due and proper to him. What I see is not he but his 'claim,' his 'right,' his place in the whole structure."

Now this association of man with man and with the areas of human life is a matter within the special competence of the Christian faith in creation. And since faith knows that all things have their origin in the Creator, it must, according to Brunner, also be able to know and state the order of creation in which all creatures have their place by the act of the Creator. He writes:

"With the creation, and with the order of being manifesting itself in creation, every creature has been given his law of life; he has received his right, his province has been staked out, his due has been determined and what is not his due. In creation, the *suum cuique* has been defined. The order of creation as the principle of all justice alone allows us to understand why both our common manhood and our single individuality contain something that in all justice must be recognized—a claim, a right whose recognition constitutes justice. If we bypass the order of creation we shall find no relation between the norm of justice and the identity of the creature."

Here Brunner has brought out something that is, after all, analogous to the old law of nature: an original order to which all human thought can turn as to a final source of justice. It differs from the old natural law in that it is within the province of faith. And since faith in creation achieves full clarity only through faith in Christ, this new natural law may be called "Christological," that is, a law which finds its only legitimate ground in the Christian faith. And since, as Brunner has shown, the revelation of faith lays claim also to human reason, the new doctrine of Christological natural law is bound to demand that secular human reason, in its search for the order of justice, be guided by faith.

From the "No!" with which revelation rejected man's rational self-assertion, Brunner has now led us to the point at which faith demands the consent of human reason. His road is consistent with itself—the road of a thinker and theologian who explicitly addressed his theological labors to the problem of the structure of knowledge implied in faith, and to the application of that knowledge. But his road is bound to take him further and further away from his initial alliance with Karl Barth. Barth, even when dealing with dogma, always remained the preacher of God's word, to whom a knowledge of Christian thought-structure is of minimal importance, a man who would admit no other duty of theology than to proclaim the word of God. In 1929, criticism begins to pass back and forth, until finally in 1934 Brunner issues his *Nature and Grace,* in which he draws the dogmatic consequences of his position in specific opposition to Barth. Brunner no longer thinks it possible that the "No!" which revelation addresses to fallen, sinful man should be extended indifferently to cover all of what it means to be a human being. He no longer thinks it permissible to deny to fallen man that he is God's image, as the Bible testifies; something which in his opinion Barth *is* doing.

"No one who agrees that only human subjects but not sticks and stones can receive the word of God and the Holy Spirit can deny that there is such a thing as a point of contact for the divine grace of redemption. This point of contact is the formal *imago Dei,* which not even the sinner has lost, the fact that man is man, the *humanitas* in the two meanings defined above: capacity for words and responsibility. Not even sin has done away with the fact that man is receptive to words, that he and he alone is receptive of the word of God....

"This possibility of his being addressed is also the presupposition of man's responsibility. Only a being that can be addressed is responsible, for it alone can make decisions. Only a being that can be addressed is capable of sin. . . .

"The word of God does not have to create man's capacity for words. He has never lost it; it is the presupposition of his ability to hear the word of God. But the word of God itself creates man's ability to believe the word of God, i.e., the ability to hear it in *such a way* as is only possible in faith."

The Reformation doctrine of salvation by grace alone is not affected, according to Brunner, by this postulate of man's power of the word. On the contrary, the doctrine presupposes that power since it alone precludes a magical interpretation of grace. But if man's power of the word is given in creation, and remains unimpaired by sin, then we must also with the Bible assume God's original revelation in creation. For, as Brunner puts it, "Wherever God does anything, He leaves the imprint of His nature upon what He does. Therefore, the creation of the world is at the same time a revelation, a self-communication of God." There exists also a natural knowledge of God's decrees, a *theologia naturalis*. Like all knowledge of God, it is pure and perfect only within faith. But this must not prevent us from admitting its existence outside of faith as well.

"For this reason there lies over these ordinances a twilight which cannot be dispelled. They are given by God. They are realized naturally. For their realization not only the natural impulse is necessary but also the *humanum*. They can be recognized as necessities and as goods by natural man. But—and this is the critical point—only by means of faith can their significance be perfectly understood and, therefore, it is only by means of faith that they can be realized according to the will of him who instituted them."

Here Brunner has replaced the mutual exclusivity of nature and grace with a relation of coordination, but a coordination that does not remove the sovereign and sole efficacy of grace in the advent of salvation. Yet Barth's answer to this challenge, given not much later, is a resounding "No!"

The very title of Barth's essay makes the point: "No!—Answer to Emil Brunner." He declines to accept the problem as Brunner has posed it in his attack. Writes Barth:

"For 'natural theology' does not exist as an entity capable of becoming a separate subject within what I consider to be real theology....If one occupies oneself with real theology, one can pass by so-called natural theology only as one would pass by an abyss into which it is inadvisable to step if one does not want to fall. All one can do is turn one's back upon it as upon the great temptation and source of error, by having nothing to do with it and by making it clear to oneself and to others from time to time why one acts that way."

Barth does not, of course, deny that questions such as that of revelation's point of contact may be raised. But he does deny that this question carries any weight of its own in the task of proclaiming the Gospel.

"If we are prepared to call the fact that man is man and not a cat, the 'point of contact,' 'the objective possibility of divine revelation,' then all objection to these concepts is nonsensical. For this truth is incontrovertible....But be that as it may: what is the relevance of the formal responsibility to make decisions to a 'capacity' which man possesses and which exists in him anterior to divine revelation? Is the revelation of God some kind of 'matter' to which man stands in some original relation because as man he *has* or even *is* the 'form' which enables him to take responsibility and make decisions in relation to various kinds of 'matter'?"

Barth denies further that there is any missionary significance to the apologetic and eristic dialogue between faith and the faithless reason, the dialogue that Brunner has made his own special task:

"In my experience the best way of dealing with 'unbelievers' and modern youth is not to try to bring out their 'capacity for revelation,' but to treat them quietly (simply remembering that Christ has died and risen also for them), as if their rejection of 'Christianity' was not to be taken seriously."

This is the parting of the ways. Brunner is unable to accept Barth's reply as an answer to his questions. Of course, contact recurs between the two former fellows-in-arms. In the anthropological volume of his *Dogmatics,* Barth accords to Brunner's anthropology, *Man in Revolt,* a sensitive discussion; and Brunner, reviewing the volume, acknowledges that he has been well understood—only to follow up with renewed doubts about Barth's theological method. Again and again, the vast difference in the thought processes of Barth the great preacher, and Brunner the great pastor and apologist, becomes evident. It shows up also where theological thinking leads to taking a political position. Both write on the Church between East and West. Brunner comes to this conclusion:

"The totalitarian state ... is lawlessness on principle. Hence it is also inhumanness on principle, the denial on principle of human dignity.... The totalitarian state is in essence atheistic, antitheistic, because by definition it claims the whole man for itself."

And now Brunner turns directly upon Karl Barth who does not wish to assume a theological position that is on principle against the East:

"I ask: Can the Church, faced with this totalitarian state, say anything other than a passionate and unconditional 'No'? Must it not react against a 'communist,' that is, a consistent totalitarian state, exactly as against the dilletante totalitarian state of Nazidom?"

This necessity is precisely what Barth the preacher denies in his reply. Addressing himself in turn directly to Brunner, he says:

"The Church is called upon to take a confessionally, spiritually, and theologically binding position in matters of politics whenever and wherever things come to a head—that is, where in the concrete conflict with a specific event the word of God calls the Church to perform its service by standing up for the faith. But the Church has no timeless dealings with this or that 'ism or system—only with the historical realities as from instant to instant they enter into the light of God's word and of faith. The Church is beholden not to any natural law but only to its living Lord. That is why the Church never thinks, speaks, or acts 'on principle.' It judges spiritually, hence only from case to case. It has no truck with any systematization of political history and its own role in it."

Brunner, however, continues consistently on his way, the way of reflecting on the problems of the insights of faith, the way of missionary care for those outside the Church, the way of the world of the mind in search of its order and foundation. This deep concern prompts him—the man who was one of those that renewed a conscious Church theology—to grow in time more and more critical of the tradition that proclaims the Church by proclaiming the truth of the Gospel in the form of an objective doctrine. For, as he points out especially in his lecture *The Divine-Human Encounter,* the word of God and the dogma of the Church are not simply objects which man faces as the subject. God's revelation, by the witness of the Bible, is not an objective announcement that man could employ like the provisos of a law code or a scientific theory. God's revelation absolutely cannot be understood in the way knowledge is understood:

"Knowing and *happening* are in this instance a single process. God communicates Himself in love: and this happens in the fullest sense only when His love is known in responding love. Unless this happening takes place, self-communication cannot consummate itself. It does not reach its goal. This act of divine self-communication thus brings together within itself the dual event of revelation and knowledge."

Nor can statements about God be separated out of the totality of this event as theoretical truths:

"All that the Bible has to say about God's being and doing, about time and eternity, about the divine purpose and creation, about sin and redemption, about grace and works, about faith and penance, about Church and Sacrament, is said within this basic structure and also formulates in a specific way this basic relation.... We call this basic formal relation, which at the same time is identical with the contents of the whole Bible, *personal correspondence.*"

"Personal correspondence," then, is the name Brunner gives to the event of the encounter between God and man that occurs wherever revelation occurs. Truth can be predicated only of the event as a whole. For truth resides in the encounter of the revelation of the God of grace with man's faith of trusting obedience.

There is no truth of revelation by itself alone, independent of faith, because there is no truth independent of this personal correspondence. In Brunner's words:

"*Faith is the truth.* For what God wills is that His name be hallowed, that His love find reciprocal love in man. To this end He gave His Son, that this could happen, *that by means of His self-giving, man would be led to self-surrender.*"

What the Church tradition hands down in objective dogmatic doctrine can be only a reflection of this primordial event, a sign by which to speak of the event. For that purpose doctrine, to be sure, is indispensable:

"God indubitably says 'something' to us in order to be present as Lord and as Father in the Son through the Spirit. Similarly the direct address in its very simplest form—'I am the Lord, thy God'—when conceptually comprehended conceals doctrine, 'theology.' God, to be sure, does not deliver to us a course of lectures in dogmatic theology or submit a confession of faith to us, but He *instructs* us authentically about Himself. He tells us authentically who He is and what He wills for us and from us. And likewise that which is simplest and most direct, i.e., immediate personal answer to prayer, also has its abstract form: 'Our Father, who art in Heaven.' Consequently we can never separate the abstract framework from the personal Presence contained in it, although certainly we must differentiate them."

But if the essence and the truth of faith are so entirely contained in the living event of personal encounter, then criticism is bound to arise of all churchly and Christian forms of life that no longer clearly show their origin. Brunner's criticism attacks wherever objective aspects—dogma, sacrament, office, church institution—have become sacred to themselves. This is the century-old *Misunderstanding of the Church*, which he attacks sharply in his book so titled. Against the historically grown church institution, Brunner opposes the living community in faith of the New Testament, the *ecclesia*:

"The Church is a historically evolved form, a vessel of the *Ecclesia*; not to it, but to the *Ecclesia* alone, was given the promise of invincibility and eternal durability. . . . The essence of the New Testament *Ecclesia* (is) the oneness of communion with Christ by faith and brotherhood in love. . . . Not the hostility of the unbelieving world, but clerical parsonic ecclesiasticism has ever been the greatest enemy of the Christian message and of brotherhood rooted in Christ. *Ecrasez l'infame* is not only the cry of hatred uttered by the rationalistic enlightenment, it is also the cry of humanity oppressed by the Church and therefore the warning sign—never to be ignored—given by Christ Himself to a Christianity which is betraying Him in the interests of the Church."

Let there be no misunderstanding: Brunner at all times held an active position in the Church. His sermons in the cathedral at Zürich—some of which even appeared in print—drew large audiences. Yet he—the theologian on the very forefront of theological investigation, the university professor whose researches are ecumenical in scope, the writer whose works have appeared in many languages—cannot conceive of Christ's community confined within the narrow walls of the institutions of the moment. He does not reject the institution of the Church, but—and here he shows himself a true Christian of the Reformation—he does insist that the subservient character of all those outward signs must never be forgotten; that the Giver of the Church, the saving gift, should never be forgotten for the sake of the gift itself—the Giver whose gifts are no more than an invitation to commune with Himself. Only in that community, which is also the living community with our brothers, only there lies salvation.

PAUL ALTHAUS

BY

Wenzel Lohff

At times the characteristic strength of an outstanding intellectual achievement may be reflected in a simple and seemingly trivial circumstance. So with Paul Althaus. After a few short years at Rostock, and disregarding many calls to posts of high distinction, Althaus devoted a lifetime, rich in teaching and research, to serve the theological faculty at the University of Erlangen. This quiet, simple ·Frankish town boasts of a glorious theological tradition which has remained unshaken by the divers currents in modern Protestantism of the last hundred years. Erlangen's theology is conservative, yet close to the realities of the present. In the words of Hofmann, one of the great teachers of its early days, Erlangen aims to teach old truth in a new way. Thus it was spared the abrupt break in theological development that elsewhere led to radical neo-Protestantism, and on to a neo-orthodoxy at odds with the present. This Erlangen tradition, a Lutheran theology fully in touch with the present, is what Althaus, together with his great comrade-at-arms Werner Elert, has represented for a generation.

Althaus himself was not a product of the Erlangen tradition. The son of a Lutheran professor of theology, he came in his student days under the influence of the great biblical theologians Schlatter and Kähler. This experience led him beyond a full awareness of his own confession, on to a free, personal attentiveness to the message of Holy Writ. Most of all, however, he was captivated by the study of Luther himself. All through his life he remained engaged in an intensive dialogue with Luther's thought—and this, no doubt, became one of the most important sources from which his own theological work drew its strength. It found expression in that imposing body of writings on Luther, which places Althaus among the leading Luther scholars of our time. To be sure, the mind of a systematic theologian is at work in these writings; and so there emerges from them not a reformer seen across a philological-historical distance, but a living Luther who can speak to the present situation. To take but one example: as Althaus writes on obedience and freedom in Luther's attitude toward the Bible, he brings out clearly in the end how Luther's loyalty to the word and his critical freedom can point the way for present-day theology toward the right use of scripture.

Yet Althaus' thought shows another influence, wholly different from that of Luther and the theology of Holy Scripture. Early in life Althaus comes to grips with the questions with which modern theological trends—and especially the theology that bases itself on historical criticism and the history of religions—have challenged the conservative theological tradition, and which would place the Gospel into the great chain of history-bound phenomena of mankind's religious evolution. Fighting his way through the implications of the historical approach for the traditional doctrine of the Church, Althaus works out his own theology. It is not a theology in which seemingly timeless doctrines are handed down unchallenged from age to age. For, once theology has grasped that all human thinking is historically determined, it must accept Paul's certain conviction that even in theology we see through a glass darkly, not face to face. The manner of theological thought that follows is developed in Althaus' programmatic essay on *The Theology of Faith (Theologie des Glaubens)*:

"The watch-word 'theology of faith' contrasts with orthodoxy. By orthodoxy we mean, not a specific confessional trend, but a certain view of dogmatics. Orthodoxy in the sense of our method existed not only among the confessional churches but also among the 'liberals' and speculative thinkers. The essence of orthodoxy as a theological attitude lies in its view of theological substance as the quintessence of 'objective' facts and 'unchanging truths.'"

Althaus' opposition to orthodoxy, then, springs not from any lack of interest in doctrine but, on the contrary, from a burning interest in a doctrine that corresponds, even in form, to the reality of faith in all its purity—something which the old orthodoxy of unchanging truths of faith cannot achieve. Says Althaus:

"The truth of God is His living word that will be heard. It is the address, the call, the living relation. It cannot be contained in a timelessly valid objective thought-system detached from the very act of knowing, and independent of the person of the knower. For it is the word addressed *to him*, the truth *for him*. He cannot 'own' it, lay it down, place it before himself and look at it. The truth that is here known, therefore, cannot be separated from the act of knowing nor from the knower—it is living truth, personal relation and bond."

Such an understanding of the truth of faith as entirely referred to the person, entirely actualistic, raises the question whether it leaves room for a dogmatic in the traditional sense of a system of Church doctrines. Althaus supplied the answer in 1929-1932, in his brilliant *Fundamentals of Dogmatics (Grundriss der Dogmatik)* which has gone through one edition after another right up to the present. In 1947, its terse and pregnant statements of Church doctrine were followed by a large dogmatic under the title *The Christian Truth (Die Christliche Wahrheit)*. Both works expose in detail all the Christian doctrines, but without ever losing sight of their origin in a theology of faith. Althaus gives an account of this connection in these words:

"Christian knowledge has its *origin* in faith. Faith depends on God's revelation. But revelation is not the communication of a factual truth, a 'doctrine,' it is a person-to-person encounter of God with ourselves. Accordingly, the substance of faith is God in His self-manifestation, and not a concentrate of truths. God and faith are as one, not doctrine and faith. Strictly speaking there are no *credenda* but only the *credendus* God who calls for and brings forth faith in His reality. That faith then, to be sure, contains the fullness of knowledge. For God manifests Himself as our Creator, Lord, King, Judge, Savior. There is no 'revealed doctrine' that must be believed; there is only the self-manifestation of God who must be believed. When faith expresses what it receives as truth in its surrender to God's self-revelation, then the concentrate of Christian truth, the 'doctrine,' comes into being. It is not doctrine that must be believed in faith—doctrine comes to be when faith finds expression."

The tradition of the Church, too, must be understood as a witness of this God's self-manifestation. Tradition cannot claim truth for itself, but refers back to God's self-manifestation, and herein lies its limitation but also its dignity and inescapable authority. Althaus' existential determination of the truths of faith does not leave Church tradition to one side—far from it. He, on the contrary, develops dogmatic understanding of faith in a constant give-and-take with Church dogmatics. He devotes a group of books to testing the solidity of classical Lutheran doctrine, including such works as *Luther's Doctrine of Justification and its Present Critics* (*Die Lutherische Rechtfertigungslehre und ihre heutigen Kritiker*), or *Luther's Doctrine of the Two Kingdoms Under Attack* (*Luthers Lehre von den beiden Reichen im Feuer der Kritik*). He squarely faces out the current challenges to Luther's position: Are the central Reformation doctrines time-bound, conditional upon a specific historical-intellectual situation? In short, are the presuppositions of Luther's doctrines dead? Has perhaps the whole Lutheran confession even caused dangerous aberrations in the history of faith and thought, and in the social and political formation of the West? With all these critical questions, raised today from

51

many quarters, Althaus deals head-on. Again and again he comes to the conclusion that the Reformation doctrines are in their ultimate intention dogmatically beyond challenge, and that any criticism, at most, touches misunderstandings and false starts. Nor does he ever deal with such criticisms in a facile fashion, or defend the confessional traditions for their own sakes. The Lutheran confession must not, he says, be understood to mean that the Lutheran Church is the only true and only saving Church:

"As a church structure, it is of the same kind as all confessions, an individual formation with its particular advantages and disadvantages and, like all others, subject to earth's laws of being one-sided and fragmentary. But from the Lutheran Church we must distinguish the Lutheran *confession*. We believe that the confessions to which Luther's Reformation gave rise are in their substance a witness to the Gospel so pure that no other symbol, no other *confessio*, can equal them. These confessions are not the separate property of particular churches; they are a sign to the entire Christian Church to look toward the Gospel. Their meaning is ecumenical. They are not meant to raise up a Lutheran Church, but that the Gospel might be powerful in all Christendom."

Within the confessional tradition, Althaus maintains very precise distinctions. Luther for him is greater than the confessional Lutheranism of subsequent centuries, and the Reformer often carries the day over the later ecclesiastical constrictions of his teaching. But even Luther does not hold office as the bearer of revelation; he is merely a witness to the truth of the Gospel.

Reformation doctrine must, therefore, be tested against the witness of the New Testament. Althaus turns to New Testament exegesis. His commentary on the Letter to the Romans is no doubt used more widely today than any other. A number of books are devoted to a comparison of the texts of the New Testament with their reformatory interpretations; the best-known of these is *Paul and Luther on the Nature of Man* (*Paulus und Luther über die Menschen*). Here Althaus confronts the anthropology of the Reformer with that of the Apostle, and comes to the conclusion that the Reformer—with his view of a natural man who can only hate God's law—has simplified the New Testament view of man beyond what is admissible. Here is Althaus' description of Paul's view:

"Man's misery does not lie in that he does *not* take joy in the good, that he does *not* like it and want it, but in that he *does* affirm it, like it, want it, and yet he, the same man, does *not* at the same time will it, and therefore does *not* do it. . . . Man both loves and hates God's command. . . .

"Theology and the proclamation of the Church will do well to seriously recall these thoughts of the apostle Paul about man, and once more to make them their own. Paul's thoughts have been covered over and largely pushed aside by Augustinianism, especially so in the theology of the reformers. The image of man as drawn by Reformation theology is simpler and less complex than that of Paul, but also less complex than reality will allow. It no longer lets us recognize God's creature in the sinner. In Paul, man, as he really is, still senses himself more fully discovered and much better understood in his self-contradiction and inner discord."

Himself fully committed to Reformation doctrine tested against Holy Scripture, Althaus now turns upon all theological doctrines that seem to him to impair this fundamental connection with the doctrines of the Reformation and the Bible. Again and again he objects to early dialectical theology and, later, especially to Karl Barth. He is fully aware of his own ties with the movement of theological renewal, and has often stressed in gratitude Barth's importance in giving a new direction to theological inquiry. But where, in Althaus' opinion, the new theological teaching does not do justice to the full breadth of the tradition of Christian doctrine, he raises his objections. Always receptive to new doctrinal formulations, he denies them recognition as soon as they lay claim to exclusive validity and appear to grow narrow and self-willed. Thus, he champions the old Lutheran sequence Law/Gospel against Barth's doctrine of Gospel and Law, which sees the Law of God as merely the form of the Gospel, the command of God's grace. Only if the Law stands on its own, outside the Gospel, only then can it impress itself upon us as the result of God's wrath and God's judgment. Faith in the saving act of Jesus alone cuts through God's wrath and judgment.

Most of all, Althaus champions the traditional Christian doctrine of a general revelation of God outside the history of salvation, the doctrine to which Karl Barth and his circle were the first to oppose their resolute "No!" To them, all divine revelation springs only from the revelation of Jesus Christ and from the proclamation of His word. For Barth, who in this respect has largely determined present-day theology, the rejection of a general revelation apart from Christ is merely the consequence of the fact that there can be no unbroken, upward progression from reason to the revelation in Christ. Whoever advocates general revelation thereby becomes also the champion of reason against faith, of natural man against the scandal of revelation.

Althaus, undismayed by attacks from every side, opposes that position, in favor of the claims of the traditional doctrine of *revelatio generalis*. A letter to a reader of his dogmatics shows his passionate concern:

"It goes without saying that my book is in decisive respects flatly opposed to the ruling theological fashion in Germany. . . . But here I cannot theologically repent. You have known me since we both began our researches. Even in those days, I found the narrowness of the predominant doctrine of revelation unbearable. It seemed to me unbiblical and cramped. I never could understand how we as theologians and churchmen could surrender the whole world of nature and of history to skepticism and secularism, and parrot what atheistic philosophy had done to strip our lives of God—and all that while claiming to preserve the honor of Christ, the only way to the Father. Once it had renounced 'general revelation,' theology, for decades following the current fashion, abandoned a task it should never have given up: the task of pointing out the marks of creation and God's order in our natural and historical life as, for example, in marriage, in the legal order, in man's very being, in his soul. It is a message we owe to those to whom we are to proclaim the Gospel, so that they may understand what the Gospel really does say."

And so Althaus teaches an arch-revelation, by which he, in keeping with the New Testament, means an original self-manifestation of God in creation and in the reality of man, which all men know already even before they encounter Jesus Christ and the proclamation of the Church. The universal claim upon all men made by the revelation of the history of salvation is well-founded only if the same God, who in Jesus Christ acts to man's salvation, is also active and knowable in creation itself. Every man who encounters the Christian Gospel has already become guilty toward the God of original revelation—and knows it. That is the only reason why the Gospel of Jesus Christ can address man in terms of his guilt. It is precisely the universal validity claimed by the revelation of the history of salvation which, according to Althaus, makes the doctrine of original and general revelation a necessity. For example:

"The guilt of unbelief lies in the fact that the man who encounters Christ does know, *should* and in God *could* know, whom he encounters: the word of God that is for him and concerns him. This knowledge, by which it is sinful to turn away from Jesus, points back to the original revelation. Since every man knows of God by God's original manifestation to his spirit and his conscience, he cannot be blind to Christ. He is bound to recognize the divinity of His word because he has heard God's word once before. He must perceive that through Jesus the word continues to be spoken which God began to speak; he must perceive that Jesus is the same as that consciousness of God which has been given to every man together with his very existence. . . . In this sense, men must *recognize* God in Jesus."

The objection has been made to the doctrine of original revelation that in the final analysis it subordinates the biblical knowledge of God to an extra-biblical philosophical God-idea, which is then *ex post facto* passed off as revelation. It has been said further that the doctrine of original revelation artificially fuses knowledge of God drawn from two totally heterogeneous sources—reason and revelation—to the detriment of a clear Christian knowledge of God. Althaus denies these objections. Their argument, he asserts, overlooks the fact that all clear and theologically legitimate statements about the self-manifestation of God rest entirely upon the revelation of the history of salvation. And besides, the objections fail to see fully the radical nature of the doctrine of original revelation. The doctrine asserts nothing less than that the God attested by biblical revelation directs man toward his own reality as a created being, and intends to be revealed in that very reality. Revelation in that reality means: the God who on the strength of biblical revelation could be taken for a God speaking in a distant, though powerful, historical tradition, this God is now close by. Here and now in our own creaturely reality He wills to be revealed and experienced.

"Insofar as the revelation of the history of salvation is 'revelation of the word,' insofar as it occurs in the witness of God, it always relates to a *specific reality* of man's life and experience of the world. The reality to which the witness relates is therefore not, first of all, and not only, the person and the history of Jesus Christ, but even prior to it nature and history, human community, the experience of conscience, man's self-encounter all in all. The word of the Bible that deals with God signifies largely nothing else than just this, that the arch-revelation of God is illumined and expressed in man's reality. To understand it one must take thought of the reality to which it belongs, and of the manifestation of God that takes place in that reality."

Elsewhere Althaus draws the consequences still more sharply:

"Faith wants to obey the true reality into which God placed man. Faith fears nothing more than it fears the imaginings of self-willed religious man. It is wholly concerned with distinguishing God's work and God's will from the wishful visions of the human heart. Hence faith carries within itself the strictest critical sense and the courage to put itself and its foundations to the test of truth. Nor is faith ever completed. It must forever penetrate and conquer new realities of the world."

"Faith and reality" is the watchword. The theological thinking that stands behind that motto has ever since gained ground against the neo-orthodoxy of the theological renewal movement. Dogmatic theology here is very close to the task of proclamation in practice: to Althaus, university preacher and the author of numerous volumes of sermons that made him known beyond the scholarly world, that connection has always been obvious. At the same time, however, the words "faith and reality" bring dogmatics close to the modern hermeneutic movement in theology which raises the remorseless question whether present-day man, such as he understands himself, can still accept the traditional dogmatic propositions. Althaus is well aware of these radical consequences. His letter to his friend goes on:

"It seems to me that, for example in Christology and in the doctrine of reconciliation, we are compelled to a far greater freedom from dogmatic tradition and its concepts, and to a far more resolute reconstruction, than have been practiced so far. As for myself, I have attempted it especially with regard to these two issues—perhaps still not radically enough, still not close enough to life; I don't know. But that is the direction of my theological endeavor. I don't have to point out that here, too, it is the pulpit which sets to me the tasks that I must then face on the lectern. At bottom, it is a struggle for the full presence and life of the proclamation, something of which all of us still fall so short. By the way, I must confess to you my amazement at the loud noise that marks today's discussions of 'demythologization.' Even without mentioning that hazy and unfortunate concept itself—whatever in it is right and necessary, dogmatics has long since practiced as a matter of course: the attempt to recover the living meaning of the theology of the early Christians, the truth of the Gospel that concerns us today in the spiritual situation of our present, and to recover it untrammeled by the theological form that for us belongs to the past."

At this point the second fundamental characteristic of Althaus' dogmatic work emerges: the resolute orientation of his dogmatics toward the present situation, toward life. The theology of faith moves within the tension of a twofold obedience: obedience to the tradition of the Church, and obedience to the critical conscience of one's own mind. Althaus contributes the Erlangen tradition of teaching old truth in a new way. To him there is no such thing as dogmatic thought detached from the present faith, and no such thing as faith independent of the critical conscience of one's own mind. This critical conscience leads Althaus to an unconditional approval of historical Bible criticism. At first, his position caused a measure of consternation in those circles of Church theology to which Althaus is close, and there was even talk of "open unbelief within the Erlangen faculty." Althaus is all the more intent on stating that the right critical inquiry, in spite of all the trouble it might cause to the representatives of Church tradition, is not a threat but on the contrary a vital function of faith—a function without which faith cannot remain faith. If it is true that faith fears nothing so much as the imaginings of self-willed religious man, critical inquiry must be applied over and over to the testimony of the Bible. Althaus replies to his attackers:

"I understand the shock only too well. I, too, have had a taste of the misery caused by our first encounter with biblical criticism. . . . But the decisive thing is that dogmatics may not for any reason whatever circumvent these questions with all their misery (as dogmatics so often did, and in some places still does today). It must pass *through* them. Else Christianity will fail to render to the present an essential service: to lead man to Christian liberty in dealing with the Bible."

Nor can criticism stop at the human reality of Jesus himself. Since Martin Kähler's famous work on the historical Jesus, it had for a generation been customary among theologians, by an appeal to the new reality of Jesus in the resurrection, to reject the critical problem of the pre-Easter Jesus as untheological, a problem posed by unbelief. Even theologians as critical as Rudolf Bultmann shared that attitude. Althaus, by contrast, calls resolutely for critical inquiry into the historical reality of the life of Jesus. If we are serious about His becoming man, we cannot shy away from that problem. Historical criticism, by removing many dogmatic accrescences from the earthly image of Jesus, returned the faith in Jesus to its proper intensity as a faith in the true man Jesus. Besides, Althaus asserts with confidence, historical criticism has established that our picture of the first community of the man Jesus is trustworthy in every essential respect. And even if it were not, faith must take the risk inherent in this critical inquiry, because it cannot bypass Christ's human reality and still remain faith. In his book *Fact and Faith in the Kerygma of Today*, the very title of which suggests its opposition to a famous work by Kähler, Althaus writes:

"The affirmation of the proclamation of Jesus Christ also implies a judgment of reason: the view of the reality of the figure and history of Jesus in its essential traits, real beyond the powers of invention—a judgment which even the unbeliever can make and, experience shows, does in fact carry within him consciously or unconsciously."

Althaus' *Dogmatics* sums up the significance of historical criticism for Christian faith:

"We have no right to put historical criticism aside as irrelevant on the grounds that its presumptive results are always changing, or are not universally accepted. True, research picks its way through a maze of experience and through many a controversy, but it makes headway nonetheless and yields genuine results which none of the researchers can or will ever again surrender. Nor can we throw the whole enterprise out as 'unbelief.' The scientific investigation of tradition, including religious witness, to test the genuine reality behind it, is our spiritual fate and inescapable task. We cannot take refuge in a dogma of the Bible, in the concept of canon—in other words, we cannot take refuge in the authority of the Church that set up the canon. To do so would be nothing else than to surrender the true humanity, that is, the historicity of Jesus."

An openness toward human reality, a faith accountable to the world, a missionary view of the Christian message: together they suggest a further main theme in Althaus' theological work, and that is the confrontation of revelation with the problems of human thought and action—the apologetics and ethics of the Christian faith. His slim volume *Outline of Ethics (Grundriss der Ethik)* here lays the foundation. Once again, revelation does not appear as a doctrine, a legal injunction to act; rather, the commandment of the revealed God stresses the imperatives that arise in human reality. Ethics, then, is concerned with this human reality.

"At stake here is reality such as *conscience* understands it, the reality, that is, which is our unconditional concern and obligation. This consciousness-perspective of reality, the presupposition of theological ethics, opens up to us in no other way except through *God's revelation.* That is the theological meaning of 'reality.' God's reality is the ground of all reality, and hence the measure of what we must respect as imperative reality."

We are placed, then, under an obligation of conscience to understand the imperatives of our present human life in the light of God's command. Althaus fully accepted that obligation. Again and again he spoke his mind on cultural, legal, moral, and political issues—arguing not from some abstract natural law but from the concrete responsibility which seeks to discover God's will from case to case in the tasks at hand. He is aware, of course, that we can never see God's will in reality face to face. Conscience can be led astray, conscience can err. Although it would be sinful to act counter to the insights of conscience from case to case, yet conscience because of this fallibility must ever be open to better insight, better knowledge. Indeed, Althaus himself never hesitated to retract any statement which he had come to see as an error. He writes:

"Conscientiousness turns into sin when it loses humility, when it asserts its views to be definitive, and shuts its doors to God's new teaching. On the other hand, God's teaching can take root only in conscientiousness, in the unbroken will to accept and obey what from case to case it sees to be right. The obedient conscience, therefore, includes both loyalty and flexibility, both resolve and openness, as one."

Besides the ethical problems there is an endless variety of problems on which a missionary-minded theology must take a stand: problems of ideology, of the interpretation of human existence in poetry and myth, of guidance in basic attitudes and rules of conduct. Althaus met the demands from these quarters with a staggering number of pamphlets and papers, and yet never neglected his large scholarly books. A partial bibliography of his writings, down to 1957, lists 349 titles dealing with almost every area of theology but especially with ethics and apologetics. Many of them bear the mark of the occasion to which they were addressed. That does not lessen their theological value; on the contrary, through them, theology assumes its true essence as a theology of faith. For according to Althaus, no theology possesses the unconditional truth of the Gospel in the form of a never changing doctrine. For him, as for the great reformers, theology is *theologia viatorum*—a theology of voyagers who must describe their travels in faith ever anew.

Althaus discusses the same truth in what is perhaps his most important book, the great work on *Eschatology* (*Die Letzten Dinge*). Twice he revised it from end to end, in grateful acceptance of criticism he had received, until he found nothing further to improve; in this he himself gave a demonstration of that truth. But more important: in the discussion of resurrection and eternal life, where theological propositions exceed and set limits to the powers of the human imagination, the willingness to verify theological tradition by the measure of human reality must meet its final test. Althaus, accordingly, considers it impossible to 'biblicize,' that is, to derive his statements about the after-life from a system of biblical statements. Equally impossible appears the attempt of philosophy which would derive statements about eternity from a contemplation of the values that shape man's spiritual life. Such a philosophy, over-reaching itself in its self-will, encounters nothing but the eternal, while Christian faith comes face to face with the Eternal One, who in His sovereignty meets and lays claim to the life of man. The theology of life after death can start only from this God's claim to the life of man, never from mere postulates of immortality. Althaus writes:

"We know nothing about the immortality of the 'soul,' only about the immortality of our relation to God. Our certainty of a new life arising out of death is grounded, therefore, in the certainty of God's relation to us, in hearing Him speaking to us, in two ways: in our experience of God's judgment, and in our experience of God's love."

The discussion of what lies beyond death would seem to set an end to all testing of theological propositions against reality—and indeed today's critical theologians are inclined to fall silent at this point. But Althaus does not feel free, here no more than elsewhere, to shun the preacher's task of bearing clear and concrete witness to God's reality that conquers death. At the point at which theological language seems bound to grow unworldly, disembodied, purely verbal—at just that point Althaus achieves the greatest power and fullness of language, and in the same breath his greatest scope and worldly concreteness. God lays His claim to this concrete worldly life of man; this very fact renders the concept of worldliness problematical for Althaus:

"Faith in the unworldliness of the Kingdom has nothing to do with a surrender of the created earthly world in return for a beyond called 'heaven' that lies beyond the created world. The Kingdom is not beyond the world of creation, it is beyond the world of sin and death. The Kingdom of the beyond enters this our reality. According to the New Testament, the Kingdom is a new eon, but the eon now and the eon to come are not like earth and heaven, not like a 'Here' and a 'Beyond'; rather, the new eon irrupts into our world, into history, and transforms them. Religious language may go on calling the world to come by the name of 'heaven,' as long as it is clearly understood that what is meant is merely its transcendence of the 'form of this world,' the world of sin and death, but not the abandonment of this world as the world, the creation, of God."

The Christian hope for the future world of God knows that that future world irrupts into this present world and takes possession. This is why Christian speech about God's world here does not fall speechless, but now too takes possession of this world in order to bear witness, in its terms, of the world of God. God's world is the beauty, the fulness, the splendor of this world, when God by His act frees it of the aspect of sin and the threat of death. Yes, even death itself is by faith deprived of its terror of the end, the judgment, the great upheaval. To Althaus, even death turns into a gift of God's world, which Christian faith experiences in the death of Christ.

"In giving the gift of mortality, God gives occasion for the highest human proof of love. Therefore we must recognize His love in the order of mortality. . . . In that mortality lies the pre-condition of total sacrifice, and so we must accept it in gratitude and love as we must accept God's good and gracious creative will in our whole life. . . . God's creative will is visible and becomes reality in Christ. For by that He gave proof of His love, that He laid down His life for us. . . . Love must have death to become fully real. In this way the creative meaning of human death is revealed through Christology."

In the face of the loving God death loses its terror and becomes for Althaus the completion of man's divine service.

"To die willingly means to accept God as God, to honor Him as the One who alone has immortality, who is God by the very fact that He gives us life and has the right to take it back. We die to honor God. This is true all the more because He wants to be praised through our faith, and nothing calls for faith as much as dying. There is no other divine service like that in which man, with all his hopes and desires, with all his thirst for life, obediently submits to God's call to die, and in his own end relies on God, commits himself into the hands of the Invisible when all things visible fade away. The perfection of the Son of God lies in His obedience to death. So we, too, must joyfully accept as God's grace that He calls us to the divine service of dying. By our death we are allowed to give praise to God."

His eschatology leads Althaus to the dogmatic theme that is his very own. It is the point that shows most compellingly the inseparable connection of dogma and faith, doctrine and life, thought and experience. Here the tasks of the dogmatist, the preacher, the apologist, the pastor, the exegete, and the patrologist fuse into the one task of giving voice to the Christian faith in living, convincing, truthful, comforting words. The final sentences of his eschatology, spoken from the high vantage point of hope, hark

63

back to this position where man must prove himself from day to day:

"We cannot wait for the new world and the new mankind, for the Kingdom and for eternal life, in any other way but 'in practice,' that is, by our quest in this our world, by deeply suffering its misery and doing battle with it. Christian hope is not a theory—it takes the whole man. To wait is a whole stance of life. To wait means to suffer, to search, to labor, to live with eyes open through the conflict between Christ and world, to push on to the outermost limit, to knock on closed doors. If we do not forever in prayer and in work strain to escape from captivity into the endless freedom and splendor of the Kingdom of God, if we do not do battle against the misery and injustice on earth, if we do not struggle for sanctification, if we do not work to bring together and prepare the community of God—how will we know what it means to wait for the Lord! Hope is truly alive only in the act, daily renewed, of our soul and our whole life."

PAUL TILLICH

BY

Horst Bürkle

Paul Tillich: Philosopher and Theologian, is the title of a recently published biography of this man. He does indeed seem to belong equally to both disciplines. Born the son of a Lutheran pastor, he received the degree of doctor of philosophy and turned immediately to working on his theological licentiate. In the First World War he served as an army chaplain. After the war he joined the theological faculty of the University of Berlin. Professorships at Marburg, Dresden, and Leipzig followed. In 1929 he was called to Frankfurt to succeed Max Scheler who had held the chair of philosophy and sociology. With the advent of Nazism in 1933 he was dismissed—and Reinhold Niebuhr called him to New York. Once again he is both a philosopher and a theologian: he is a member of the philosophical faculty of Columbia University, as well as that of Union Theological Seminary.

The years that followed were years of vast activity. His influence grew beyond the borders of the United States. He still publishes and lectures extensively. Since 1948 his travels have been taking him to Europe more and more frequently; he has visited Marburg, Berlin, Hamburg. At about the same time (1948) he brought out the first volume of his *Systematic Theology,* summing up his work, scattered until then in nearly a hundred separate essays.

The stages of Tillich's career reflect to some degree the character of his thought, which never shied away from crossing over into other areas nor feared to meet the tension between existence and revelation, knowledge and faith. His very heart is in that tension— a quality that places him among the great in the history of Christian theology, those who each in his own time succeeded in relating the reality in which they lived to the reality opened up to them by faith.

It must be admitted that Tillich's enterprise has often been misunderstood. The liberals among the theologians have never thought him liberal enough. The orthodox and neo-orthodox wings of today's academic theology take scandal in the structures of his thought because these correspond to no traditional scheme. His theological system will not let itself be fitted into any of the historically developed groupings, although some genuinely Lutheran traces may perhaps be discerned in it. But he is basically an ecumenical theologian who has, for once, succeeded again in seeing and understanding the immense coherence between things that essentially belong together. At one place or another in his work he renders justice to every true confessional formulation and theological trend in its partial validity, and pays respect to its intention. In this respect Tillich differs from many other theologians of the day, who stress their own direction and narrow their own presuppositions to a degree that blocks their understanding of all other systems. This is the very point at which the great significance of Tillich's theology emerges. The extent to which his thought manages to absorb and interpret the intellectual currents of our time is striking; and he does the same for a number of theological formulations: Tillich will incorporate them insofar as they are expressions of a specific intellectual development. From the very start of his writing career he has shown again and again his astounding capacity to absorb into his theological view the reality that passes before his eyes. The titles alone of his numerous books and papers tell the story: he deals with economics and politics; socialism and sociology; education and ethics; psychology and psychotherapy. On principle there is no segment of life that does not have a place in his theology. This draws him into intellectual dialogue with men from many other areas of life and scholarship, who sense the understanding with which Tillich comes to their encounter. Here lies the secret of what Tillich in another context calls the "Protestant principle":

"It is a presupposition . . . that no realm of life can be understood and formed without a relation to the Protestant principle, as it is a presupposition also that Protestantism cannot be undersood and formed except in relation to all forms of life."

The first impulse to practice theology in such a way that it would always keep in view the full reality of experience, that impulse Tillich received from his teacher Martin Käehler. He learned from Käehler that no theological endeavor must ever lack that correlation. The more closely theology kept in touch with the experience of the reality surrounding it, and the more it made the problems of the day its own, the better did it carry out its proper task:

"*The task of theology is mediation,* mediation between the eternal criterion of truth as it is manifest in the picture of Jesus as the Christ and the changing experiences of individuals and groups, their varying questions and their categories of perceiving reality. If the mediating task of theology is rejected, theology itself is rejected; for the term 'theo-logy' implies, as such, a mediation, namely, between the mystery, which is the *theos,* and the understanding, which is *logos.*"

On this assumption it is possible for Tillich once again to open the conversation among the various theological trends and positions. For him, the very essence of theology is in this conversation, in which the divers points of view discourse about their common object of inquiry.

"One of the methods of mediation in theology is called 'dialectical.' Dialectics is the way of seeking for truth by talking with others from different points of view, through 'Yes' and 'No,' until a 'Yes' has been reached which is hardened in the fire of many 'No's' and which unites the elements of truth promoted in the discussion. It is most unfortunate that in recent years the name 'dialectical theology' has been applied to a theology that is strongly opposed to any kind of dialectics and mediation and that constantly repeats the 'Yes' to its own and the 'No' to any other position. This has made it difficult to use the term dialectical to denote theological movements of a really dialectical, that is a mediating, character; and it has resulted in the cheap and clumsy way of dividing all theologians into naturalists and supernaturalists, or into liberals and orthodox. As a theologian who sometimes has been dealt with in this easy way of labeling somebody (for instance, by being called a 'neo-supernaturalist'), I want to state unambiguously my conviction that these divisions are completely obsolete in the actual work which is done today by every theologian who takes the mediating or dialectical task of theology seriously. Therefore, I would not be ashamed to be called a 'theologian of mediation,' which, for me, would simply mean: a 'theo-logian.' "

This liberation of theological endeavor to pursue changing inquiries prompted by new realities is balanced, in Tillich's thought, by a strict adherence to the Reformation doctrine of justification. That doctrine remains for him the starting point of every Protestant theology. But he makes clear that this, the heart and center of his thought, must itself be also understood in a new way. He senses the embarrassment of modern man who does not know what to do with this insight of the Reformation. Today, Tillich assumes, it is hardly understood any longer and to make it at all intelligible has become almost impossible. "This whole complex of ideas," he writes, "which for more than a century— not so very long ago—was discussed in every household and workshop, in every market and country inn of Germany, is now scarcely understandable even to our most intelligent scholars. We have here a breaking-down of tradition that has few parallels."

But Tillich is prepared to go along into the changed world. This step leads him to the point which is the very seat of modern man's temptation, where modern man awaits the answer that a theology of justification through God can give him. Tillich sees that the principle of justification by faith refers not only to the religious-ethical but also to the religious-intellectual life. Not only he who is in sin but also he who is in doubt is justified by faith.

"The situation of doubt, even of doubt about God, need not separate us from God. There is faith in every serious doubt, namely, the faith in the truth as such, even if the only truth we can express is our lack of truth. But if this is experienced in its depth and as an ultimate concern, the divine is present; and he who doubts in such an attitude is 'justified' in his thinking."

His interpretation of the doctrine of justification allows Tillich to attack the very core of most men's real embarrassment: the agonizing question of the meaning of this life. Doubt at this point means to him an indication of the sense in which man is still alive. Here, in the experience of being altogether cut off from God, he who is struck by such doubt learns God's presence. Tillich stresses again and again that it is this radical and universal interpretation of the justification doctrine which has made of him a conscious Protestant. What Luther came to realize through his temptation as a sinner, and through his question for the God of grace, is here applied in a new way to man tempted by the question of the meaning of existence itself. Tillich had sought close communication with the philosophy of our time, in order to learn what basic questions about man's existence we are faced with today. The mere acceptance of some traditional self-image and self-understanding was for Tillich fully as impossible as the mere repetition of pre-formulated answers of the past. His radical and universal interpretation of the doctrine of justification by faith points to further decisive consequences of his theology.

"If it is valid," he writes, "no realm of life can exist without relation to something unconditional, to an ultimate concern. Religion, like God, is omnipresent; its presence, like that of God, can be forgotten, neglected, denied. But it is always effective, giving inexhaustible depth to life and inexhaustible meaning to every cultural creation."

Tillich can now turn to the history of religions and of Christianity, to its fullest extent, and give it a new interpretation. His re-appraisals and re-interpretations that now follow reach far back into intellectual history—something that in Protestantism had not been customary before. He contrasts the theonomous epochs of the early Middle Ages with the heteronomy of the late Middle Ages and the autonomy of self-conscious modern humanism. The transparency of the divers cultural periods is recognized again, and they are once again seen, through their creations, as vessels of what is essential—vessels of spiritual contents.

"The Protestant principle as derived from the doctrine of justification through faith rejects heteronomy (represented by the doctrine of papal infallibility) as well as self-complacent autonomy (represented by secular humanism). It demands a self-transcending autonomy, or theonomy."

To understand why Tillich, after the First World War, became one of the founders of the religious-socialist movement, we must look once again to the Protestant principle. With the help of that principle he undertakes to achieve a new understanding of a historical situation verging on chaos:

"History became the central problem of my theology and philosophy because of the historical reality as I found it when I returned from the First World War: a chaotic Germany and Europe; the end of the period of the victorious *bourgeoisie* and of the nineteenth-century way of life; the split between the Lutheran churches and the proletariat; the gap between the transcendent message of traditional Christianity and the immanent hopes of the revolutionary movements. The situation demanded interpretation as well as action. . . . My entrance into the religious-socialist movement meant for me the definite break with philosophical idealism and theological transcendentalism."

He does not stop with that break. The discarded views are replaced by a positive answer, a new interpretation of the events of the times that gives them meaning: a theological interpretation by which Tillich demonstrates that no understanding of contemporary history is possible if the question of God is left out. The link is his new insight into the meaning of what the New Testament calls "*kairos*":

" 'Kairos,' the 'fullness of time,' according to the New Testament use of the word, describes the moment in which the eternal breaks into the temporal, and the temporal is prepared to receive it. What happened in the one unique kairos, the appearance of Jesus as the Christ, i.e., as the center of history, may happen in a derived form again and again in the process of time, creating centers of lesser importance on which the periodization of history is dependent. . . ."

"The Protestant principle demands a method of interpreting history in which the critical transcendence of the divine over against conservatism and utopianism is strongly expressed and in which, at the same time, the creative omnipresence of the divine in the course of history is concretely indicated."

Again and again Tillich turns the critical function of his theological thought upon the Church itself. He accepts the doctrine that prevailed between Luther and Melanchthon as the correct understanding of grace: justification by grace alone, which in our relation to God makes us dependent upon God alone and in no way upon ourselves. From this position he criticizes two misunderstandings of the meaning of the Church:

"The interest of early Protestantism was, however, so much centered around individual justification that the idea of a 'Gestalt of grace' in our historical existence could not develop. This development was also prevented by the fact that the Catholic church considered itself as the body of objective grace, thus discrediting the idea of a 'Gestalt of grace' for Protestant consciousness. It is obvious that the Protestant principle cannot admit any identification of grace with a visible reality, not even with the Church on its visible side. But the negation of a visible 'Gestalt of grace' does not imply the negation of the concept as such. The Church in its spiritual quality, as an object of faith, is a 'Gestalt of grace.' "

There is no mistaking the fact that Tillich here calls for a form of the Church. He strives to recover proper sacramental thinking in the Protestant camp. Calling on the findings of psychotherapy, he reassigns to symbols their indispensable place in the life of the Church:

"The decrease in sacramental thinking and feeling in the churches of the Reformation and in the American denominations is appalling. Nature has lost its religious meaning and is excluded from participation in the power of salvation; the sacraments have lost their spiritual power and are vanishing in the consciousness of most Protestants; the Christ is interpreted as a religious personality and not as the basic sacramental reality, the 'New Being.' The Protestant protest has rightly destroyed the magical elements in Catholic sacramentalism but has wrongly brought to the verge of disappearance the sacramental foundation of Christianity and with it the religious foundation of the protest itself.... Protestants often confuse essential symbols with accidental signs. They often are unaware of the numinous power inherent in genuine symbols, words, acts, persons, things. They have replaced the great wealth of symbols appearing in the Christian tradition by rational concepts, moral laws, and subjective emotions. This also was a consequence of the Protestant protest against the superstitious use of the traditional symbols in Roman Catholicism and in all paganism. But here also the protest has endangered its own basis."

Behind this statement stands Tillich's experience with Protestant preaching, which seemed to him to place almost exclusive emphasis on the individual personality. The individual was being overburdened and isolated with the demand for continuous, conscious decisions and experiences. What the Reformation had understood the experience of faith to be—an immediate and personal attitude toward God—seemed to have withered down into an individualism that threatened to degenerate into a personality cult. Modern psychology and sociology helped Tillich to find the needed corrective. His theology absorbs the findings of medical psychology with its rediscovery of the unconscious, and its insights into the unconscious drives of the mass psyche, and the evidence of sociology concerning the deep involvement of the individual in the society of which he is unconditionally a member. His main concern is whether the Church can keep step with our age, whether it is capable of making the changes that are due.

"Personal experience, the intimate observation of many individuals, the knowledge provided by psychotherapy, the trend of the younger generation in Europe toward the vital and pre-rational side of the individual and social life, the urgent desire for more community and authority and for powerful and dominating symbols—all these seemed to prove that the Protestant-humanist ideal of personality has been undermined and that the Protestant cultus and its personal and social ethics have to undergo a far-reaching transformation. This impression was and is supported by the general development of Western civilization toward more collectivistic forms of political and economic life. The demand for a basic security in social, as well as in spiritual, respects has superseded (though not removed) the liberal demand for liberty. And this demand can no longer be suppressed, for it is rooted in the deepest levels of the men of today, of personalities and groups. . . . The question of whether Protestantism as a determining historical factor will survive is, above all, the question of whether it will be able to adapt itself to the new situation; it is the question of whether Protestantism, in the power of its principle, will be able to dissolve its amalgamation with bourgeois ideology and reality and create a synthesis, in criticism and acceptance, with the new forces that have arisen in the present stage of a revolutionary transformation of man and his world."

Tillich has taken the first steps to deal with the problem. But even his beginnings have shown clearly the direction in which a new Protestant social doctrine must develop. To Tillich, the assignment means that he must work out an ethic for a changing world.

" 'Changing world' . . . does not mean the general change implied in everything that exists; neither does it mean the continuous change connected more fundamentally with history than with nature; but it points to the fact that we are living in a historical period, characterized by a radical and revolutionary transformation of one historical era into another one. Nobody can doubt this fact seriously, and nobody who has even a minimum of historical understanding would do so after what has occurred in recent years. We are in the midst of a world revolution affecting every section of human existence, forcing upon us a new interpretation of life and the world."

What about an ethics in this connection? Does it represent a realm above change? Is it suprahistorical in its foundation, and its commands? Or does it follow the stream of historical becoming, and will it be transformed as rapidly as the other realms of life are transformed in our days? If the latter be the case, what authority, what power of shaping human life, is left to it? It is in the tensions between these extremes that Tillich attempts to find a new theological foundation of ethics. He moves from the alternative of absolutism, which must fall before any genuine change in history, to that of a relativism which adopts change as its own principle, and rejects both.

"Is there a possible solution beyond the alternative of an absolutism that breaks down in every radical change of history and a relativism that makes change itself the ultimate principle? I think there is, and I think it is implied in the basis of Christian ethics, namely, in the principle of love, in the sense of the Greek word *agape*. This is not said in an apologetic interest for Christianity, but it is said under the urge of the actual problem in our present world situation. Love, *agape,* offers a principle of ethics which maintains an eternal, unchangeable element but makes its realization dependent on continuous acts of a creative intuition."

Here Tillich's interpretation of the historical *kairos* touches upon *agape,* his fundamental principle of ethics:

"Ethics in a changing world must be understood as ethics of the kairos. The answer to the demand for ethics in a changing world is ethics determined by the kairos; but only love is able to appear in every kairos. Law is not able to because law is the attempt to impose something which belonged to a special time on all times."

"Love is above law, also above the natural law in Stoicism and the super-natural law in Catholicism. You *can* express it as a law, you can say as Jesus and the apostles did: 'Thou shalt love'; but in so doing you know that this is a paradoxical way of speaking, indicating that the ultimate principle of ethics, which, on the one hand, is an unconditional command, is, on the other hand, the power breaking through all commands. And just this ambiguous character of love enables it to be the solution of the question of ethics in a changing world. If you look at the principles of natural law as embodied in the Bill of Rights, you will find that, taken as the concrete embodiments of the principle of love in a special situation, they are great and true and powerful; they represent love by establishing freedom and equal rights against willfulness and suppression and against the destruction of the dignity of human beings. But, taken as eternal laws and applied legalistically to different situations, for instance, to the early Middle Ages or the decay and transformation of economic capitalism, these principles become bad ideologies used for the maintenance of decaying institutions and powers. This is the reason for the extremely profound struggle of Paul and Luther against the 'Law' and for their insistence on the mortifying consequences of the law and the vivifying of love. *Love alone can transform itself according to the concrete demands of every individual and social situation without losing its eternity and dignity and unconditional validity.* Love can adapt itself to every phase of a changing world."

It sounds almost as though Tillich were proposing here an ultimate reduction of theology to the bare principle of love—a principle altogether lacking in final concreteness. But a look at his publications will show much more clearly than do our short excerpts what a wealth of correlations opens up for the theologian who dares expose the dynamic content of his message to reality. It is indeed a daring enterprise. How much simpler it would be to adhere to tried and true, though traditional Christian formulations and thought structures. Nothing is easier than the mere repetition, the simple following along, that avoids all the unavoidable—the trouble of making ideas of your own. In this age when it is fashionable once more to use Christian formulae, Tillich's thought is like the tearing down of false claims and facades. And that is his intention: to keep the Church from losing sight of the world into which it has been sent, and from taking refuge in a cloud-cuckoo-land of doctrines that no longer bear any relation to life.

On the other hand, he is also concerned with a world and an age in which many people no longer know what to do with this phenomenon, the Church—an indifference arising from the fact that no longer does anyone expect help from the Church in dealing with the problems posed by life itself. To correlate the two—God, and man in his worldliness—in an indissoluble fusion, is the aim of Tillich's theology. "Method of correlation" is what he calls this concept crucial to his thinking.

"The divine-human relationship is a correlation also in its cognitive side. Symbolically speaking, God answers man's questions, and under the impact of God's answers man asks them. Theology formulates the questions implied in human existence, and theology formulates the answers implied in divine self-manifestation under the guidance of the questions implied in human existence. This is a circle which drives man to a point where question and answer are not separated."

If we keep our eyes firmly on this correlation, it is no longer possible to make unqualified, flat statements about God and Christianity. Only that remains valid which has been understood because it was first perceived as God's necessary answer. The *word* is opposed to the tide of words that have lost their currency. Truths which are merely known are set straight by the truth that reveals itself in the perception of the *logos,* because that truth is at the same time experienced as a living force:

"The answers implied in the event of revelation are meaningful only in so far as they are in correlation with questions concerning the whole of our existence, with existential questions. Only those who have experienced the shock of transistoriness, the anxiety in which they are aware of their finitude, the threat of nonbeing, can understand what the notion of God means. Only those who have experienced the tragic ambiguities of our historical existence and have totally questioned the meaning of existence can understand what the symbol of the Kingdom of God means. Revelation answers questions which have been asked and always will be asked because they are 'we ourselves.' Man is the question he asks about himself, before any question has been formulated."

Tillich has been accused of making God, in this correlation, dependent on man's prerogative to ask the question. That is a misunderstanding. It is God Himself who prepares the question since He shares in bringing about the historical situation from which alone the question springs.

"The Christian message provides the answers to the questions implied in human existence. These answers are contained in the revelatory events on which Christianity is based.... Their content cannot be derived from the questions, that is, from an analysis of human existence. They are 'spoken' *to* human existence from beyond it. Otherwise they would not be answers, for the question is human existence itself."

We need not remember more than these words from Tillich's work to realize wherein lies his importance for theology—and emphatically not only for Protestant theology. He, Tillich, made the much needed attempt to create the conditions that would allow us once again to understand and believe in the message of Jesus as the Christ. There are, on the one hand, churches that are content to recite a ready dogma, and on the other hand there is a world grown worldly that tries to get by with pseudo-answers to the most pressing questions of existence because it cannot grasp God's answer. This is the chasm that alarmed Tillich, and from the start he was passionately concerned to bridge it. The response he got has confirmed the urgency of his attempt. Hardly any other theologian has had as much dialogue with and cooperation from artists, scientists, writers and philosophers, of the Old World as well as the New. His sermons show his basic theological insights into the practice of proclamation and preachment. And the sum of his theology is now before us in the three volumes of his *Systematic Theology*.

What sets Tillich apart is the unconditional character of his historical thinking. He has, for once, shown again an understanding for growth and for change. To use a phrase coined by Rosenstock-Huessy, Tillich may make it possible for us again not only to catch up with the modern world but to *outrun* it.

REINHOLD NIEBUHR

BY

Heinrich-Constantin Rohrbach

"I cannot and do not claim to be a theologian. I have never been very competent in the nice points of pure theology. I have been frequently challenged by the stricter sects of theologians in Europe to prove that my interests were theological rather than practical or 'apologetic,' but I have always refused to enter a defense, partly because I thought the point was well taken and partly because the distinction did not interest me."

With these remarks Reinhold Niebuhr introduces a volume in which a score of leading scholars—theologians, sociologists, philosophers and political scientists from the United States and Europe, Protestants, Catholics, and Jews—devote long critical essays to the discussion of his work. The mere existence of the book shows Niebuhr's extraordinary importance for theology in our time.

The best approach to his writings is to recall the living experience that went into their making.

Niebuhr grew up in the America of the turn of the century, the golden age of unbroken prosperity in a country which had seen no foreign war within the memory of living men. It was a proud age, filled with the conviction that democracy made men good, and that those new sciences—psychology and sociology—would overcome man's evil inclinations, once so dangerous, much as the machine had yoked the mountains and spanned the vastness of a continent. God remained of interest only as someone who had presumably arranged everything so well that America had come to be "God's country."

In this intellectual climate, then, young Niebuhr, born in Missouri as the son of an historian from Germany, Barthold Georg Niebuhr, and reared in a home filled with the spirit of the great Adolf Harnack, began his theological career. Characteristically, he declined the prospects of academic life, for what attracted him more was the practical work of a parish pastor, and not as much, the fine points of systematic theology. In 1915 he was assigned to a very small new parish in Detroit, then a rapidly expanding city. In the thirteen years of his pastorate his parish had grown to eight hundred members.

"During my pastorate of thirteen years," he writes, "Detroit was to expand from a half to a million and a half population. The resulting facts determined my development more than any books I may have read."

"The social realities of a rapidly expanding industrial community," he continues, "before the time of the organization of the workers, and under the leadership of a group of resourceful engineers who understood little about human relations, forced me to reconsider the highly moralistic creed which I had accepted as tantamount to the Christian faith."

All the world at that time admired the generosity of Henry Ford's five-dollars-a-day wage; but Niebuhr, who knew the economic plight of the automobile workers in his own parish, openly dissented by publishing a highly critical article, "How philanthropic is Henry Ford?" Heavy pressure occasionally brought to bear upon the churches by the Detroit Board of Commerce, to discourage invitations to labor convention speakers from unions branded as communistic, taught him "the irrelevance of the mild moralistic idealism, which I had identified with the Christian faith, to the power realities of our modern technical society."

The pastor was also deeply stirred by what he saw of the day-to-day life and death among the common people of his parish.

"Two old ladies were dying shortly after I assumed charge of the parish. They were both equally respectable members of the congregation. But I soon noted that their manner of facing death was strikingly dissimilar. One old lady was too preoccupied with self, too aggrieved that Providence should not have taken account of her virtue in failing to protect her against a grievous illness, to be able to face death with any serenity. While my own simple idealism would have scarcely been equal to the test of facing the ultimate issue, I found myself deeply disturbed by the fact that faith was evidently of so little account in the final test.

"The other old lady had brought up a healthy and wholesome family, though her husband was subject to periodic fits of insanity which forced her to be the breadwinner as well as homemaker. Just as her two splendid daughters had finished their training and were eager to give their mother a secure and quiet evening of life, she was found to be suffering from cancer. I stood weekly at her bedside while she told me what passages of scripture, what psalms and what prayers to read to her; most of them expressed gratitude for all the mercies of God which she had received in life. She faced death with the utmost peace of soul.

"I relearned the essentials of the Christian faith at the bedside of that nice old soul. I appreciated that the ultimate problem of human existence is the peril of sin and death in the way that these two perils are so curiously compounded; for we fall into sin by trying to evade or to conquer death or our own insignificance, of which death is the ultimate symbol. The Christian faith holds out the hope that our fragmentary lives will be completed in a total and larger plan than any which we control or comprehend; and that a part of the completion is the forgiveness of sin, that is, the forgiveness of the evils into which we fall by our frantic efforts to complete our own lives or to endow them with significance."

Against the background of such experiences began Niebuhr's

merciless criticism, aimed at the very roots of the intellectual, moral, and religious attitudes of his nation. He dug deeper and deeper into the presuppositions of its blustering optimism, rooted in the Enlightenment, the French Revolution, and the Renaissance. He drew upon the writers of the Reformation, on Augustine, finally on the apostle Paul, the Gospels, and the Old Testament to show the stark contradiction between the proud convictions of liberalism and the profound insight of the Bible into the discord in the mind of man. His critical studies of American intellectual and theological history—enriched by his experience with the social struggles of the industrial metropolis in which he lived and with the problems of the people to whom he was pastor—made Niebuhr the champion of biblical realism against the cheap faith in progress that dominated church and academy, government and industry.

"My early writings were all characterized by a critical attitude toward the 'liberal' world view, whether expressed in secular or in Christian terms. For years I commuted, as it were, between ecclesiastical and academic communities. I found each with a sense of superiority over the other either because it possessed, or had discarded, the Christian faith. But this contest was ironic because the viewpoints of the two communities were strikingly similar, and both were obviously irrelevant to the ultimate realities, whether in terms of mankind's collective behavior or in terms of individual man's ultimate problems."

In 1928, after thirteen years in his Detroit parish, Niebuhr was invited to join the theological faculty of Columbia University in New York. By now, countless lectures and many important articles in leading magazines of every kind had made him known far beyond the borders of the United States. The topics of his writings ranged from "The Threat of the R.O.T.C." to the pointed question of "What are the Churches Advertising?"

Until the call to Columbia University, Niebuhr's commitments as lecturer and preacher had kept him from the quiet of the scholar's study. But even now, a professor of theology, he remains the relentless critic of the ethics and social life of church and society. From his first major work, *Moral Man and Immoral Society,* down to his most recent works, his main concern was not so much with a systematic presentation of Christian faith in its timeless validity as with the actual proclamation of the Christian faith in the intellectual discussion of his time—and that is, of our time.

It can be said with confidence that it was Reinhold Niebuhr who after the First World War made theology once again a fit subject for conversation among thoughtful Americans. He commanded a hearing because he heeded, analyzed, and critically applied the thought of psychologists, sociologists, historians, political philosophers and practicing politicians—and that with an intellectual astuteness far from customary in the Church. Paul Scherer, commenting on Niebuhr's sermons, wrote:

"From hearing him, professors and students alike, doctors, lawyers, politicians, authors, editors, long unaccustomed to take seriously anything that emanated from the pulpit, began to read his books and discuss his theology."

By sermon, publication and lecture Niebuhr carried his remorseless attack to the very walls of a stronghold in which, he felt, the churches and other social groupings of the nation were concealing themselves from the call of God. The horrors of the First World War, and perhaps even more the crumbling of America's faith in progress under the impact of the Great Depression, with all its misery, opened the hearts of many to Niebuhr's words.

Still, Niebuhr's battle against the whole century-old fabric of philosophical and Protestant traditions in America was anything but easy.

"In America, where the viewpoints of the French Enlightenment and the idealism of sectarian Christianity became strangely compounded, the achievements of a liberal culture and society seemed very impressive. It had emancipated the individual from irrelevant social restraints and inequalities; it had unloosed the initiative of the common man.... It had established a democratic political order and vanquished ancient tyrannies.... The wide opportunities of an advancing frontier and of a consistently expanding economy had destroyed class distinctions, and had made the 'liberty, equality, and fraternity' of the French Revolutions seem to be a present reality and achievement. The sentimental views of human nature were so endemic in a liberal culture, and its democratic achievements were so great, that it became popular to regard mild illusions about human virtue as prerequisites for democratic success."

While the fundamentalists accused Niebuhr of sacrilegious criticism of the Bible word, so-called progressives in and outside the Church charged him with a grim pessimism because he pointed out relentlessly that all human action was inescapably streaked with evil. Yet Niebuhr could keep an audience spellbound with his keen analyses of the intellectual movements of the day. Many of his sermons have dealt incisively with a whole cluster of such movements.

Even Niebuhr himself is unable to tell whether it was the critical analysis of contemporary philosophy that led him to a deeper understanding of biblical teachings, or whether it was the other way around:

"It is difficult to know whether the criticism of both liberal and Marxist views of human nature and history was prompted by a profounder understanding of the biblical faith; or whether this understanding was prompted by the refutation of the liberal and Marxist faith by the tragic facts of contemporary history which included two world wars and the encounter of a liberal culture with two idolatrous tyrannies, first Nazism and then Communism."

Even the two massive and most systematic works of Niebuhr, published between 1941 and 1949, *The Nature and Destiny of Man* and *Faith and History,* maintain their sharp focus upon the meaning of the Christian faith in man's quest for the purpose of human existence and human history. He never developed a systematic doctrine of the Christian view of God and Christ. For many years his work drew down upon him criticism from all sides. It is, therefore, perhaps in keeping with the apologetic character of Niebuhr's work, which expounds the Christian faith by means of a running controversy, that his position is presented through such criticism. His central concern should emerge all the more clearly.

Niebuhr has been especially criticized for offering man's radical freedom as the one and only ultimately valid mark of man's humanity. Some critics doubted the very existence of such a freedom, in the face of the evidence of natural science, for the countless ways in which man is determined by his environment. Others wanted to discern man's specific humanity in some other trait, of somewhat more positive content than this radical freedom—a freedom of which Niebuhr said expressly that its results could be positive as easily as negative. Niebuhr replied:

"When we speak of man's 'radical' freedom, we do not suggest that his creaturely limitations should be obscured: he is subject to the necessities of nature, of sexual and racial limitations, of geography and climate, and of the dominant drives of his own creaturely nature. His freedom must be defined as 'radical' to indicate that, when man rises above the necessities and limits of nature, he is not inevitably bound in his actions to the norms and universalities of 'reason.' Therefore the growth of his power and freedom over nature does not make for freedom over self and does not automatically make for wider interests and more inclusive harmonies."

Here Niebuhr points to the incontrovertible evidence gathered in the observation of man's individual and social behavior, that man is after all not an object in nature that could be manipulated at will. Nor is man a being whom nothing but his physical nature prevents from developing his mind, which sits inside him like the kernel in the shell, to a condition of pure reason that would automatically give him greater and greater control over his sub-rational impulses.

"The common sense of the traditional man in the street seldom gives way to the illusion that jealousy and envy, which poison even the most personal of human contacts, are no more than a weakness of undisciplined reason. He knows they are temptations afflicting the saint no less than the sinner. Practicing politicians do not look on the strong man's will to power as the last vestige of a barbarism of past ages. All sound political wisdom will attempt to harness and contain that urge for power, to use it, and to render it harmless. No sound economic policy will treat the drive for economic success as a force that is about to vanish from the context of an enlightened mankind. It knows that this drive represents a part of human egoism which must be watched and controlled and transformed for the common good, but which can never be completely suppressed."

Niebuhr, then, contends that man simply cannot be pressed into a system by naturalistic or idealistic or any other categories. The one and only way to speak meaningfully of man is the dramatic, historical, personal manner of the Bible: man is a person; his personality is determined by the personal being of God who created him by making him man.

Niebuhr is well aware that here he disagrees somewhat with Paul Tillich, for decades his friend and colleague at the same seminary. But he maintains, against Tillich, that we must deal with the person of God and with His action in history and in the life of the individual, without seeking the protection and support of an ontology. He answers Tillich:

"Tillich is a great metaphysician, but he will not think too much of my gratitude because he feels that I have not learned the philosophical lessons too well.

"The point at issue between us is the old and yet ever new problem of the relation of faith to reason. I think that is what he means by saying that I have inadequate epistemology. I can find no way of proving by an epistemological method that God, the creator, is revealed as forgiving love in the drama of Christ's life, death, and resurrection. Upon that faith the Christian Church is founded. I think this faith may be validated in experience. . . . But I know of no way of inducing this faith by purely rational argument."

All Christian discourse about God which attempts to make faith in God accessible by calling God the Being Itself, in whom all concrete being is rooted, arouses Niebuhr's distrust: it seems to him to confine God within the categories of human philosophies.

With the same passionate stress upon man's inescapable and un-

85

deniable freedom, Niebuhr counters those critics who assert that the essential humanity of "man the enigma" is a virtue of a specific sort, and not just that freedom:

"The division of man's self into a rational and a natural, or a rational and an instinctual self, leads to a false estimate of human virtue. Man's true self, in its unity that defies all division, is always completely involved in man's every evil act, especially in the evil of egoism. Man always has sufficient mastery over the promptings of nature so that he is not compelled to follow in his actions the promptings of egoism. If he does nonetheless, he is guilty in the general judgment, as he is guilty in the judgment of his own heart. The human self knows itself to be free, but not free to do the good, as Augustine has already seen. Man seeks his own advantage even though he has the freedom to see goals that are superior to his own advantage. This use man makes of freedom is just what makes the increase of human powers so dubious a matter.

"New technological advances begin by serving private interests. A long and painful process is needed to bring them under the control of the larger community or of a superior value. The capacity of the human self to imagine a world larger than his immediate surroundings causes imperialism long before it brings about the limitation, or the equalization by global planning, of this or that private interest.

"The truth of the matter is that human nature is strongly inclined to seek its own advantage, but it also has a dimension of self-knowledge which makes it impossible for man to explain this inclination as merely a fact of nature. On the other hand, whenever man aspires to a higher goal he subtly confuses his own interest with any value to which he aspires."

Another, and in some ways opposite, criticism of Niebuhr's thought comes from so-called dialectical theology which developed in post-First World War Europe and is associated especially with the name of Karl Barth. Niebuhr's European critics object that it is senseless to attempt to lead men to the Christian faith by proving to them how untenable are their various theories on the nature and destiny of man. Faith, these critics say, is always reached only by the grace of God—and Niebuhr's conclusions are rendered inescapable from the outset simply because he starts from the Christian faith as his premise. In consequence, his conclusions must remain unconvincing to anyone who does not also from the outset share that faith.

Niebuhr's response to this criticism, and the way in which he here interprets man's reality in terms of his theology, touch upon new depths in our spiritual-theological situation. From the start, his thought is inspired with the urgency of a faith that has grown from his own contacts with living problems, both personal and social. Niebuhr's defense is the defense of his own way to Christian faith in God. He starts with an admission:

"Since a guiding presupposition, held by faith, acts as a kind of filter for the evidence adduced by experience, it would seem that the theologians are right, and that the modern scientists are wrong in making 'experience' a final arbiter of truth. But the matter is more complex. Guiding presuppositions do indeed color the evidence accumulated by experience; but they do not fully control experience. Presuppositions are like spectacles worn by a nearsighted or myopic man. He cannot see without the spectacles. But if evidence other than that gathered by his sight persuades him that his spectacles are inadequate to help him see what he ought to see, he will change his spectacles."

Niebuhr then proceeds to show how modern secularism and skepticism arise because both the Christian and the Jewish faith seem to be in conflict with the clear evidence of science. And he goes on to show how often science has every right to object to the blindness of the churches toward the rightful claims that science makes within her areas of competence.

But most important, Niebuhr shows that the various philosophical and pseudoscientific answers which are offered as substitutes for the Christian faith are in turn not as free of all presuppositions as they pretend to be. They, too, look at the world through spectacles—spectacles that are patently incapable of showing the world as it is.

87

"The refutation of one set of presuppositions," Niebuhr admits, "does not, of course, rationally compel men to accept an alternative faith. Indeed, we have already confessed that no ultimate sense of the meaning of life is rationally compelling." However, "our apologetic task as proponents of the Christian faith must include the analysis of experience which proves alternative faiths to be mistaken."

Niebuhr conceives the proof as follows:

"There is a dimension of human existence which makes all purely rationalistic interpretations, not to speak of purely naturalistic ones, inadequate. That is the dimension of the eternal in the human spirit, which reveals itself in the capacity of the self to transcend not only the processes of nature but the operations of its own reason, and to stand, as it were, above the structures and coherences of the world. Whenever typically modern men become conscious of this dimension and seek for an interpretation of life which will do justice to this dimension, they elaborate a mystical doctrine in addition to the rationalistic one." He offers Bertrand Russell and Aldous Huxley as examples, and continues: "Man's uneasy conscience, his awareness that in the ultimate instance he is judged for making too much of himself . . . this experience is interpreted by mysticism as a judgment upon all temporal particularity, including man's own individuality. By the definition of mysticism, only the undifferentiated unity of the divine is good, while all particularity is evil. The sin of man is thus absurdly interpreted as an ontological fate, whereas every experience must persuade us that our conscience is uneasy not because we are egos but because we are egotists."

Niebuhr, then, holds that the validity of Christianity is inextricably bound up with the idea of the historical character of man. We can describe man because we can have knowledge of ourselves —but we can never force ourselves into a system, since any system would be of our own making. Man's freedom prevents him from subordinating this freedom to an ontological system. In the last analysis, the concept of man's personality defies rational understanding.

And yet, even though man's reason cannot rationally grasp the concept of God's "personality," and even though the notion of a personal God is repugnant to man's bent toward systematic, rational thought, we must speak of God's *personality*, of His action in the history of mankind through Jesus Christ, and of His action in the life of every single man. The philosophy that God is "absolute," and therefore cannot be a person, "involves itself in an absurdity in the effort to escape an absurdity; it defines God in terms of all kinds of 'absolutes'; but its God lacks the simple majesty of freedom which man undoubtedly has."

Niebuhr thus tries to analyze common human experience as an aid to the understanding of Christian faith. He does not, after all, intend by subterfuge to systematize and degrade the logically inconceivable existence and activity of God—he means to demonstrate only how straight and honest thought will show us that even our own essence is beyond our comprehension.

Accordingly he attacks in turn those orthodox theologians who charge him with excessive indulgence in social and ethical analysis. ". . . a type of religious orthodoxy betrays man's natural skepticism about the truths of love and faith, and also the natural human inclination to avoid a genuine encounter with God, by transmuting *Heilsgeschichte* into a series of miraculous events, miraculously attested, so that one need not appropriate them existentially, but merely claim some special knowledge of historical miracles."

But Niebuhr's supreme concern is that the Christian and the theologian must have the courage to understand and proclaim God's essence, God's will, and God's action of judgment and grace, in his own life as well as in the spiritual movements of his time.

Here Niebuhr's thought may serve us as a guide. The question of what man truly is arises with ever growing urgency in the most divers areas of thought. There are, no doubt, differences between the intellectual situation of Western Germany, where these lines were written, and the intellectual situation of the America of Reinhold Niebuhr. There are still large sections of the American public, among them scientists and theologians of renown, who either maintain an unshakably optimistic liberalism, or else propose a naturalistic explanation of man and man's history. In Europe this turn of mind has by and large vanished, and in the United States, too, it may be on the wane. Physicists, biologists, medical scientists and psychologists have grown quite humble, and at times they admit quite frankly their helplessness to explain man's true nature, and man's future. Pronouncements on the matter now tend to end with a simple period, rather than the proud exclamation mark of firm conviction—and quite often there follows a question mark after the essential, the really important points: who are we, really, and what ought we to be?

Such inquiries, of course, also mean an entirely new inquiry into the Christian faith and what it has to say about the meaning of man's life and history. In order to give the answers we must have the courage Reinhold Niebuhr has displayed, the courage to enter into the thought processes of every kind of intellectual discipline.

And from the very start we must face the fact that our judgment will have to be revised now and again. Niebuhr himself, for example, stood very close to a Marxist interpretation of social justice during certain phases of his protest against the cheap optimism of economic leaders—but today he criticizes Marxism as sharply as he does liberal ideology. Throughout his life, Niebuhr has preferred to expose his understanding of Christianity to the corrective impact of the actual events of the day, even if these were not yet fully assimilable, rather than to withdraw behind the apparently assured dogmatic formulae that say flatly: "This is what the Christian faith says, because it has always said so: Take it or leave it!"

His unflagging willingness to take a position—often a daring position—has made Niebuhr the living symbol of a theological revolution in the United States. Only so could he become a favorite companion of historians and politicians, physicians, psychologists and others. They feel here was a man who thought that he as a theologian had something to say to them, who in turn took pains to study their fields with care, and who had the courage to deal concretely with their problems.

This manner of taking theology seriously into the arena of intellectual issues must exact a price. The price is that theology, by virtue of an infallible interpretation, can no longer pronounce on every detail of the Christian faith. To quote once more Niebuhr's own words:

"I was aware constantly . . . of the problem of why anyone should pay any more attention to what I have to say than to what I once said and have since repudiated or amended." And then, after criticizing himself, he applies his criticism with equal vigor to the whole Church: "We must admit that there is no guarantee in any theology or form of worship that a community of faith, which intends to bring men into contact with the true God, may not be used for essentially idolatrous purposes. Men may use it to claim a special alliance with God against their foes. We must confess the significance of the long history of religious fanaticism, and must admit that a religion which has triumphed over idolatry in principle may in actual fact be made an instrument of partial and interested perspectives. Without such admission, the humility of a genuine scientist and the measured common sense of the man of affairs, who knows his ends to be in conflict with other legitimate ends, are superior to the wisdom of Christians."

Such is the courageous and critical attitude of a theology which deals with the realities of our day—the attitude that is needed if we are to escape from the confusion of inadequate thought systems, and from the sterility of Christian doctrines which are true in theory, but in fact are dead.

KARL ADAM

BY

Jakob Laubach

"The most successful theologian of our age," is what Karl Adam has been called. While success is no proof of genuine merit, it is a fact that Karl Adam has shaped the view of Christ and Church held by a generation of German Catholics; his works have been translated into nearly every Western language, and are being read around the world.

There is another side to Karl Adam's impact. Whether he speaks or writes, he always finds the right word—alive, heart-piercing, inspiring. His theology never smacks of anemic scholarship but always is a proclamation, in the best sense a sermon, a ministering to the souls of men. His aim is to set forth the vital values of theology, to bring the truth of revelation within the reach of living man, to show the moral, ordering, informing power of faith. To him, religious doctrine and right living, dogmatics and moral theology, are of a piece.

His academic career: in 1917, the University of Strasbourg invited him, though a dogmatic theologian, to teach moral theology. But two years later, he accepted an invitation to assume the chair of dogmatic theology at Tuebingen.

Adam's inaugural address at Tuebingen presented his view of the nature of theology: Theology is the science of faith. It is rooted in a faith that strives for understanding. Its starting point is faith, the "Church in its self-consciousness," its goal the scientific investigation into the faith held by all the Church in its essence, its growth, and its effects. Adam says:

"Catholic theology, then, is *bound*, but bound only to its subject, which is the faith of the Church in its self-consciousness. On close inspection this bond formally parallels that of the profane sciences. They, too, acknowledge no other bond but that imposed upon them by their subject, and by the methods that derive from the subject. In the same way the theologian acknowledges only the bond that necessarily follows from the specific nature of his subject, his task, which is the scientific investigation of the faith of the Church in its self-consciousness. What binds the theologian is not an exterior, heterogeneous authority, a *ukase* from the outside, but the particular nature of his subject and the method it demands; his task is to interpret the Church in its self-consciousness. As soon as the theologian detaches himself inwardly from that self-consciousness, and begins to direct his investigations beyond it or against it—without any *a priori* assumptions, to use a psychologically untenable term—from that moment on he may be a philologist, a psychologist of religion, or a religious historian, but he is no longer a theologian."

For thirty years Adam worked in Tuebingen as scholar, teacher, and minister of souls. The lovely Suabian town straddling the Neckar river had won his heart, even though the first forty years of his life had been spent in Bavaria: the son of a teacher from the Palatinate, he attended the Gymnasium at Amberg and the seminary for philosophy and theology in Regensburg, and read dogmatics and history at Munich. He will never lose his Bavarian touch, and still knows how to use the earthy Bavarian idiom to good effect. But it was at Tuebingen where he found the climate—especially the intellectual climate—for which he had been looking. And even the honor of an invitation to the University of Bonn in 1925 could not draw him away. His love for this town on the Neckar, one of Germany's intellectual capitals, rings in the words he wrote for the 450th anniversay of the university:

"The special character of Tuebingen's spirit is this: its haunts are everywhere, in the professor's study and the student's garret, in the painted brick-and-timber fronts of its houses, the plane-tree promenade along the Neckar, the Old Auditorium, the two convents. Its *genius loci* is the majestic influence of the past upon the present, the deep awareness of our ties with our forebears whose portraits greet us from the university's walls and who will not die. Let the horns honk and the antennae sprout—behind the white-curtained windows our Hoelderlins and Uhlands, Hegels and Strausses, Baurs and Möhlers are still sitting."

The name of Möhler conjures up a tradition to which Adam feels himself especially indebted: that of Tuebingen's school of theology. The distinctive feature of that school is its close synthesis of speculative and historical theology, a combination of the morphological study of dogmas with an open awareness of the vital currents and problems of the present.

"However much Tuebingen's school of thought differed from the purely static analysis of scholasticism in the stress it laid upon the dynamism of revelation and of faith, and in its method of a dialectic of faith, it yet was akin to scholasticism both in its starting point and in its goal, as well as in its conscious reference to Thomas Aquinas. Its theology was a *theology of life*—not only in that, like every Catholic theology, it handed on living truths, but also in that it tried to throw into relief the surging inner life of these truths as they have grown in their organic interaction and in their oneness with the highest ultimate forces of revelation. Even while Tuebingen's theology tried to bring out the vital force of revelation, its driving, moving, inspiring energies—and so to lead toward the study of dogma in its historical development—even so its theology has not failed to come to grips with recent philosophy and the radical findings of historical theology."

Karl Adam himself has also come to grips with contemporary philosophy. His profound study of the problems of the natural knowledge of God owes much to the phenomenology of Max Scheler. It is the old problem of philosophy: in what manner, and under what conditions, can God's reality and essence be known? Adam adopts the basic principle of all phenomenology:

"The *what* of an object of knowledge, its essence stripped of all modes of being, determines also in some way the *act* by which it is grasped: both the manner in which it is grasped, and the subjective presuppositions, the conditions in which the act of grasping it takes place."

But God is in reality and essence different from the world of phenomena; He is immeasurably superior to it. Knowledge of God —that is, the act by which God can be known—must therefore in its totality differ from any of the acts of knowing by which we take possession of the world of empirical things. Adam draws the conclusion:

"Because God is absolute personality, superior to this world, and because natural revelation is thus not due to us in any way, it follows that humility, reverence, purity, and love are the only attitudes of the human spirit that are correlative to the majesty of the gracious God of revelation—they are the proper and essentially necessary disposition for a natural knowledge of God. . . . Where this disposition is lacking, the *logical, objective force* of the arguments for God's existence, drawn from natural revelation, remains unimpaired; but the arguments no longer carry *subjective conviction*, they can no longer affect *life*."

Natural knowledge of God, besides these ethical presuppositions, has, for Karl Adam, also an ontological *a priori*. Man has no innate idea of God, but he does have a firm feeling for the absolute, the unconditional. He experiences his own conditional, limited, contingent nature. This experience opens man's mind and makes him receptive to the divine. Such an opening-up precedes, and prepares the way for, all conscious knowledge of God.

The function of the proofs for the existence of God is not, then, to create subjective religious experience, or the substantive experience of God, by means of logic. Their function is merely to legitimize religious faith before the tribunal of reason—to prove that it is not an unfounded and irrational faith; the proofs merely present those factual qualities and realities of the world which tend to direct the inquiring mind toward an effective metaphysical causality.

Yet the rational demonstration of God's existence and essence is not totally independent of the inner feeling of experiencing God—or, as we would say today, of the existential experience of God. This inner feeling is here considered as one of man's capacities: the capacity whose metaphysics Theodor Haecker meant to describe but unfortunately only sketched in a short essay. Adam, then, sees the most intimate connection between the knowledge of God that is based on the world's reality and on our judgment of what exists, and man's weighing, evaluating inner feeling.

"The inner feeling of religious knowledge can be appreciated properly only if we are clear about the special function of 'feeling' in the economy of the human spirit. Feeling is an immediate experience, a sampling and tasting of what helps or hinders my life, and so it is of necessity associated with pleasure and displeasure. As a *spiritual* over-all feeling, it is an experience, an immediate perception of my momentary vital, over-all condition, of the measure of value of that which at this moment fills my life: that is, it expresses a condition. And it is original, *primary*, in that it *precedes* the other acts of the soul. When impressions enter from outside, they are at once sampled by this feeling for their value content, and entered as if on a weather chart with the labels 'helpful to life' or 'hurtful to life.' Nor is that all. If the newly entered impressions are helpful, the satisfaction they produce at once and automatically sets off all other spiritual powers, by virtue of the oneness of our inner life, and these actively pick up the scent of the good impression. The satisfaction prompts the will to send out reason, too, after the good that has been felt, to test the good and perhaps turn it into a consciously held possession. Feeling thus turns from a mere recording instrument of pleasure and displeasure into a *motor* that moves the will, and a *prompter* of knowledge."

To Karl Adam, then, the whole man—feeling, will, and reason —is involved in the search for the existence and essence of God. Adam keeps sight of man in the concrete, with his questions arising within him and in their relatedness to his own self. It is thus no surprise that Adam early in his studies encountered Augustine, and ever after showed a tender affinity with the thought of this great confessor and theologian of antiquity. In 1930, on the occasion of a celebration in honor of St. Augustine, Adam said:

"Augustine thinks and inquires as a living human being, as a man who draws his questions first of all from his own inwardness, and who deals ever with external objects that pose problems to him, never only as external objects *per se*, but always in their relatedness to his own self. In this respect his theology is a theology of experience. Not in the sense, of course, that the holy and the divine exist for him only as an event in experience or a fact of consciousness, but in the sense that to him there is no truth *per se*, no science *per se*, that is not also truth and science for him himself, and that does not grow vital and fruitful only by its relatedness to his own self."

His very first scholarly studies led Adam to early Christianity, and to Augustine. After an analysis of Tertullian's concept of the Church, Adam investigated the early Christian doctrine of penance, and the Augustinian doctrine of the Eucharist. Augustine, Adam feels, more than any other of the Church Fathers, has brought out the essential core of Christianity: the mystery of the Incarnation.

"Augustine prompted the Christendom of his age to vigorous self-appraisal and, so to speak, rediscovered Christianity for many of them. As he steeped himself in St. Paul and in the best of the patristic writings, that which is new in Christianity struck him in all its full significance. Christianity in essence is redemption, and is in essence grounded in the mystery of the Incarnation. To be a

97

Christian does not mean just to accept in faith the divine truths and to obey God's commandments—to be a Christian means to be reborn through the Holy Spirit, reborn in the new man which is Christ. That is Augustine's good tidings, that is what makes his life strong and triumphant, that is the joyful outcry of his heart: 'My source is Christ, my root is Christ, my head is Christ!' "

The message of Jesus Christ, the Son of God and of man, the message of the single Mediator, the man Jesus Christ, and the message of the Church as the mysterious body of Christ: they are the center of Adam's theological thought, and the goal of his priestly labors.

But what, precisely, is the message of Jesus as the Christ? Adam gives its outlines in the introduction to his *The Christ of Faith*:

"*Christianity is Christ.* This is the message that gives foundation and content not only to the moral imperatives and ethical standards, but also to the dogmas, the truths of our faith. Only in the Son do we attain certainty of the Father and the Holy Spirit. Only the belief in Christ produced the belief in the Trinity. Christology, the doctrine of the person and the work of Christ, comes prior in the history of revelation to the dogma of God the one and three-in-one.

"Similarly with the dogmas of the creation, of the first state of man, of original sin, and salvation. The same holds for the Church's doctrines of grace, the sacrament, eschatology, and, last but not least, the idea of the Church itself. All these dogmas grow from the seed of the Christological dogma. What they do is to describe the intensive and extensive influence of the mystery of Christ, both in the individual soul and in the bosom of the believing Church. Without Christ there can be no grace, no sacrament, no Church, no hope for the future."

Karl Adam stresses it again and again: the most exalted and also the most responsible task of the Church is the proclamation of Christ. If the Church does not start from here, and return to here, then the very heart and core of its proclamation is missing.

But Jesus Christ is not only the center of the Christian message, He is also the ground and cause of our faith:

"It is always the living Christ Himself who makes us believers—an ultimate, incomparable, personal impression of Him who touches upon the center and core of our being whenever we hear Him speak or see Him act. From Him emanates the touch of life."

Karl Adam sets before us the living Christ, Christ our brother, the Son of God and of man. The source of this picture of Christ is the faith of the Church. Adam draws the picture line by line—by a careful exegesis of scripture, theological tradition, the teachings of the Church, and with a psychology adapted to modern man.

Christ is the great divide of the spirit—Christ confronts every man with a decision. Karl Adam does not tire of stressing this existential significance of the Christ problem. But the problem of the historical personality of Jesus Christ does not thereby become secondary for Adam as it does for Rudolf Bultmann, who recognizes as significant only "the act of God in the crucifixion of Jesus for my sake." According to Adam, the decision for Christ is possible only if man is confronted fully with Christ's figure, the mystery of His person, the extraordinary and unheard-of phenomenon of His life, His actions, and His fate.

What are the main traits of this picture of Christ? Adam turns first to the four gospels. They attest with one voice that Jesus, from the beginning of His public life, lived in the consciousness of His unique task—that He had been sent by the Father. "I have come" —the frequent use of this apocalyptic formula stresses that Jesus has a public task to fulfill which is to introduce the new era. Christ is higher than all the prophets, higher even than the Law of Moses; He is the one who fulfills all prophecy. Yet He is more: He is of one essence with Jehova, is Himself Jehova, He is the Son of the Father. But side by side with this testimony of the Lord's majesty we find equally clear statements of Jesus' human lowliness and weakness. He was exposed to temptation from outside, from the Fiend, and at times from men also. His struggle on Mount Olivet is a struggle for the will of the Father. Jesus' human sensibilities recoil before the dreadful manner in which the Father's will threatens to realize itself for Him. Among the miserable of Israel the most miserable—that is the Gospel picture of the Lord.

"If we put this picture of humbleness and simplicity side by side with the ideas the ancients had of their sons of God in human form, we become aware of the enormous difference that separates the picture of Christ in the Gospels from the ancient ideas of the Savior: the pagan Hellenists regarded Him as a walking miracle, a sort of heavenly phantom, but in contrast to this, Jesus reveals the purest, simplest humanity, the smell of the earth, praying, struggling, suffering out of the depths of His perfect humanity."

The early Church, too, proclaims Him as God become man, Adam points out. For the early Church, Jesus' resurrection is the decisive fact: the apostles bear witness to it. The powers of the Trinity—the God of Abraham, He who is exalted to sit at God's right hand, and the Holy Spirit—are the fundamental divine powers of the proclamation of the early Church. The early Church, then, starts not with a Son of man prior to history, but with one who became man; it starts not from the divinity but from the humanity of Christ. But it states emphatically: This humanity has been taken up into the divine glory. Jesus' divine eminence is expressed more clearly even in the name "the Lord" than in the name "the Christ." For, both in Jewish and in Hellenistic usage "the Lord" is the true name of God in His outward manifestations.

At this point Adam takes issue with Protestant Bible criticism. The eschatological and mystical school especially, and above all Bousset, have tried to demonstrate that the early Church only gradually did arrive at confessing the divinity of Christ. After carefully weighing and refuting the various arguments, Adam states:

"The belief in Christ cannot have been born either of the Hellenistic divine Savior figures themselves or of the Hellenistic idea of salvation; between the Hellenistic and the Christian Saviors yawns an unbridgeable abyss. The convert from Hellenism to Christianity comes from a world of fantastic excess into a world of clearly delineated bright reality, into daylight—and history. And he comes from a world of naïve superficiality and coarse sensuality into the inner world of the soul and the spirit, where forgiveness of sins, love, and peace are the reigning powers. There is no unison between these, only stark opposition. It is impossible for Christianity to have arisen from something so essentially antithetical to it.

It can only have developed not dependent upon the Hellenistic mysteries, but in opposition to them. We need only recall the bloody martyrdoms of the first three centuries. They are overwhelming proof that the first Christians knew how sharply opposed they were to pagan myth and cult, and that they would sooner give up their lives than ally themselves to such imaginings."

Christ's picture is clarified further as Adam undertakes to describe the self-consciousness of Christ layer by layer. He first examines His consciousness of being the Messias; His entire attitude proves that He knew and confessed Himself to be the Messias King. But how, then, are we to understand the biblical passages in which Jesus explicitly forbids any public announcement of His being the Messias? Adam shows that Jesus, it would seem, did not wish to be called the Messias by the Jews, because they would have misunderstood His mission to be that of a political Messias. But among the heathen—in the neighborhood of Decapolis, say, or in Samaria—where He had no misunderstanding to fear, He confessed Himself from the beginning as the Messias, the bringer of redemption, of rebirth to eternal life.

Yet Jesus is most fond of calling Himself "the Son of man." Let us note well: never *a* son of man but always *the* son of man. No one else ever speaks of Him as the son of man. The name is always the Lord's own designation of Himself.

How should the term as Jesus uses it be understood? The Greek and Latin Church Fathers understood it as a reference to Christ's human origin. But the majority of the new interpretations—indeed almost all of them—understood the "Son of Man" in messianic terms.

Primarily, we must have a clear idea of the early history of the term. The book of Daniel first spoke of "one like the son of man." He is the symbol for a new people and kingdom of God, which will take the place of the kingdoms on earth symbolized by four great beasts in Daniel's prophecy. What are the elements of this prophetic symbol, "Son of Man," that Jesus took into His self-designation, in what sense did He use it?

By all textual evidence, Adam says, Jesus wanted first and foremost to claim that Daniel's "one like the son of man" and his kingdom of God had been made manifest in Him:

"The heart of His claim was that 'the sign of the Son of Man' will appear in heaven. On the clouds of heaven He will come with the power and the glory, to set up His kingdom and hold the Last Judgment. Here, His office as *ruler* and judge over all mankind at the end of time is proclaimed. And Jesus decides the fate of all mankind, not simply that of the Jews. Jewish nationalism no longer had any place in this idea. Moreover, it also raised Jesus' claim that the true place and home of the Son of Man was in heaven at the right hand of the Ancient of Days. Jesus is, in His one who 'has come,' come from a higher supernatural reality. The idea of pre-existence, which is explicit in Daniel's image of the Son of Man, is implicit in this 'coming.'

"But Jesus' consciousness of being the Son of Man also contains elements that cannot be explained by the Book of Daniel. He is fond of calling Himself the Son of Man when He is speaking of His coming suffering. Jewish dogma of the time of Jesus had no conception of a suffering Messias, only a Messias of glory. But Jesus knows that He is called to suffer. . . . Jesus has rather subsumed Isaias' man of sorrows into His idea of Daniel's son of man. This is His *original* creation, the expression of His own awareness of His nature, going beyond all the prophets, and concentrating their scattered illumination into one consciousness that He is the judge and Lord of mankind, called to rule by His messianic deeds and sorrows, the divine redeemer *in via crucis*, by way of the cross.

"Thus the name, 'Son of Man,' as Jesus understood it, is for its period the most profound expression of His consciousness that He was the Messias. In its sequence of the Son of Man pre-existent, humiliated, and then exalted, it contained the seeds of the entire history of our redemption."

Adam sees the high point of Christ's messianic self-consciousness in His self-designation as the "Son of God." The idea of a son of God was greatly familiar to the Jews, but they applied it to especially chosen created beings. To prevent misunderstandings, it would seem that the authors of the synoptic gospels avoided speaking of Jesus' self-designation as God's Son. But there are several passages in John where Jesus calls Himself "Son of God" even before His enemies. Once again it is Christ's original deed to fill the theocratic concept of "Son of God" of His Jewish environment with the metaphysical meaning that He is indeed the Son of God.

The various layers of Christ's self-consciousness are to Karl Adam the true foundation of every Christology. It was Paul and John, the two "theologians" among the apostles, who elaborated upon the meaning of Christ's self-revelation.

The foundation of Paul's belief in Christ is his experience of Christ at Damascus. The "Christ according to the spirit," the God Christ who here overcame him, completely overshadows in Paul's proclamation the human and historical Jesus.

There have been attempts to discover the true source of the Christology of Paul, apostle to the nations, in the Hellenistic mysteries. No doubt, says Adam, that Paul's proclamation should have made use of those ideas understood by his contemporaries. The concepts of truth, life, rebirth, and illumination can be found in Paul's thought, just as they can in the mystery religions. But in Paul they have a precise theological meaning, not the magical one of the Hellenistic nature myths.

To Paul we owe the first systematic Christology. He even touched upon the problem of how Christ's divinity and humanity are related. His doctrine may be summed up as follows: Christ, Son of God, the pre-existing celestial being, was sent to earth by God to deliver mankind. He "emptied" Himself of the form of God and took upon Himself the form of a servant. Christ emptied Himself not of divine existence, but of "being equal to God." It is not a transformation of divinity into humanity, but rather the contrary: the divine glory is suspended, so that only the humanity is visible.

John the Evangelist enlarges and enriches Christology. If we want to know how Jesus spoke, not as a public preacher on the streets or at the lakeside, but as friend among friends, we must turn to John.

"When St. John wrote his Gospel, towards the end of the first

Christian century, the first hard pioneer work had in essentials been achieved. The enormous strength of Paul's mission had established the new Christianity in the Jewish as well as in the Hellenistic world. He placed Christ's divinity so emphatically at the center of the Christian faith that, in the context of Hellenistic Gnosticism, there was the danger of regarding it as the exclusive element, and denying the humanity of Jesus—which is why John is solicitous to present and illuminate the *humanity* in Christ too. . . . Christ's divine glory shines through His humanity. Any dualism in the image of Christ is vanquished. Paul had eyes only for the divine Christ; to him, Christ's humanity was the crass antithesis of His divinity. John had eyes—and love—for His humanity too. . . . The eschatological expectation of the future disappears. The 'glory of God is already present in Christ.' . . . Jesus, our life, our bread of heaven, the light of the world, the vine, the Good Shepherd—these are the motifs of St. John's Gospel. Everything in our Lord's life is conceived in its essence, and illuminated with the light of eternity. This is concentrated into the confession: 'And the Word was made flesh, and dwelt among us. And we saw his glory —glory as of the only-begotten of the Father—full of Grace and of truth' (John 1:14). . . . The prologue to the Gospel according to St. John is a hymn to the working of the Logos through the entire cosmos. Paul is aware of Christ's pre-existent working (I Cor. 10:3 f.). But it is only an influence upon the children of Israel. Paul goes deeper only in the Epistle to the Colossians. In Christ, 'all things hold together.' But where Paul makes only isolated allusions, John has a clear, unequivocal doctrine. There has been nothing in the world or in the entire history of mankind that does not have its life and truth from the Logos. He is the only true revealer of God."

These passages make us realize how, in Karl Adam's view, the Gospel of John goes to the very heart of Jesus Christ's message. John's picture of Christ, Adam says, is the most *consummate* picture that revelation has vouchsafed us. Later theology could add nothing essential. All it did was to clarify, conceptualize, and systematize what John had described with simple directness.

It has been justly said that the great merit of Adam's Christology lies in its discussion of biblical theology. But in his books, almost all of which carry the name of Christ in their very titles, he draws for us also the picture of Christ that is found in the early Fathers and the Scholastics. And he often follows Scotist doctrine, on points not yet absorbed into dogma, especially when dealing with Christ's human nature in all its fullness.

One of Adam's students, the dogmatic theologian Fritz Hofmann of Wuerzburg, once summed up the scholarly and apologetic importance of Adam's work in these words:

"At the center of the Christian proclamation, and therewith also at the center of the living theology of Karl Adam, is the *divine-human person of Jesus Christ.* . . . It was Adam who brought out the foundation of faith in inward emotion, the importance of the living Church to the understanding of the living Christ, and the roots of the conviction carried by Holy Scripture as they are laid bare by the form-critical method. It was he who exposed, in principle, the anti-revelatory assumptions of a presumably 'assumptionless' liberal theology; who established the validity, and the limitations, of the so-called eschatological school; who drew the sharp divide between Christian belief in the Son of God and in redemption, and the Jewish idea of the Messias as well as the Hellenistic idea of a divine savior; he who by an *exact* exegetical investigation of the sources for Christ's resurrection could refute the modern version of the vision theory. All this he accomplished with a thoroughness that could forego scholarly adornments without risking the charge of superficiality. Nobody else has done as much. And still we have not mentioned the principal fruit of Adam's work. It lies in the vigor with which he places into the very center of theological discussion the *mediatory, redemptive significance of Jesus' humanity,* on the basis of liturgy and patristic doctrine—and the compelling force with which he portrays through the Gospels the sublime majesty of Jesus' human nature."

The mediatory and redemptive significance of Jesus' humanity, then, is the point upon which Karl Adam laid the greatest stress.

It also serves him as the starting point for his reflections on the Church. The Church as the body of Christ, the revelation and epiphany of Christ's saving power, is the second idea basic to Adam's theology. Today, after the encyclical *Mystici Corporis Christi*, that mysterious dimension is no longer altogether unfamiliar to us. But for many centuries the Church had been thought of only as an institution; it had been seen, so to speak, only from the outside. It is owing largely to Karl Adam that our age does once again perceive, give deep assent to, and experience the reality of the spiritual inwardness of the Church, the mysterious body of Christ.

In his inaugural address at Tuebingen in 1919, Karl Adam made this avowal:

"I confess that when I became familiar with the thought of the early Christians, two ideas were borne in upon me. One was the clear consciousness of the believers of the indwelling of the Holy Spirit with them *in its essence*; the other, the high estimation of the *ecclesia*—the *solidarity* of the early Christian consciousness of faith. And that faith—it was nothing purely conceptual—was love and life; and love and life will form community. Thus it was a conviction inherent in the early Christian consciousness of faith, reaffirmed over and over from Paul to Ignatius to Cyprian to Augustine: the Spirit acts in and through the community—the community is the true and proper organ of the Spirit. *Not the 'I' but the 'We' is the bearer of the Spirit.*"

Adam has been charged with promoting a veiled "solidarism." But he means only to bring out the intensive solidarity of men in sin and in grace, such as had been taught before him by Augustine and by Möhler. To Adam, mankind is not a mere conglomeration of individuals, but an organic unity, a single "we." Only in that light can we even begin to understand that the fate of all mankind is wrapped up in the fate of Adam the first man.

"Because He who became man as the new Adam, the personified 'We' of all the redeemed, embraces in His person all the multiplicity of those that need redemption—that is precisely why Christianity is in essence a bond of the members with their head, a holy community, a sacred body. In His 'I' all mankind which had gone astray, man who had been altogether torn from his divine root, was once and for all reunited with divinity, with the life of all life, the fountain of all power, truth, and love. In Him all mankind is now once more raised from negation to affirmation, from nothingness to fullness, from unworthiness to worth. Thus, in all the breadth and all the depth of its being, mankind became *a new oneness in Him*."

From this central idea of the Christian proclamation springs Adam's concept of the Church. The Church is nothing else than Christ living on and growing in space and in history:

"The Church is the body permeated through and through by the redemptive might of Jesus. So intimate is this union of Christ with the Church, so inseparable, natural, and essential, that St. Paul in his Epistles to the Colossians and Ephesians explicitly calls Christ the Head of the body. As the Head of the body Christ makes the organism of the Church whole and complete. And Christ and the Church can no more be regarded separately than can a head and its body. . . . Nor could this intimate connection of Christ and the Church, this their intimate oneness, receive more profound or plainer expression than in the figure of a marriage of Christ and the Church which St. Paul, inspired by the language of several of the prophets, is the first to employ."

Karl Adam does not overlook the human, all too human side of the Church. This side, too, he interprets in the light of the mysterious oneness of Christ the Head with the Church His body. Just as Christ by becoming man took upon Himself a shattering self-abasement from crib to cross, so His "body" the Church, by entering into the accidents of history, underwent of necessity a self-impoverishment. Only indirectly, only imperfectly can she reflect that mysterious glory which is hers in her essence.

The imperfection of the members of Christ's body, and, in particular, the failure of the theologians, Karl Adam readily acknowledged. On the occasion of his seventieth birthday, he addressed his friends and students:

"*Ut omnes unum sint*—that all may be one! That was the last wish of the Lord, His legacy to Christendom. How shamefully we have used that legacy! . . . And we theologians are guilty above all others. For we have cast in hard and rigid forms the things that divide us, and so have made the division to endure. It is our duty, then, and our responsibility above all others to do our share so that the old unity may return."

If we try to sum up the lifework of Karl Adam, now eighty-seven, we can do no better than to apply to him the words he said of St. Augustine: "He prompted the Christendom of his age to vigorous self-appraisal."

Karl Adam assumed his place in the stream of Church tradition and, in the words of John, drew from it living water. He proclaimed and glorified Christ in everything—Christ become man, Christ our brother, our friend; Christ the Lord and Redeemer; Christ the mythical head of the Church which is His body, living on. In this lies Karl Adam's true contribution to the theology of our time, in his new interpretation of Christian tradition, which is the interpretation, too, of our life:

Jesus the Christ of Faith.

ROMANO GUARDINI

BY

Jakob Laubach

Hardly another Catholic theologian in our day has become so widely known and recognized as Romano Guardini. His writings, published in the course of half a century, represent an opus of extraordinary scope and substance. There are lectures and essays on problems of the times and on cultural matters; a series of monographs on the great figures of Western intellectual history—Augustine, Dante, Pascal, Hoelderlin, Dostoevsky, and Rilke; and many works in the field of religion, philosophy, and ethics. Guardini has rightly been called "one of the few universalists who, amid the specialization of our day, feel a commitment to the totality of the life of the mind."

This very diversity, however, these forays into so many areas of the intellectual life, also has been held against him. He has given us too many attempts—so the objection goes—and has given in too often to the claims of the moment, instead of offering a synthesis and a system.

That objection mistakes the individuality of Guardini and his special gifts. For the specific characteristic of his thought and work is simply this: that he is "on the way," forever starting afresh; his work is, and means to be, a pointing of the way.

There is another objection of seemingly greater weight: Just where—in all the critical, philosophical, spiritual, and ethical writings of Guardini—can his theology, his contribution to the theological discussion of our age, be found? Indeed, he is neither exegete nor liturgist, neither dogmatist nor moralist, neither philosopher nor historian of religion—though his writings touch upon all of these. Nor does it prove much that his doctoral dissertation is devoted to Bonaventure's doctrine of redemption, nor that his inaugural dissertation of 1922 in Bonn deals with the Franciscan theologians.

But we mean to show here that the basis of his thought, the recurrent themes of his life's work, cannot be understood unless they are considered as theology. We shall cite passages from every phase of his work, especially from the publications of the 1930's when his mind found expression in quiet, clear formulations, contrasting with the immediacy of emotion of his early years, and the reticent, complex, and, at times, resigned, diction of later life.

Guardini's work shows the mark of his origin, his historical situation, and his intellectual affinities.

Romano Guardini was born in 1885 in Verona, of Italian parents. While he was still in his tender youth his parents removed to Germany, to the city of Mainz. There, in the town of Gutenberg and Ketteler, he grew up amid the monuments of a great mediaeval tradition. He attended the gymnasium, met his friend Karl Neundörfer who later died in an accident, and in the Schleussner family found a circle of vital mysticism. Latin in origin, German in education—in Guardini this contrast produced a fruitful tension; an essay of 1928, *Thule and Hellas* (*Thule und Hellas*), shows that he is well aware of it.

Beginning even during his years at the gymnasium, later in his student days at Tuebingen, Berlin, and Freiburg, and later still as a young priest, Guardini took an active part in the German youth movement. This movement, which in protest against bourgeois narrowness and hypocrisy proclaimed a free, natural, responsible community among the young, had received its initial impulse from the naturalistic, no less than the irrationalist, revolt against the positivist desert of the nineteenth century.

Nor was Guardini long to discover this current of Western thought to which he felt akin—the current that leads from Plato to Augustine and on to Bonaventure. The Platonist world view and method of inquiry are for him closely related to the phenomenon of spiritual light which he appears to have studied first in Freiburg while working on Bonaventure. His collection entitled *Reflection and Parable* (*In Spiegel und Gleichnis*) refers to it more than once. Here is one example:

"In my studies at that time...I learned what the concept or, more correctly, the phenomenon of spiritual light means, how it makes its appearance within a certain intellectual and contemplative experience. For the moment, the insight remained purely theoretical; yet I knew that there had to be more—until, fifteen years later, I was traveling in the Engadine and saw its light. . . . It was then that I came to understand a few things of Plato that are not written in any books—except his own; but there you read them only after you have seen that clear light and after it has made your heart to overflow—overflow with what is also the innermost spirit. I understood also a few things of Plotinus, and again of Augustine, because it is alive in all of them though in each according to his special nature. And when I saw how that light embraced the trees, the edge of leaf and branch and shape, and what it did to the mountains, in the late afternoon, when all things are transmuted; then it dawned on me what the doctrine of transfiguration must be about."

This sensuous-spiritual experience gives Guardini access to St. Bonaventure's doctrine of knowledge:

"When I grasp something only with the senses, I have not known its essence but have only a passing impression of something that passes. True knowledge means that I, with the organ of the spirit, seize the eternal content of meaning of that which passes, that is to say, that I grasp its idea. How does this occur? This is the point where Bonaventure develops, with something close to passion, the Augustinian concept of knowledge: that grasping occurs *in lumine mentis*, in an event of light, *per irradiationem aeternarum*, by the radiance of the eternal idea into the spirit.

"As with every specific striving for an absolute, so here in the idea of a spiritual light we encounter something pre-conceptual. ... For Bonaventure, there in this 'light' the idea, the eternal vision of essence, value, and meaning lights up the spirit. But since the idea 'is' in God, knowledge means a 'contact' of some kind with God. In knowledge, God touches the spirit with the idea which is His living, archetypal thought of the thing in question, of its plenitude of essence and value."

This unmistakably Platonist-Augustinian structure of knowledge and thought Guardini makes his own—it is his own. But to know one's own type of thinking also makes it possible critically to overcome its one-sidedness. Guardini is well aware of the dangers of Platonist thinking. The Platonist, being sensitive to value, perfection, the idea, is also especially sensitive to all that is imperfect, dark, base, ugly. And this might lead him into melancholy, disorientation, or phantasy. The Platonist must remain on the road to history, into ever renewed actualization, if he is to overcome melancholy and the inclination toward death.

And Guardini does face history, he grapples with it, he attempts to read the signs of the times and the indications of the future. His writings since the 1920's in social and cultural criticism—*The End of the Modern World*, to name but one of them—are evidence of how well he knew that he was living in a time of change. And they show further that he has always taken part in the historical change.

As early as 1921, under the impact of the turbulent war and postwar years, Guardini in his essay on Anselm of Canterbury has this to say about post-modern thought:

"In contrast to the thought of the most recent past, wrapped up entirely in concept and abstraction, we witness today a tremendous awakening of the sense of reality. True, the past, too, had something which was called a 'sense of reality' in natural science and technology, in social and political science. But that was in fact only a familiarity with the surface, joined to a well developed technique for mastering that surface. . . . The small realities were seen, the large ones overlooked; did we not manage even to overlook that there is a God, a soul, a world with objective meaning and purpose?

"But now there seems to dawn an age when that is no longer possible. Now man—and most of all the man who is most true to his time, most open and most clear-eyed—will once again feel the hard impact of reality. Apparently, thought once again tends reverently to be guided by being. . . . A manner of scientific thinking seems to be springing up that starts with the clear perception of the concrete, and keeps its eyes fixed on the problems posed by the concrete. . . . It also emerges clearly that thought, the organ of science, is itself a concrete event, whose bearer is a living subject, not an abstraction. . . . This new way of thinking, akin to that of the Middle Ages, reveals itself especially . . . in the principle of phenomenology by which the various areas of being call for specific attitudes in the knowing subject, so that an object is known really and fully only when the knowing subject assumes the attitude that corresponds to the object."

The outer and inner facts that we have sketched—Guardini's origin, his Platonist-Augustinian mode of thought, his intellectual situation—must be kept in mind if we are to understand his theory of knowledge and his philosophy of the living-concrete. The rediscovery of concrete reality that he discerns everywhere after the First World War calls for concrete thinking which, as he puts it, "is not conceived as the purely theoretical occupation of the intellect with objective data, but presupposes being and issues in being."

Knowledge, says Guardini, does not operate "like a camera which when cocked mechanically snaps whatever is in front of the lens." There is in reality no thinking *per se* directed at an object *per se.* There is only "the concrete thinking of this living man directed toward this specific object. And that is a concrete, living act."

Knowledge, then, cannot be divorced from the concrete act of the knower. This fact in turn presupposes a specific concept of "truth," in contrast to a mere "correctness" of knowledge. To Guardini the old classic definition of truth, *adaequatio rei et intellectus*— as he translates it, "the agreement between the object and the inwardly reflecting image"—is still the best. But this agreement contains a double dimension: the controllable, objective agreement, that is, "correctness," and the "truth" which arises only when the thinker "lives" the agreement, when he experiences and inwardly appropriates it.

Guardini's major work, *The Antithesis* (*Der Gegensatz*), published as early as 1914, deals in particular with the problem of knowledge. The living-concrete, he says, because of its suprarational character can be known only by an act of knowing which is at once conceptual and intuitive, and which thereby embraces the antithetical structure of human thought. This act of knowing, which takes place in the extreme tension between the opposing poles of human life, he calls *'Anschauung'*—intuitive perception. It is that act "of which we hear again and again in the history of the mind: the catching sight of the essential form, the sudden illumination of meaningful coherence, the being-struck by the vision of value." Such knowledge encompassing opposites, Guardini says, can be accomplished only dialectically. Much of his work is indeed in the form of dialogue, conversation, interpretation, statement and counterstatement, showing clearly to what extent it rests on the dialectic manner of thought and expression.

This, then, is Guardini's theory of knowledge: that the knower is always a concrete man, with his specific structure of thought, who knows "truth," and not merely "correctness" only, when his knowledge is directed toward actualization. Guardini develops this theory of living and concrete knowledge in order that he may apply it to the most concrete: Revelation, the self-unveiling of the living God. For theology, to Guardini, is a science of the concrete.

But what happens to thought when its object is the living God in His self-communication? Guardini's work, *The Essence of Christianity (Das Wesen des Christentums)*, of 1953, formulates the basic answer: All our thought is cast into crisis by Revelation, for Revelation means that we do not think "about God" but "from God." This crisis leads to a turning, a "conversion" of thought.

"Revelation . . . means that things are back in place, in order. And to believe means to take one's own place in that order. To know, 'from God,' that the world is in the light; that in essence it was never dark, but is built of truth; that it was never shut off, but transparent to the view that rises from a pure heart; that it was never alien but God's own, who gave it into man's trust.

"In the light of Revelation thought grows humble and at the same time confident. Knowledge is not the illumination of what in itself is dark, but the entrance into that light which in essence, from God, is in the world. Knowledge is not the opening-up of what is in essence closed off, but the path into that freedom which belongs to the creature as long as he remains in the order. Knowledge is not a struggle with a silent, alien nature, but a knowledge following in the footsteps of God's own knowledge."

"The essential structure of Christian truth," then, is that it is revealed. This concrete revelation tells us that we can reach the living God only through Christ. He, His historical personality, is the category of all that is Christian, and therewith also of Christian and theological thought. Thought in the realm of Revelation is under the sign of Christ's mediation.

The person of Christ in His historical uniqueness and eternal glory as the category of thought: that is a paradox to those who do not perform the "conversion" of thought, since the position otherwise occupied by general concept—which is what category here means—is now taken up by an historical personality.

In his book *The Lord*, as well as in many other published writings, Guardini tries to draw the picture of Jesus the Christ in the New Testament.

"Who Jesus the Christ is or can be, I cannot judge out of myself nor out of the world. Neither psychology nor philosophy, neither experience nor history supplies a measure. He can confront me only out of His own sovereign freedom. And I, in a critically precise attitude, can do nothing but look, listen, and obey.... For here, in form and speech and fate, speaks the essential word of God. Here is neither 'personality' or 'idea,' but 'the beginning' from which all that is true takes its beginning."

It is only from Christ, from that tremendous reality which is beyond all measure, that an answer can be given to the question of the "essence of Christianity":

"This essence cannot be determined in the abstract. There is no doctrine, no basic structure of moral values, no religious attitude and order of life that could be divorced from the person of Christ and of which it could then be said that this is Christian. Christian is *He Himself*; that which reaches man through Him, and the relation which through Him man can have to God.

"A doctrine is Christian in so far as it issues from His mouth. Existence is Christian in so far as its movement is determined by Him. In everything claiming to be Christian He must be implied....

"From this there follow far-reaching problems. The difficulty of the practical demand made on man, to surrender that freedom which assures his relation to the norm and to submit to a person as the final value, finds expression in the danger of scandal: a danger of which Christ Himself was well aware.... The theoretical problems are suggested by questions such as these: If Christ is the category of Christian thought, in what manner are the contents of this thought given? How do the matters-of-fact of existence fit into that basic personal form? What is the structure of the Christian proclamation, the Christian consciousness, and so on? These problems are exceedingly difficult, and it would seem that theological thought has not yet truly come to grips with them. It would appear that theology seeks to establish its scientific character by following the scheme of the historical or the philosophical discipline, which is based upon abstract categories, and to see its specifically Christian nature only in the special qualities of content, or in the authoritative character of Revelation. But no one raises the theoretical question as to what the nature of Christian consciousness must be, the nature of the Christian act of knowing and its methodical course—that is, the science of a Christian—once Christ is the category of this consciousness and this knowing. That question is left to our religious posterity."

If the essence of Christianity cannot be derived from natural, worldly presuppositions, then it can only be derived from faith. "Faith is the attitude of knowing which corresponds to Revelation," says Guardini. At the outset of every Christian—and every theological—thought there are, then, two interrelated archphenomena: the living God, who in His own free initiative reveals Himself in the person of Christ; and faith, the capacity granted in grace by the same God to accept that Revelation. Neither phenomenon can be derived logically, nor can either be reduced to something else.

"But even 'converted' thought, whose starting points are these archphenomena, and its scientific formulation, theology, remain structure-bound because they are concrete thought. Since no thought structure is 'Christian' as such, whatever thought structure is proper in each case must submit to criticism—and thought after 'conversion' must submit not only to the criticism of its antithesis but also to the criticism of Christ.

"No human attitude is Christian as such. What is Christian is 'not of this world'; but all structures *are* of this world, inasmuch as they belong to the world's ordered structures. Thus what is Christian is not a type in contrast to others, but is what every type becomes when it comes to Christ, believes, and is baptized. This way to Christ is open to any kind of mind—including that of the Platonist. And, any kind of mind might miss the way— even the actualistic or the personalistic kind; if it does so, it becomes itself pagan."

Beginning with the publication of his book, *On the Meaning of the Church* (*Vom Sinn der Kirche*) in 1922, Guardini continues to express his thoughts on the meaning of the Church in ever new formulations. The essential relation between Church and faith is the subject of his book *The Life of Faith,* published in 1936. Certain excerpts follow:

" 'The Church' means the 'us' in faith; it is the sum-total, the whole community of believers; it is the believing collectivity. It is not merely Christian prayer which ought to say 'us,' but also faith. The latter is equally rooted in 'us,' understood as a whole. The true 'us' is more than a mere sum of individuals. It is a movement proceeding from them all. A true collectivity or totality is something more than a simple grouping of a few individuals; it is a vast living structure of which each individual is a member. A hundred men who stand before God as an *ekklesia* represent something more than the mere addition of a hundred individuals; they constitute a living and believing community—we do not mean merely a simple 'community' in the purely subjective sense of the term, a convenient designation for a feeling arising from the communal needs of the individual. No, the origin of the community we are referring to here, its consistency and its value, are drawn from something outside the communal needs of the individual; they come from elsewhere, they derive consistency and value from elsewhere: I refer to the 'Church.'

"The Church is the institution planted by Christ in history amidst mankind. It embraces not 'several individuals' or even 'all individuals'—these are mere numerical aggregates—but the whole human race as such, humanity in its entirety. The latter has been called to a holy life and to a new birth on the day of the Pentecost. This Christian totality is something concrete and real, and would continue to exist even if it were, from the point of view of numbers, reduced to but three members. It is not the result of the will or thought of men—the existence of the Christian is neither—but it exists by virtue of a divine decree, by a holy institution and creation according to the will of Christ.

"The Church is the original principle from which the life of the individual comes; it is the ground which supports him, the atmosphere which he breathes.... The Church is a living whole which penetrates the individual."

For decades Guardini has been proclaiming to his hearers and readers alike the riches of a Church newly awakened in the souls of men—evidence of a very special kind as to how his thought on Revelation urges toward "realization," in the sense of Cardinal Newman's use of the term. Realization of this kind expresses itself also in Guardini's intellectually and spiritually leading role in the Catholic Youth movement in Germany, of which the ancient Castle Rothenfels has come to be the center and, as it were, the symbol. In this context belong also his numerous writings of a contemplative nature, his sermons, Bible commentaries and prayers, as well as his educational and in the deepest sense "informative" writings. But what has yielded the richest fruit is Guardini's participation in the liturgical movement. By providing explanatory texts, and by his personal living practice, he has led a whole generation of young Catholics to the very heart of the Church, the liturgy, the Eucharist, the great feasts of the Church year.

His book, *The Senses and Religious Understanding* (*Die Sinne und die religiöse Erkenntnis*) of 1958 sums up his thoughts on how the reality of the holy may be understood in its epiphanies:

"What man desires is not so much intellectual truth as truth in being—more precisely, illumined truth. In an age when concepts and formulae rattle and clutter on the one hand, while on the other hand a demonic materialism drags all things down to a mere sensual level, in such an age man desires to grow aware of reality —entire—which is body and spirit, form and light, being and meaning, the world which is whole.... But that means: consciously or unconsciously man tries to find the epiphany in the liturgy—in the events of the cult he seeks the sudden radiance of the holy reality; the sound of the eternal Word in speech and song; the presence of the Holy Spirit in the body of the tangible. The liturgy ... goes out to meet redeemed man in the redeemed world. Thus we must discover anew the acts that tend to express those realities in time and space and tangible form, that is, the element of epiphany in the liturgy. And with equal resolution as well as deliberation, we must inquire whether the concrete form of the liturgy is in fact such that those acts can tend in that direction. We must relearn to see, to perceive, to grasp in our hands, to deal with living existence—and besides, we must account to ourselves where our liturgical activity has grown poor in imagery, where abstract, where decorative; we must ask ourselves how it might recover that richness of image and active energy which might lead the people of our time into the realm of Revelation with a more alive, more humane guidance than mere instruction and mere admonition can provide."

"Converted thought" not only depends on the concrete thought structure of the individual; it not only is realized and set free in the wholeness of the Church; it is also, and remains, within the specific situation of the times. And that situation, at *The End of the Modern World,* poses very special tasks for theology.

The first task is to achieve a clear distinction of what is Christian. Guardini asks that the essential content of the Christian consciousness be freed of the "overlays, conformities, and falsifications" of modern thought. By that he means "weakening of the faith to a point where it is no longer able to penetrate the vast number of phenomena and to create the 'world' "; the withdrawal into an "airtight" inwardness, into defensiveness and apologetics, which abandons the interpretation of existence to thought without faith. And again, Christian thought, in adopting the methods and accepting the results of modern science, had succumbed all to easily to the temptation of surrendering the substance derived from Revelation.

The true task of theology, as Guardini sees it, is to elaborate upon that which is essentially Christian. A true biblical theology must give up its rationalistic and historicizing attitude; the fact that its subject is the word of God, Sacred Scripture, proclamation, calls for a corresponding way of inquiry, a way which all the faithful can follow in principle.

"It has always been in the Christian consciousness that the individual human being in his time faces the living word of God, Christ and Christ's life and word, the event of redemption and of revelation, in a manner different from that in which he faces any other historical event, and that he faces them 'immediately.' It is true, of course, that Christ existed in His time as a real, historical figure. He is not an idea, nor a myth, nor the projection of a religious or metaphysical experience into the historical past. He is history who took place at that time. But at he same time He co-exists in all times because He is the living Son of God, the essential word of God, and comes from eternity and is eternal life. . . .

"And so the word of God addresses Himself to every age and demands faith—addresses Himself also to our time, to me. And each one has the right, nay, the proper duty, to hear it directly as it speaks out of his own time; out of the historical understanding of his own constitution and surroundings. God's word in scripture is 'all-historical' and all history demands that its meaning be drawn from it. In this total demand each age finds its special task."

In the New Testament, especially in the Pauline idea of "the new man coming into being in the old," Guardini finds the presuppositions for a psychology of existence in holiness, for a theological psychology that he tries to define more closely in *The Lord, The Lord's Mother (Die Mutter des Herrn)*, and *The Human Reality of the Lord (Die Menschliche Wirklichkeit des Herrn)*.

The definition, the distinction of what is Christian—that, in Romano Guardini's view, is the one central purpose of theology. Another purpose follows: to grasp the totality of the world and of existence. In *Freedom, Grace, and Destiny,* which appeared in 1948, he has this to say on the relation between Revelation and the world:

"Revelation has a special relation to immediate existence. Its communication to man comes from the pure generosity of God. It is not a higher level nor is it a deeper inwardness in the possibilities of this world; it differs from any this-worldly aspect that can be imagined. To employ a somewhat indefinite term, it is 'supernatural.' But the God of revelation is the same God who created the world and, therefore, the relation between revelation and the world is not merely one of difference. The Creator ordinated the world towards revelation, and this fundamental reality of existence has not been suppressed by sin. Scattered throughout the world are premonitions from which, in themselves, no single detail of revelation could be deduced but, once revelation has taken place, the Logos, as John declares, 'without whom was made nothing that was made' comes 'unto his own'; and created being remains His property, even though it has turned against Him in sin and 'his own received him not' (John 1:3-11). Thus a light is cast by revelation also on the things of the world. The paradox is in fact true that the real significance of these worldly things issues not from the things themselves but, in the first instance, from revelation. In other words, the reality and values of this world of our immediate experience are finally understood and made operative through the providence with which the redemption has surrounded them."

Guardini maintains here that all created things are ordered toward Christ, the Logos, and remain His own even if they oppose Him in sin. This is the fundamental assumption of that part of his work which he himself calls the "science of the Catholic world view." His book *Religion and Revelation* (*Religion und Offenbarung*) of 1959 thus defines the Catholic world view: "the picture of the world as it appears when the world is seen from Revelation." The Catholic world view combines those clarifications which "the immediate problems of the world receive from Revelation," and it gives those answers "to which Revelation is prompted by the questions of the world."

This science of the Catholic world view bears a close relation to Guardini's academic career, which brought him an audience far beyond the circle of Catholic students. After his qualifying examinations at Bonn in 1923, he was called to the university at Breslau to assume the chair of dogmatic theology; at the same time he received a permanent appointment at the University of Berlin which simultaneously set up a special chair for "Philosophy of Religion and the Catholic World View"—a chair abolished by the Hitler régime in 1939. After 1945 at Tuebingen, and since 1948 at Munich, Guardini, now on the philosophical faculty, has lectured predominantly on problems of the Catholic world view.

To achieve the full vision of the coherence of all Christian existence, as Guardini himself says in *Freedom, Grace, and Destiny,* is the ultimate goal of all his labors:

"The time has come to take our stand again, to think and live in Christian existence as a whole, in the sense of the Pauline words: 'All is yours but you are Christ's' (I Cor. 3:23). It is time to realize that all divisions have only a methodological value and that what really exists is the world and man in the world, as called by God and judged and redeemed. It is time for us to consider the whole as a whole. In the process we shall preserve all that has been won in the long, sustained effort of previous centuries: a critical conscience, careful differentiation, and the serious discussion of scientific questions. Our formula is in no sense one of 'Back to the past,' whether to the Middle Ages or the early Christian period. It can only be a forward movement, transcending divisions to attain to the whole, with the approach which once was that of Western man but which now, after an interval of five hundred years, has become more critical, more earnest, and more detached.

"As far as reflection is concerned, we must study a phenomenon not merely as it appears by itself but as it runs through all the dimensions—depth, breadth, and height—of existence understood in the Christian sense, and we must endeavor to grasp its significance from the combined standpoints of psychology, philosophy, and theology, in such a way, however, that we incur no charge of crossing frontiers unduly or confusing the territories in which we work."

This view of existence, understood in the Christian sense in all its depth, breadth and height, means to Guardini, first of all, the view of man who has existence only in the relation "from God, toward God." In this light we must understand Guardini's interpretations of the great men of Western intellectual history. Through them he develops the basic outline of a Christian anthropology, maintaining a clear distinction between Christian characteristics and those of a this-worldly sanctity such as may be seen, for example, in Hoelderlin or Rilke.

Guardini's concern with man, and with the truly necessary 'definition' of the human person caught between the mass and vast totalities, also provides the impulse for his studies in intellectual and cultural history. Their ultimate objective is a sober clarification of the Christian situation today. Thus he says in *The End of the Modern World,* published in 1950:

"To be a Christian means to take a position toward Revelation, and such a position may be taken in any period of historical development. In this respect, Revelation is equally close to, and equally far from, every period. The Middle Ages, too, knew unbelief of every degree of intensity—just as the modern age has known a fully Christian faith. But the faith of the modern age has differed from that of the Middle Ages. The modern Christian has had to develop his faith under the historical conditions of individual self-reliance, and has often succeeded in a manner full worthy of the manner of the Middle Ages. But in the process he has encountered obstacles that made it difficult for him to accept his age as easily as could the preceding epoch. The memory of man's revolt against God was still too much alive; the way in which it had brought every sector of cultural activity into conflict with faith, and had crowded faith itself into a position of inferiority, was still too dubious. Besides, there is what we have called modern dishonesty: that duplicity which on the one hand rejected Christian doctrine and the Christian order of life, while on the other hand claiming as its own their human and cultural effects. This situation has rendered the Christian uncertain in his relation to modernity. At every hand he encountered in the modern world ideas and values whose Christian origin was patent, but which were asserted to be public property. Everywhere he came upon property of the Christian heritage that was now being turned against him. How could he have been confident? These ambiguities are about to end. The coming era, wherever it turns against Christianity, will do so in full earnest. It will pronounce secularized Christianity to be sheer sentimentality—and that will clear the air. Full of hostility and full of danger, but clean and in the open. . . .

"Christianity has often been charged with being a hiding place for modern man where he takes shelter against the modern situation. There is a good deal of truth in this charge—not just because dogma, by its objectivity, establishes a firm order of thought and of life, but also because in the Church there has remained alive a wealth of cultural traditions which have elsewhere died out. In the coming age, there will be less and less cause for that charge.

"The cultural heritage in the possession of the Church will not escape the general decay of all tradition, and where it does endure it will be weakened by many a problem. But as concerns dogma, while it is of its essence to endure through the changes of time, since it is founded beyond time, we may yet expect that its character as a rule and guide of life will once again be felt with special clarity.

"The more clearly Christianity proves itself once again to be that which does not go without saying, and the more sharply it is compelled to set itself apart from a predominant non-Christian world view, the more strongly dogma, side by side with its theoretical dimension, will bring to the fore its practical-existential dimension."

His resolute emphasis on what is distinctly Christian is one of the striking characteristics of Guardini's work. The other is his openness in every direction: he is open to the living tradition, to this-worldly holiness, and to the currents of the times. Out of this fruitful tension grows his life's work: particularly where it is reflection and activity rooted in faith—a faith that seeks to achieve scientific understanding. Guardini's many-faceted thought —rooted in its basic understanding of the living, concrete world, in that application of the understanding to Revelation which he called "conversion," and in the rewarding challenge raised against various tenets of faith—is in fact a systematic theology, with its clear inner logic and its unity of theme, method and motivation.

Among the writings of the octogenarian scholar are contributions to the problems of religion and revelation, the Church and the liturgy, the psychology of Jesus, the phenomenology of Christianity; to a Christian anthropology; and to a science of the Catholic world view. Many of his ideas today are almost taken for granted—a sign of his profound effect.

Nor can Guardini, the theologian, be separated from Guardini the great religious educator; the preceptor who stimulates and moves minds; the Socratic teacher of thought; the interpreter of the sacred signs and the signs of the times.

His work offers a new reading of Christian theology because it brings clearly to the fore that which is unique in Christian life and Christian consciousness, yet without rejecting the world and the things of the world; and because it throws Christianity wide open to the world—a world that itself is never 'sin' but is merely 'in sin'—that Christianity would draw into this truly catholic openness.

HEINRICH SCHLIER

BY

Jakob Laubach

Heinrich Schlier's theological position is perhaps best described in a remark he made in the "short account" of his conversion to Catholicism: "How much there is that is admitted in Protestant exegesis and history, only to be rejected when it comes to dogma and the Church!"

These words imply, for one, that Protestant and Catholic exegesis of recent decades have in many points arrived at identical results. But the words imply further that what prompted Schlier (in 1933) to join the Catholic Church were the conclusions he found himself compelled to draw from his New Testament exegesis. Therefore, his work and his contribution to today's Christian theology can be understood only in the light of that personal decision—which is the only reason why it is mentioned here at all. In passing, it might also be mentioned that his collected essays, published in 1953 under the title *The Time of the Church* (*Die Zeit der Kirche*), have all received the imprimatur even though, with the exception of one paper written before his conversion, they had originally appeared in Protestant publications.

Heinrich Schlier was born in 1900, in Neuburg on the Danube. He tells us that it was the atmosphere of this little Bavarian town, rich in tradition, which kept him from developing an anti-Catholic bias. On the completion of his theological studies he became a pastor, later a lecturer at Jena University, until finally he was appointed to a professorship at Marburg. He mentions Karl Barth, Rudolf Bultmann and Martin Heidegger as his great, revered teachers.

Even his earliest publications present the two main themes on which his exegesis and thought are focused, and which he identifies by the words "the world," and "the Church." And indeed there was no mistaking the "world" that faced him in 1933, the year of Hitler's rise to power. Schlier joined the German Confessional Church,* and in 1935 became the head of its theological seminary in Wuppertal; later, he assumed the pastorate of a Confessional parish in Elberfeld.

His intellectual and theological search for the meaning of the "world" led Schlier to inquire into the New Testament view of the essence of the state, the essence of history. Here he encountered Antichrist, who will come at the end of time, as well as the powers and forces of the *seculum;* and here he came upon God's word about the Jews and Gentiles, and the *mysterium* of Israel.

In the thirties, when many students—and not a few teachers of theology as well—fell victims to the worship of the state, Schlier published an article on "The New Testament view of the State" (*Die Beurteilung des Staates im Neuen Testament*). The essential truth about the state, Schlier says, is to be found in the words of Jesus before Pilate. Jesus Christ, in the world, raises up a kingdom that is not of this world. The worldly state can in no way pass judgment on that kingdom or its representatives. Pilate's question

* The group of German Evangelical Christians, established under the leadership of Pastor Martin Niemoeller, which opposed the Nazi-sponsored German-Christian Church Movement, 1933-1945.

"What is truth?" is not, as Schlier sees it, the question of a skeptic, nor that of a realist who does not think much of truth. Rather, Pilate, the representative of state power, is asking for the truth that he himself does not possess. For the state is not that truth on which our life is founded. It is true, of course, that the state has been entrusted by God with supreme power over man. But it can exercise that power in justice only if its refers back to something other than its own authority. Schlier writes:

"The theologically primary answer to the question of how the New Testament judges the state, is not that of Romans 13:1 ff., which is commonly cited in this context, but another and in fact prior answer: to wit, that the real state rightly so called is in heaven—that the worldly state is not *the* state as such. This is cited clearly, more clearly than it emerges from current translations, in Philippians 3:20. The community, the citizenship—for that is the correct translation of *politeuma*, rather than 'conversation'—to which we individuals are from our first origin indigenous, and to which we are thus ultimately obligated, is not the worldly but the heavenly community.... We who are within the Church are already living in the true *polis,* for that is what is meant; we are living by its laws and can no longer accept the worldly state, nor this world generally, as the foundation of our existence. Insofar as the state has any importance at all ... it is only that of a tent soon to be struck, a town whose walls will soon be razed again."

But does not this eschatological reservation in face of the worldly state force the conclusion that the state is superfluous, that we are not bound to obey it? Peter and Paul, the apostles, say on the contrary: it is a sign of true unworldliness, true abstinence from the works of the "flesh," to obey the state, and even evil authority, since it too was instituted by God.

This interpretation of the New Testament texts concerning the state, which was published before 1933, is remarkable in two respects. First, in that it underlies the eschatologically grounded unworldliness of Christians, warning them not to make the state their god; and second, because it maintains with Luther absolute obedience even to evil authority. Other theologians, under the impact of the unspeakable brutalities of the Hitler régime which led to a discussion of the right to resist, have challenged this absolute obedience.

In an article of 1935 Schlier continues in depth his inquiry into the nature of the state and of the world. In the thirteenth chapter of the Apocalypse, John's vision turns to the historical world after Christ. In the figure of the two beasts he portrays Antichrist, a creature of the end of history over which Christ is Lord.

"That creature seen all in all is a misshapen and unholy earthly power. We can grasp only some of the characteristic features of this shape that is now spreading across the world: the litheness of the panther, the strength of the bear, the huge maw of the lion. It is an apparition no longer human but, precisely, beastly—it is the cunning, crude, all-devouring *imperium*, the worldly power ruled by bestial instincts and taking bestial forms. It is not 'the state' as such, political power in the service of the order of this world; it is the political power that has refused its mission to keep order—*perverted political power* in its concrete inhuman shape.

"To this distorted reflection of its nature, which is not an idea outside of time but which comes crawling across the horizon in the shape of an imperium sunk into blind self-worship, Satan lends his strength, his throne, and his great might. For despite its terrible size this political power does not derive its peculiar life from its own self but receives it from its creator. This 'world state' is not only satanically created, it is also satanically endowed. It is thus both the fruit and the instrument of him whom it resembles. It accepts what Jesus the Christ had rejected in the desert, and therein shows its antichristian nature. Its action no longer represents the 'ordinance of God' (Rom. 13:2) but the decree of the devil. Its thrones are Satan's thrones. Its executive power is not political service to God but to God's enemy."

It is hardly possible to carry exegesis closer to the times than this. Exegesis, to Schlier, is never a "purely historical" discipline; he has always insisted on its "actualization" in the hermeneutical performance of existence and on its independent function within theology as a whole.

John's Apocalyspe not only tells us of the end of time—it is also the only book in the New Testament that has history for its theme. In an essay, "On Understanding History" (*Zum Verstaendnis der Geschichte*), drawn from the Apocalypse, Schlier sets out the Christian view of history. Research and reflection, he states, allow man to know the course of events, certain internal and external connections and, perhaps, even some part of the laws of history. But the secret of history, Revelation tells us, can be known "only in a spiritual break-through of history." We must let ourselves be enraptured in the "spirit" to the vision of history's patent events.

"This does not mean that history could be understood in disregard of its concrete historical events, as if 'in principle.' The spiritual transport out of history is in a certain sense also a transport toward history. History is not understood from itself, though through itself and by means of itself. It reveals itself only to the eye that concentrates on the course of events. That means: the truth of history emerges in history only in the historical encounter. History appears—in history—only through the medium of the events in time, not apart from them. Thus the illumined vision of the enraptured prophet who sees through and across history's whole extent rests upon historical persons, institutions, conditions and occurrences of his place and his time, to discern and to make known in them the reflection of the real and all-timely happening. Through the events of his time, he illumines the decisive traits of real history beyond events. In this way every event is for him a kind of symbol, a 'type.' "

But what, according to John, does happen in all the happening of history?

History is the world that happens, in which and through which God asserts for the time being His future domination—the domination which the crucified and risen Jesus Christ has assumed. A somewhat schematic comparison of the Greek, the Jewish, and the Christian views of history might look like this:

"The mark of the Greek view of history is that *circuitus rerum* which carries its meaning within itself. The mark of the Jewish view of history is that process pointing toward an end whose meaning resides and becomes apparent in the end alone. But the peculiarity of the Christian view is this, that neither the circle of becoming and decay itself, nor the end alone, exhausts the meaning of history and so represents the real happening of history—but that the end has irrupted into the circle and has broken it; that it has pointed the course of events toward the end which may in a preliminary fashion become event in every here and now of history. History accordingly is the moment-to-moment preliminary resolution of history's forever impending future."

In this preliminary resolution, the historical events are "pangs" that punish what is past and give birth to what is to come. The spiritual and political positions and institutions of history always take shape in resistance to the forces "that hold open Christ's future in history." These forces bear witness to Him. It is especially in the martyrs that, as Schlier puts it, "the future of Christ occurs historically." These witnesses have faith, love, and hope; they practice vigilance and patience. The extreme rapture of the apostle represents the Christian with a sober, and sobering, situation:

"Confronted daily with the supreme possibility of history, with the love of Christ which, truly concealed now but also truly real, calls from this history which denies it, we are bound to abandon all illusions about history. We will no longer dream of being able to plan and guide and direct its course. Not only because history, even in the narrowest circle of life, fades away into a distance beyond the vision of most men, but because its day-to-day concrete claim is so great and so hard to meet that those who hear it soon run out of time and inclination and power to do more than stand up to the moment, to the momentary vision of the present future of God's love that history offers them."

Another characteristic of the time and the world of our history, Schlier states, is that it is the concrete history of the Jews and the pagans—the history of the Jewish people chosen by God and hardening their hearts, the history of the gathering of the pagan peoples into the Church.

The *Mystery of Israel* (*Das Mysterium Israels*), to which Schlier has devoted several papers, can be fathomed only theologically. All other approaches fail. Israel has one undeniable prerogative: God has chosen it, has given it His promise, His law, and His cult. He has come near to this people as He has to no other. But Israel, as a people, has been unable to bear this nearness of God. Paul describes it thus: "For they stumbled at the stumbling-stone, as it is written: 'Behold I lay in Sion a stumbling-stone and a rock of scandal. And whosoever believeth in him shall not be confounded' " (Rom. 9:33).

John, as Schlier shows, goes yet another step further. He sees the secret of the Jews' apostasy in that they sought not God, but themselves.

"At bottom they bear God a grudge for being chosen, and for the consequences in their lives of that prerogative. At bottom Israel desires to dissolve in the world like other peoples, and yet it cannot because God has chosen it. At bottom Israel wants to be innocuous and human just like the pagans all around. But God oppresses it with His word. They cannot shake the word off—it is in their blood. And so Israel attempts to deceive God and itself with the name of God. It cannot, nor can no longer, conceal God in graven idols; but it can make God an easier burden by making Him a God only for the just and not for those who falter—a God who demands this or that which one gladly gives up, but who does not demand the whole man; a God who demands performance but not love; who is a God to whom one does not need to admit failure, with whom one can remain partners, to whom one does not have to surrender for better or for worse in order to survive.

"This enmity to God runs grumbling through Israel's history in the Old Testament from generation to generation. And it comes to a head at last in the mortal hatred against him in whom God, who gives and who demands everything, has Israel at bay."

Since that time, the people of Israel is "set free in the desert of the world." Nor "will it perish by the impatience of the nations

nor by its own. It rests upon the patience of God." Among all
peoples it remains the people which God has in mind, "the
mysterious center of history."

"This, then, is the mystery of Israel: every Jew carries within
him from his fathers the radiance of God's nearness. Every Jew
is marked with the brand of God's wrath. Over every Jew God
holds His breath. Upon every Jew there also rests even now the
distant glow of that coming day when the dead arise. In all this,
every Jew is the proof of God's gracious and holy patience and
loyalty."

So understood, and that means biblically, the Jew is merely
man's ultimate possibility. Jews and pagans are alike in their
creatureliness. They differ only in their history and their apostasy.

The Jews have been unable to bear God's nearness. The pagans,
Schlier states in explicating the Letter to the Romans, have given
up their existence as God's creatures and so have lost their original
knowledge of God. And now in their delusion they seek God in
the deified image of the creature, and enmesh themselves ever
more deeply in falsehood and in guilt.

Both, then, were in need of redemption, Jews and pagans. Yet
the New Testament leaves no doubt that the mission of the early
Church to the heathen began only after the Jews had rejected the
Messiah.

Schlier's essay of 1942 on "The Mission to the Heathen of the
Early Church" (*Die Entscheidung fuer die Heidenmission in der
Urchristenheit*) is based on researches presented by Erik Peterson
as early as 1929. Schlier offers the following theses:

First, "the mission to the heathen is possible only on condition
that Israel has rejected the Messiah Jesus, and thereby has itself
been rejected as the chosen people."

Second, "the mission to the heathen is possible only on condition
that the Messiah Jesus has been awakened from the dead and
exalted to the right hand of God, has given His Holy Spirit, and
sent His apostles." By His resurrection and exaltation Jesus Christ
becomes the Lord of the world, the judge of the living and the

dead. To Israel this means: its prerogative for historic time is taken from it; the Law is henceforth not a means of salvation. And for the pagans: the *regnum Christi* extends in future over all peoples and all tongues.

Third, "the mission to the heathen is possible only on condition that the end of the world, which has begun with Christ and presses upon the age, is not immediately impending." But then it is necessary "that Christ proclaim to all nations His lordship, which has now become a direct lordship over all the nations and no longer is an indirect lordship mediated through Israel."

This formulation brings up the question of the Church. We must inquire into the biblical texts to learn how Christ meant to proclaim His lordship to all the people, how He meant to exercise it.

The Church—this is the second focus of Schlier's thought, his truly major theme. With it his exegesis of the New Testament and, in particular, of Paul's letters turned into a truly existential interpretation; every passage of the text, every word and every syllable —studied not in a historicizing or psychologizing fashion but for its factual meaning—became a preparation for Schlier's personal decision. His essays on the Church, collected in a volume entitled *The Time of the Church* (*Die Zeit der Kirche*), show his growing awareness of having joined battle with the very principles of modern Protestant theology.

For Schlier, scripture leads beyond itself or, more precisely, it leads through itself to the Church. In his commentary on Galatians, published in 1949 and dedicated to Rudolf Bultman, he shows that Paul knows a norm of proclamation. Paul, to be sure, received the Gospel by the direct revelation of Jesus Christ, and there can be no doubt of the existence of the charismatic-mystical revelation of Christ. But Paul also knows himself to be the bearer of a "fixed Logos." And the fact of the development of the apostolic deposit, which is decisive for an understanding of tradition in a wider sense, can according to Schlier also be documented from scripture:

"The self-tradition of Christ, by the Holy Spirit, within the Church, and radiating in every direction, has been caught up and documented in the New Testament in 'principle,' which means in origin and beginning. It then comes to light in connection with the apostolic deposit which is not only the written tradition of the New Testament, but resides more and more in the total tradition of the Church. There is no other way to a theological understanding of the development of the Jesus tradition into the Gospels, and also in the Gospels. It can be understood only—and this comes out quite clearly especially with the fourth Gospel—as a self-interpretation of the 'archword' of Jesus Christ, by the Holy Spirit, in the faith of the Church. The process of the unfolding of the archevent can, however, also be discerned in the letters of the apostle Paul: not only, for example, in the development of his concept of the Church, but also in the historical phenomenon of the Church. In the pastoral letters themselves, we already find reflections on the status of the unfolding tradition prompted by a new situation confronting the Church. It cannot be denied, then, that in the New Testament both the historical phenomena and their interpretation are seen in the process of development. Historical-critical research has brought this very fact to our attention. At most, the process might be variously interpreted: either as a proper, faithful elaboration at one and the same substance, a constantly new, constantly unfolding representation of that substance; or else as an improper development, departing ever farther from the archsubstance and even contradicting it, gathering up as it were ever new substance on the way, which sooner or later issues in a 'falling-away' from the archevent and the archword."

Even more important to Schlier is a second principle in the New Testament which has been stressed especially by the apostle John: that the Word became flesh.

"The Word became 'flesh,' not word, as it might be posited briefly in view of the modern Protestant, and *in ovo* even of Luther's, understanding of revelation. And since the Word became flesh, not word, there is not only preaching, there is also the sacrament; there is a dogma and not only a creed; there is finally the real presence of Christ in the Church, its institutions, its law, and its liturgy."

The word of Holy Scripture, says Schlier, points to the sacrament, a sacrament that is more than just "sign" or "word." In an essay published as early in 1938, Schlier declared baptism to be the instrumental cause of salvation by virtue of the performance of the act of baptism. This effect distinguishes baptism from a symbolic act which merely represents something which is caused in some other manner. And when Karl Barth in 1943 published an essay on *The Teaching of the Church regarding Baptism,* Schlier opposed Barth's theses in a lecture which he later elaborated into a substantial article. He sums up Barth's crucial statements as follows:

"First: Baptism is in essence an eloquent image of the saving event of Christ's death and resurrection. Its meaning is cognitive.

"Second: Baptism derives its efficacy from the free word and act of Christ and, therefore, is not effective without exception. It is not a necessary means of salvation.

"Third: Baptism has the effect of placing the baptized under the sign of Christ's death and resurrection, and thus binds him inalterably to its solace, its admonition, and its obligation.

"From these three theses follows, fourth, the conclusion: The only proper baptism is the baptism of one who freely decides for baptism, and freely confesses in baptism—but not the baptism of an infant."

Schlier can discover no such concept of baptism or of sacrament in the New Testament. His own interpretation, especially of Romans 6 and other passages in Paul's letters, allows him to state that it is impossible to describe baptism as an "image" of the saving event or to declare its effect to be "cognitive." While it is indeed a *signum,* a signifying action, it yet effects, as a *signum instrumentale,* that which it signifies by its performance, *ex opere operato.*

Schlier finds it stated in the New Testament with the same unmistakable clarity that Christ has instituted baptism, that it is necessary for salvation, and that Christ and the Holy Spirit have bound themselves to the order of baptism. In baptism the baptized is incorporated into Christ's body, receives "all grace as the fundamental grace of the new life," and is reborn.

The idea of rebirth is particularly apt to demonstrate the relation between grace mediated by the word and grace mediated by baptism:

"The rebirth that occurs in baptism is begun by the word which faith apprehends. Baptism itself is the moment when the new man comes into the world, when he is so to speak completely born. The birth begun by the word is completed and 'properly' performed in the baptism."

But, it might be objected, what role does faith play then in baptism? An examination of the apposite passages in scripture—Paul's letters and the Acts—leads Schlier to this conclusion:

"First: According to the New Testament, there is no Christian life without faith and baptism. Faith which has apprehended the word leads self-evidently and necessarily to baptism.

"Second: This actual faith is at the same time the disposition necessary for the baptism of the person to be baptized, and therewith it is a condition of baptism. It represents the personal turn toward the *Kyrios*, and the first and preparatory act of allegiance to Him in whom the faithful is objectively incorporated by baptism.

"Third: The center event, however, toward which faith is directed and for which it is the preparation, in which and by which that faith is confessed ... the event with which the Christian life begins, is the self-efficacious baptism.

"Fourth: Faith then takes baptism up into itself inasmuch as faith itself preserves and ever again reawakens the salvation experienced in baptism. Hence faith—and this is of great importance in this context—is certainly the right disposition for baptism, and in that sense is the condition under which baptism is given. But it is not that which alone renders the event of baptism, as such, effective and so replaces it."

Finally, Schlier rejects Barth's objections to infant baptism. It can be neither proved nor disproved, he states, that infant baptism was practiced in the missionary communities of the early Christians. And in Church history, only the spiritualist sects have so far attacked infant baptism on the ground of the concepts of baptism and of sacrament. Yet if infant baptism is not merely possible but even necessary, we have no right to let a child grow up as the "old man" when it could be the "new man." Beyond that, the saving will of God covers not only the new man but also the new "people," the new mankind, and the new world. And grace "wants to sanctify the individual man down to his roots, and from his roots up"; it wants to be anticipatory grace running ahead of the event.

However, says Schlier, the Word became flesh not only in the sacrament but also in the dogma of the Church that originates in the apostolic kerygma. In his commentary on I Corinthians, he shows how Paul summons the community of Corinth, which wants to recognize only a church of *charisma* and *pneuma,* "back to a church of concrete, time-embodied, final phenomena."

Further, the eternal Word became flesh in the order and the offices of the Church. Schlier finds proof especially in the pastoral letters. His interpretation— and this is methodologically most interesting—is based upon the old liberal Protestant school and yields these conclusions:

"The order of 'the Church of the living God, the pillar and ground of the truth' (I Tim. 3:15), the 'great house' (II Tim. 2:20) of God, rests upon 'office.' The 'power,' the spiritual power, lies in the hands of specific holders of office, who are called, receive the grace of their office, and are appointed to a service; who thus teach and govern the Church, and pass the office on by the laying-on of hands, by consecration. The principle of office prevails.

"This 'office' has its origin in Jesus Christ's call and appointment of the apostles to the service of the Gospel. The office passes on and develops, from generation to generation, through the handing on of the charisma of office (and through the apostolic paradosis) from the apostle to the apostle's disciple, and from him to the local presbyter-bishop. The principle of succession prevails.

"The office knows certain degrees. It shows itself in the service of the apostle's disciple placed over a Church territory where he figures also as the apostolic delegate, and in the service of several 'presiding' elders or bishops in the local church. There is further the service of the deacons and the 'widows,' both of whom perform supporting functions. In its gradation, office shows its tendency toward a monarchic top. The principle of the primate can be discerned."

Incarnation, the real presence of Christ in the Church, takes place finally in the sacrifice of the Mass, the Lord's supper. Schlier's work on *The Proclamation in the Divine Service of the Church* (*Die Verkuendigung im Gottesdienst der Kirche*) interprets this ever-renewed proclamation of the death of Christ:

"The Church is built in the community when the community assembles for the Lord's supper.

"In the Lord's supper the 'memory' of Christ is founded ever anew as it causes the realization of His presence.

"And whatever else remains to be said about the Lord's supper, in its ritual performance it surely is the proclamation and representation of Christ's death for our sakes, as He began it the night of His self-surrender, as it was preserved in the tradition of the Church 'from the Lord onward,' and as it continues to the parousia."

Schlier sees the mystery of Christ and of His Church under yet another, entirely different aspect: the eschatological-pneumatic aspect of the Letter to the Ephesians. His book on *Christ and the Church in the Letter to the Ephesians* (*Christus und die Kirche nach dem Epheserbrief*), published in 1930, first shows his efforts to clarify the exegetical and historical problems, and to define the theological substance, of Paul's letter. His learned commentary under the title *The Letter to the Ephesians* (*Der Brief an die Epheser*), which has been called "an existential interpretation of the mythical imagery and formulations" of Paul's letter, sums up the results of many years of research.

The Church, Paul writes to the Ephesians, has been chosen and preordained in Christ by God's loving will, long before creation.

"In the eternal, unfathomable movement of God's love toward His Son the Church is envisioned and preconceived; in this love rests the Church's existence, from it stems its essence. Its essence, then, does not stem from creation, but rather from the essence of the wisdom of God which was before creation and was His companion, the companion of the eternal love with which He loved His Son. But just by being of the essence of that wisdom, the Church is no stranger to creation. For this wisdom, focused upon the Son and the sons in Him, now expresses itself also and first of all in the creation and its works. Not that the Church appears in the creation, but the wisdom of God, focused on the Son and the sons, kept, as it were, the Church in view when it pronounced the word in which the world was created. And so creation is ordered toward the Church, and the Church points back to creation. And so the wisdom of creation will in the Church once again have the word—not so much as the wisdom of the creation, but in a newer and yet more ancient way, as the wisdom of the eternal providence of God's love. Thus, the Church is not grounded in the creation, nor the creation in the Church; but neither does the Church contradict creation, nor creation the Church. Rather, creation serves the Church by being oriented toward the Church, and the Church serves creation by repeating it in a new way. For the Church reveals creation, but in such a way that the meaning of the wisdom of creation grows clear in the reflection of the Church: the sonship of the sons, and the fatherhood of God in Jesus Christ."

Paul's letter bears unmistakable witness to something further: the "Unity of the Church" (as one of Schlier's essays is entitled). In the one single body of Christ upon the cross, Jews and pagans, all men, are reconciled with God. And this one single body of Christ lives historically and concretely in the Church:

"To the apostle, the unity of the Church is a *mark of its essence.* The Church fulfills its essence, that is, its being, what it is, only if it is *one.* The reason is that the Church owes its essential being to *one body of Christ upon the cross,* that it is the effect and the elaboration of that vast realm of life within the power of the one Holy Spirit which opened up in the death of Christ. This unity of the Church, now, is in essence *historical-concrete*. The Body of Christ has its essence nowhere else than in the real presence of the Church. The Lord has established His presence here on earth in us as members of His body. He has done it by means of the concrete Gospel and of concrete, effective signs. He has made use of concrete implements and institutions. In the same way He has joined concrete unity in concrete faith, thought, hope, and love. 'One body and one spirit: as you are called in one hope of your calling. One Lord, one faith, one baptism. One God and Father of all, who is above all, and though all, and in us all" (Eph. 4:4-6).

The search for the Church determines the way of Schlier the theologian. Protestant exegete, student of Karl Barth and Rudolf Bultmann, he finds after many years of unprejudiced study of the New Testament, and in particular of Paul's letters, that the Catholic Church has remained in essence evangelic, faithful to Holy Scripture.

There is another thing about Schlier's work: he retains the arch-evangelical heritage of the word, but he renews, refreshes it by means of the at once enlarging and compressing stylistic power of Martin Heidegger, to make it render service to the Church's proclamation. His language thus is incredibly tight, weighty because charged with meaning—a language that carries a new force of witness and conviction. His short essay of 1958, *God's Word, a New Testament Recollection* (*Wort Gottes—eine neutestamentliche Besinnung*), may be read as a sketch for a theology of the word.

"The word that God speaks, and the word that Christ speaks, is the 'word' *per se,* that which in reality and truth is the 'word.' ... Since God's word, or respectively Christ's word, is *the* word *per se,* we can conclude further that any word is word insofar as it participates in the word of God.

"Yet we pass over, by mere force of habit, another simple situation of fact which is far from self-evident, nay, is extremely strange and even incredible: that the New Testament, and especially Paul the apostle, also calls God's word and the Lord's word—and even God's Gospel and Christ's Gospel— 'my' or 'our' word, 'my' or 'our' Gospel.... Both God's word and the apostle's word, the apostle's word and Christ's word, patently coincide or at any rate are so imbedded one in the other that hearing one, the apostle's word, we can hear the other, God's or Christ's word."

But the apostle whom Christ has empowered to proclaim "his" Gospel as a witness of the risen Christ is conscious that he must proclaim it in utter simplicity and must bear witness to it by his own existence. The only thing that matters is that Christ be present in it and Himself confront the hearers. And how does Christ's presence occur in the word of post-apostolic times, in the course of history? Here we are face to face with the question whether and how the word, the epiphany of Jesus Christ, continues within the Church.

"The Gospel as the word of God on the lips of man, in being given to the Church through the hands of the apostolic successors not only did not lose its essential nature, but on the contrary has only now reached the fullness of its essence. For only now it becomes evident that it has entered completely into the word of the apostolic witnesses, entered really into history. The word of man does, after all, live in history not by being said once and then disappearing—to be at best remembered as fixed in its own time, to be dug up in its old form and presented in its distant shape. The word of man lives in history rather in such a way that what has once been said is interpreted and so, safeguarded in the interpretation, is handed on. And this manner of living in history, of man's word, has been achieved fully by God's word or the Gospel only when it became the apostolic tradition of the Church, understood in ever new ways and so unfolding in the performance of its ongoing service."

The proclamation of the word in the Church and through the Church occurs in the sermon which, understood biblically, is the prophetic word; in the liturgy; and most concentrated, in the Lord's supper. At the Lord's supper, says Schlier, the community lets the word "fall silent and turn into sign." The verbal proclamation of Christ's death at the Lord's supper—"Whenever you shall eat this bread and drink this wine, you proclaim the death of the Lord"—this proclamation by the word cannot be separated from the proclamation by the act that takes place there.

"In this proclamation of the death of Christ, which itself is centered in the repetition of the (transubstantiating) words of the Lord, the Lord in death does in effect appear and communicate Himself in the sign, the sign into which the word has let the word fall silent, and in which Christ in ultimate self-surrender is still present only in 'elements.' This word, then, if we may put it that way, is the 'densest' word in two respects. First, in that it reveals the death of Christ, the saving event in which all others issue and assume their purpose and foundation. And second, in that it makes present the central saving event in which everything is 'said,' in a mode in which the word beyond word is given in pure sign (bread and wine).

"But if the word of proclamation in the Lord's supper, and more precisely the transubstantiating word within this proclamation in the Lord's supper, is God's 'densest' word, *the* word of the word of God, the Gospel, then every other word that is proclaimed is merely a fore-word to it. Still it remains God's word and effects less than the presence of the Christ Jesus who reveals Himself through the word of man, in the power of the Holy Spirit, in the mode of the word. And as a fore-word in this sense, it is nothing else than the tradition of Christ Jesus Himself to those who in hearing 'receive' it and 'pass it on.'"

We said at the start that Heinrich Schlier's researches and re-flections are focused upon two themes: 'world' and 'Church.' In one sally after another he attempts to penetrate to the very center of the history of salvation. And in the process, he sees that, since the incarnation of the word, the time of the world—this eon—is truly the "time of the Church"; and that the Church is the rule, is proper to the world, is where the world is at home. As he once said: "The Church now is the world."

HANS URS VON BALTHASAR

BY

Jakob Laubach

Some years ago Hans Urs von Balthasar, as he looked back upon his published work on the occasion of his fiftieth birthday, remarked that he had written "a good many seemingly quite disparate things." And indeed, a first glance at his numerous and thematically greatly varied writings—studies in German literature and language as well as in philosophy, translations from various languages, and contributions to patristics, controversial theology and theology of history—only tends to strengthen that impression.

But, as Reinhold Schneider has pointed out, Balthasar's publications are in fact variations on a single theme, the theme of *time*. We hope to show that Balthasar's thought and work move always in three areas which might be described as follows: the revelation of the fullness of God in Jesus Christ; the Church as the fullness of Christ and the realm of Christ's message; and the radiance of the Church within the world.

Balthasar's first large publication, *The Apocalypse of the German Soul* (*Die Apokalypse der Deutschen Seele,* 3 volumes, 1937-1939), deals of course with German literature, but even here the author raises the question of "ultimate commitments." He offers a compelling survey of the Promethean stance from Lessing to Rilke, and guides us through the work of the philosophers and poets up to that very point where—willingly or against passionate resistance—it opens up to Christ. And yet he sees also with shattering clarity the catastrophe of German idealism which, in setting itself up as an absolute, was to yield so apocalpytic a harvest.

This book grew out of the dissertation which Hans Urs von Balthasar submitted at Zürich in 1929. Born in 1905, he attended the Benedictine gymnasium in Engelberg, continued at the Jesuit college in Feldkirch, and then went on to Zürich in 1923. At Zürich, Vienna and Berlin he spent nine semesters in the study of German literature and philosophy.

The turning point in Balthasar's inner development came in his encounter with Ignatius Loyola. In 1929 Balthasar became a member of the Society of Jesus. He spent his first three years studying philosophy at the seminary of the order in Pullach, where he came into close contact with Peter Lippert, and with Erich Przywara who strongly influenced the direction of his philosophical studies and ideas.

His years of theological formation, 1934 to 1938, Balthasar served with the Jesuits in Lyons. These years in France, he feels, were absolutely decisive. For it was in Lyons that he met Jean Daniélou, Gaston Fessard and, above all, Henri de Lubac, who interested him in patristics. In Lyons, too, he came to know Paul Claudel; later in Basle he met Albert Béguin, Georges Bernanos' great friend and critic.

Hans Urs von Balthasar, as he himself once put it, wants "a kneeling, not a sitting theology." Basically, theology is "adoration and sanctity, or love of God and neighbor," even if "between these two poles of Christian dealings with the word of God—poles which at once call for each other, fuse into one another—something is inserted that can be called a theoretical concern with the word." To him, theological disputations of the word, such as we find especially in the Gospel of John, are always "on their way either toward the act of faith or else toward the act of faithlessness." This is the point where philology begins—philology which does not intend to lose itself in adoration and obedience but is sufficient unto itself. However, "the theology of the Church is not permitted to remain within the epoch of theory any longer than were the Jews who walked with the Word of God."

This view has a number of consequences for the structure of theology. All occupation with the finiteness of the word—with concept, image, sentence, context—is of necessity nothing but an approach to the infinity that in the word became flesh. The formulation of a logic of the thought and expression of the word of God, though it is absolutely necessary, must grow out of the fundamental fact, accepted by faith, that God became man. In an essay under the title *What is the use of Theology?* (*Was soll Theologie*), of 1953, Balthasar writes:

"Neither history nor evolution nor philosophy is speaking here, but only faith itself, which demands that formulation of the language of theology which will lead to more profound adoration, to better obedience in the conduct of life. The theologian, then, is expected to apply the laws of human thought in such a way that they make visible the laws of faith. . . .

"In other words: any concept of theology has to be catholic, which means universal: embracing and drawing into it all truth, or opening itself to all truth, removing all division, rising through death to life in heavenly truth—and do so in faith, not in (Hegelian-dialectical) knowledge, or else in a knowledge which itself is a faith searching and finding in proportion as it has adoration and obedience and grace. A Catholic concept, therefore, is not at all the same thing as a Platonic or an Aristotelian concept, because the word of God in human form (flesh, or Holy Scripture) is not just any word. Such an 'all-inclusive' or 'all-opening' Catholic logic is not an invitation to dissolve everything in a vague, inspirational infinity— it is the intellectually most demanding attitude there is, where our thought is forever face to face with a decision for the word of God, not just in content but even in form, in the very act of thinking which, therefore, must bear the stigma of Catholic logic. Theology takes place in the tribunal where the word of God judges the word of man; the word entire of Holy Scripture, from beginning to end, bears this face: how could theology escape it!"

Balthasar's account of the function of theology is based on this: the Word, which is God, became man without ceasing to be God. His personal encounter with Christ the Word is brought about by Ignatius Loyola, whose *Exercises* Balthasar published in 1946 in a new translation because these exercises represent to him the basic structure of a theology worked out in human terms. His guide into the very depths of the mystery of the incarnation, Balthasar knows, is the Gospel of John, which grows especially meaningful to him in the interpretation of Adrienne von Speyr. Everything that is of decisive importance, he once said, takes place within the spiritual area that lies between John and Ignatius—the area of vocation, of being chosen by Christ.

Christ, the Word become flesh, is the key to all the problems of scripture, because the letter is to the spirit as the flesh of Christ is to His divine nature and person.

Christ, the concrete primal idea of the creating God, must be thought of as the basis of all ontology, because this truth holds: "Once and for all times, Being was in being."

Christ, as "the center of all the ways of God," also calls for an eschatology which makes manifest all creation as judged and redeemed by Christ—as the event which once and for all has gone beyond the God-man situation of the Old Covenant, and which is yet ever new for every man at every moment.

And the existence of Christ is, in the end, the norm of history. Christ is "the heart of the world."

These, then, are the dimensions in which Hans Urs von Balthasar sees the Word become flesh. His ideas on eschatology are to be found in an essay in the collection *Current Problems of Theology*

(*Fragen der Theologie Heute*) of 1958. Eschatology, he writes, is the "storm center" of present-day theology. The increasing radicalization of all liberal theology thus takes place under the sign of the "uneventuated" return of Christ: that is, under the aspect of eschatology. Karl Barth's counter-movement is a programmatic "eschatologization" of theology as a whole. And Bultmann's demythologizing and existentializing of theology, too, stems positively as well as negatively from the same storm center.

And yet all this plowing-up of theology under the aspect of eschatology so far has not led to a systematic, all-embracing exposition. We are today faced with a radical reduction:

"The vertiginous number of years of human history between 'Adam' and Abraham which made the heads of the nineteenth century swim, the still more unimaginable number of 'eons' from the foundation of the world to Adam, the intimation of the true dimensions of the universe and still more of its constant expansion —these seemed at first to destroy all common yardsticks between such a world and the biblical 'world's end.' They absolutely put an end to any placing of the eschatological 'places'—heaven, hell, purgatory, limbo—anywhere within that One World, since this world, once a theological cosmos whose limits touched above on the Divine, below on the demonic, had now turned into a physical cosmos; they even put an end (though this was less clearly understood) to the idea of the 'end of time' (of planet Earth, for instance) as an event of theological relevance. The 'last things' of man, of his history and his universe, all had now to be taken over into an entirely new dimension, a dimension which from the start could only be one of revelation and of faith. Two consequences followed: the last things, the *eschata*, escaped 'visualization' in thought in a completely new manner because the whole world system, and all of earthly, aborning, living, dying mankind, was now referred to a dimension thrown open only by God's revelatory action upon the world. On the other hand, all of theology was now in turn seized by the *eschata*—they eschatologized theology; they now were essentially *the* world, *the* human kind, *the* human history, in that God's decisive and transmuting action acts upon them.

"In other words: the so-called last things became only the more actual in proportion as they escaped visualization; they turned into 'last event,' affecting the being and the history of man and world. It was no longer 'last things' in a cosmos understood in the old theological sense. The cosmos now referred beyond itself, to the action of God."

This view, Balthasar admits, involves a certain danger of "a-cosmism." But, as the great French exegete Lagrange noted long before Bultmann, that is the situation which leads us directly to the center of Old Testament faith: the living God, in heaven or on earth, alone remains before the eyes of the psalmist, the eyes of the believer. For this reason, current eschatological reflection shows a pronouncedly anti-Platonist trend, because the dichotomy into a mortal body and an immortal soul misses the decisive point of the phenomenon of death. Precisely because the event in which the cosmos transcends into the "ultimate" cannot be interpreted in terms of cosmology and within history, the final act of God's salvation is an action upon the creature, the creature's redefinition. And since the turn from the Old to the New eon is identical in meaning with the death and resurrection of the son of God, his "return" to the Father is the creation of that dimension into which man and cosmos are beginning to turn by God's freely given grace.

The christological structure of eschatology has a number of consequences—for eschatology itself, for the other areas of theology, and for the encounter between theology and philosophy in the question of the natural and supernatural finality of man and cosmos as reformulated especially by Teilhard de Chardin.

All Christian reflection upon history as well must start with Christ the Word become flesh. The "nucleus" of such a theology Balthasar projects in his book, *A Theology of History*, published in 1958. In this work, Balthasar deals with Christ's mode of time, the inclusion of history within the life of Christ, Christ as the norm of history, and history under the norm of Christ.

The Son's form of existence, which makes Him the Son from all eternity, is the uninterrupted reception of everything that He is from the Father: existence as receiving, as openness to the will of the Father, as subsistent fulfillment of that will in a continuous mission. This receptivity to everything that comes to Him from the Father is the basis of *time* and *temporality* as these terms apply to the Son:

"What tells us more than anything else that Jesus' mode of time is indeed real is the fact that He does not anticipate the will of the Father. He does not do that precise thing which we try to do when we sin, which is to break out of time, within which are contained God's dispositions for us, in order to arrogate to ourselves a sort of eternity, to 'take the long view' and 'make sure of things.' Both Irenaeus and Clement consider that original sin consisted in anticipation of this kind; and indeed, at the close of Revelation, the reward which the Son bestows upon the victor is that fruit of Paradise which the sinner, to his own harm, had stolen in anticipation. God intended man to have *all* good, but in His, God's time; and therefore, all disobedience, all sin, consists essentially in breaking out of time. Hence the restoration of order by the Son of God had to be the annulment of that premature snatching at knowledge, the beating down of the hand outstretched towards eternity, the repentant return from a false, swift transfer into eternity to a true, slow confinement in time."

Christ not only has time for God and from God, but He is also the point "at which God has time for the world." "This disclosure of God through time is identical with grace; access to Him granted by Himself." It follows that the time in which we live is not a purely "natural" phenomenon. Man's time as contained within this time, which is to say Christian existence, is determined as to its content by "these three" (I Cor. 13:13): faith, hope and love. But these theological virtues must not be considered one-sidedly in the perspective of an abstract Platonist-Aristotelian or any other philosophical or mystical antithesis between time and eternity.

"Only a genuine theology of time, gained from the contemplation of Christ's existence, can provide a sound concept of eternity, consistent with Revelation, as a basis for the very ground of Christian existence, which is believing and hoping love. If we think in terms of escaping from time, faith and hope will necessarily be reduced to preliminaries belonging to this world. . . .

"The most important and the most striking consequence of this is that only a genuinely theological notion of time can show Christian faith to be a true imitation of Christ. If the central foundation of Christ's act of existence as man is seen as a timeless vision (timeless at least in content), then the followers of Christ cannot imitate Him at all in this act, and Christ's position as archetype and prototype really is called in question."

But Christ "not only has time" because the whole of His life is an openness toward the Father; he also includes history within His life by obediently accepting and fulfilling the tradition of God's covenant. It follows that grace is historical.

However, Christ's inclusion of our time and our history is not sufficient explanation of the way in which Christ becomes the norm of history. Further reflection on the reality of Christ is needed to show in what way He became not only the supreme moral exemplar but the inward and necessary norm of every life. The question is: how can the individual existence of Christ be so universalized? And the answer is: by the action of the Holy Spirit.

Balthasar considers three ways in which the Spirit acts in history. The first concerns the working of the Spirit upon the incarnate Son Himself, in the forty days after the Resurrection when the glory of His divinity, and the presence of eternity in time, radiate unbroken. The second is the working of the Spirit as He relates to the historical Church of every age, expressed typically in the sacraments and most fully in the Eucharist. A third completes this relation by creating the missions of the Church and of the individual as applications of the life of Christ.

Christ, entered into history, then, by the action of the Holy Spirit, becomes universalized, becomes the norm of history.

How does Christ place man and history under His norm? All things created have their beginning and their end in Christ, and He will come one day to judge all history. But this completion of the meaning of history in Christ is not to be understood as though created nature had in it no immanent meaning of its own, but only in Christ.

"Unless the incarnation involves the acceptance of an immanent essence conferred by the act of creation and not able to be lost, there could be no truer incarnation, no possibility of God's becoming man and becoming history. It is not a definition of the essence of man that he is a member of Christ; nor of world history that it is co-extensive (invisibly) with the history of the Kingdom of God."

If the law of the Incarnation requires that the meaning of history should not be imposed from above, but must emerge from the union of what God destines for it with its own interior line of development, we must examine what that line of development is and how the union is accomplished.

Existence, Balthasar says, since Plato, can no longer be interpreted apart from some concept of progress. "A movement of progress from earth to heaven, from subjection to death to kinship with the gods; a setting up of the image of man as one who turns away from the horizontal, animal level to the ethereal world above: such is the basic experience of the great cultures for the two or three millennia before Christ.... But the biblical experience is the first to swing the vertical interpretation over so as to coincide with the horizontal; hitherto the divine pole has always lain exclusively above; from now on it will equally, and essentially, lie in the future, in time. God is awaited in history. He will come and hold judgment on earth...."

But the history of Israel is always a twofold history; it is both secular and sacred. This raises a difficulty full of importance for the theologian—whether that other history which runs concurrently beneath the sacred history of Israel bears any relationship, precisely as history, to the historically attained "fullness of time." For Hegel, who recognizes only one history, at once sacred and secular, the answer must obviously be "Yes": so, too, for the Christian theologian of history since Justin and Eusebius. But Protestant theologians of history, such as Karl Loewith for example, object that "the relation of the salvation-event to world history can neither be demonstrated historically nor established from the data of faith."

Balthasar here returns to his starting point, the Incarnation of Christ, to clarify further the relation between secular and sacred history. The "middle wall of partition" between secular and sacred history ends at the point where the Word no longer sounds prophetically from heaven but becomes flesh, i.e., man. Since Christ, all history is basically "sacred," not least because of the Church's presence and testimony within that one all-inclusive world history.

This also throws new light on matter, which in the philosophy and mysticism of the ancients was regarded as a place of banishment and servitude from which the spirit had to liberate itself. But nowadays matter assumes another aspect—it becomes a hierarchy of successive and evolving forms of life which are inwardly oriented towards the supreme form they attain in man, who ontogenetically recapitulates in himself, crowns and transcends all the forms of nature.

Christ the Incarnate Word ultimately draws back into eternity all that exists in time. He, who as redeemer and judge rules all human and all cosmic history, by becoming man has been linked so deeply to creation, so fused with it, that He may be called *The Heart of the World* (*Das Herz der Welt*), the title of a book with 13 Christ-hymns which Balthasar published in 1945. The hymns represent a form of contemplative prayer which, for Balthasar, is an essential part of theology.

In this book "heart speaks to heart" in words inspired by the literature and poetry of many generations.

"You sense the times—how then could you not also sense the heart? You feel the current of grace that presses toward you warm and throbbing—how could you not feel, too, how you are loved? You seek for proof—and are yourself the proof. You seek to catch Him, the unknown, in the mesh of your knowledge—and are yourself caught in the ineluctable net of His power. You want to grasp —and you are in the grasp. You want to conquer—and you are conquered. You pretend to seek—and have yourself been found long ago and forever. You grope through a thousand veils for a living body—and you would claim you do not feel the hand that without veil rests on your naked soul? You flit about in the haste of your restless heart and call it religion, but in truth it is the jumping of the fish wriggling in the net. You desire to find God, even at the price of a thousand pains; what humiliation that your action was acting, because He holds you already in His hand. Put your finger on the living pulse of being. Feel the throbbing, which in a single act of creation claims you and sets you free. Which in the tremendous outpouring of existence at once sets the precise measure of the distance: how you are to love Him as the closest neighbor, and to sink down before Him as the highest of the high. How in one single act He clothes you for love, and for love strips you bare. How with your life He gives all treasure into your hands, and the most precious prize: that you can requite His love, His giving—and yet how He (not afterward, not on the second count, the second step, but at once) takes back all He has given, so that you may love the giver not the gift and in the giving know yourself to be no more than a ripple in His stream. In one flash you are at once close and far, encounter a friend—and a master. You are at once His son and His servant. This first thing you will not outrun. Such as you became, you will live in eternity; for even if your virtue, your wisdom, your love were to tower high past all measure, and if you grew past men and angels straight up through all the heavens, you never grow away from the origin. But nothing is more blessed than this first thing; and even on the widest arc of growth you would forever arch back to this original miracle; for the being of love is magnificent past understanding."

The revelation of God's overflowing fullness in Jesus Christ! That is for Hans Urs von Balthasar the one central fact. It concerns him especially in relation to a new eschatology and theology of history. But these, as he once said, call for an inclusive "theology of the Word." He thinks of his patristic studies, and his introductions to Irenaeus, Origen, Gregory of Nyssa, Maximus the Confessor, and of Augustine as elements of such a theology.

In the same context belong his reflections on the theology of the word of Martin Buber and Karl Barth.

The dialogue between Israel and the Church seems to Balthasar an urgent necessity. The Christian must finally, he says in his *Martin Buber and Christianity*, "receive something vital and alive from the Jew, something more than the letter of the scriptures as they were handed down, something that could not be divorced from the living voice, very necessary perhaps, and bearing upon salvation." In recent decades, especially, we are beginning to discern the deep roots that Christianity had in its Jewish setting, as for example, the findings of Qumran demonstrate. And in a certain sense there is validity even in Buber's assertion that the impelling power of Jesus' message stems from the ancient Jewish demand for unconditional decision, from Abraham's faith.

Buber sees no other way to overcome the dualism between spirit and body, religion and political life, than by a return to a prophetic theocracy; and all apocalyptic theology that seeks to construct a visionary beyond upon the ruins of this world is an apostasy from the sacramental, grace-given unity of people and country. He charges the Christians in particular with having promoted this dualism.

In that context Balthasar makes this shattering remark:

"Christianity re-established the dualism of sacred and profane, of Church and State, which may perhaps be regarded as a convenient way of avoiding the real task, or if it is in some sense justifiable would still have to be regarded as encouraging that form of escapism. The real task is to be converted and, by realizing the faith here and now, to make room for the Kingdom of God. The Sermon on the Mount means neither more nor less. . . ."

Having noted a number of undeniable agreements between Judaism and Christianity, Balthasar shows that the two move in opposite directions:

"One might almost say that Israel's life, the movement of its life, is an eternal return from the dispersion. The movement of the Church is the exact opposite, a centrifugal movement, going out to all the nations of the earth at all times. . . ."

His dialogue with Buber serves Balthasar at the same time to clarify his own attitude toward the Old Testament.

In a large work published in 1951, Balthasar sets out to present and interpret the theology of Karl Barth. He looks upon it as a renewal of patristics. He traces Barth's theological development down to the decisive point where Barth, from the infinite otherness between creator and creature, turned to the possibility of appropriation by faith, the *analogia fidei*. Balthasar sees the completion of Barth's turn at that point where Barth replaces his central concept of "the word of God" with the concept "Jesus Christ, God and man," and begins to draw out all the consequences. Barth's decisive insight consists in the realization that Christ is not only the redeemer but also the real ground of divine creation. In order to compare Barth's crucial positions in Christology, and in the doctrines of nature, grace, and sin, with Catholic doctrine, Balthasar also studies the specifically "Catholic form of thought" as it developed in the course of history.

Balthasar concludes that the differences between Barth and Catholic theology in respect to the doctrine of grace and to Christology are not so deep as to justify a schism; they are no greater than the differences within Protestantism, such as between Karl Barth and Emil Brunner, nor the differences within Catholicism, such as in the interpretations of Vatican I. But let us note: the same does not hold for the doctrine of the Church and of the sacraments, where views are crucially divided.

Balthasar's second central theme is the Church as the fullness of Christ and the realm of His mission. True, Balthasar deals with this subject more in the role of editor than that of author. To him, the spirit of the Church of Christ is above all a spirit of sanctity and of mission. His collection of portraits of saints, entitled *Men of the Church in Witness and Document* (*Menschen der Kirche in Zeugnis und Urkunde*), is intended to present the sense of mission, not the psychology, of the saints.

In the same sense—safekeeping what is subjective in the Church

within that which is objective—we must understand also Balthasar's works on Augustine. Especially in his introduction to a widely
distributed edition of Augustine's *Confessions*, he points out that
here, for the first time, "Christian subjectivity" raises its head, "with
all the enrapturing and questionable things that will in the future
become possible under this heading." He stresses that Augustine's
Confessions must always be read in the context of his great theological treatises on the Trinity and the City of God, and of his four
great commentaries on scripture.

Balthasar deems it proper to oppose the one-sided emphasis on
the "grandiose subjectivity" of the saints and mystics that is an ever-
present danger in monastery and Church. This view becomes perhaps clearest in his biography of Therese of Lisieux, whose life he
intentionally presents as the "history of a mission," not the "history
of a soul"; in his book on Elizabeth of Dijon; and in the introduction to the *Book of Flowing Praise* (*Das Buch vom stroemenden
Lob*) of Mechthild of Hackeborn.

The Church filled with Christ must radiate its fullness into all
the world, and in its dialogue with the world must draw toward
itself all truth and beauty and freedom of creation. Here is the
third of Balthasar's major themes. The Church, in the New Covenant, completes the essence of the synagogue to be the people of
promise, the people for all men. "As an anticipation of the universal
Kingdom of God, the Church *transcends* its visible form, founded
by Christ and indissoluble, into an (eschatological) wholeness."
Balthasar finds this concept of the Church among the Greek
Church Fathers, who see the Church "as the sacrament of the redeemed cosmos, the light of Christ that progressively illumines all
the world's darkness."

The penetration of Church and cosmos that is effective in Christ,
says Balthasar, is the fundamental experience of such Catholic
writers as Paul Claudel, Georges Bernanos, and Reinhold Schneider. These he studies with special care. It has been held against
Balthasar that he, a publishing theologian, paid too much attention
to writers and poets. However, Balthasar replies in polemic vein in

his book on Bernanos of 1954, it could be "that in the great Catholic writers, more original and great and freely growing vital thought can be found than among the narrow-chested theology of our day that is content to subsist on thin soup."

The most interesting thing about his translation of Claudel's *Satin Slipper* is Balthasar's epilogue. Claudel, says Balthasar, eager for the world as no Christian ever was, like Columbus discovers the terrible and enchanting fact that the curved line returns into itself. This is to say:

"Mankind is referred back to itself not only in terms of its geography and astronomy—no, its arrow-straight yearning upward to the angels returns upon itself: if there be paradise, it can be nowhere but on earth—an earth that may be consumed in its own yearning and guilt, consumed in God's fire of punishment and love, yet an earth reborn, transfigured as earth....

"The whole globe is the stage not only outwardly but also, of necessity, inwardly; whenever two humans love each other, the fate of the earth hangs in the balance; love makes sense only under this horizon, and its twofold movement of an infinite arrow-straight yearning that no limits can satisfy, and of an infinitely circling rest that wants nothing but itself, is the horizon of the world, and the problem of the earth.

"Claudel knows that this is a religious problem, and that the problem of the horizon can be solved only in God. He also knows that the solution must, through all deaths, embrace the unabridged fullness of the earth....

"Renunciation is not a self-chosen, self-empowered No against the Yes of the world; it means rather that we are opened completely to the searing, the division, the torture, and the crucifixion of true, yes-saying love. Read in this way, Claudel's work is something like a primer of asceticism, an intimation of a primer of mysticism by a Christian layman for Christian laymen. The cross is not a separate, world-denying stake of torture; the world itself and the love of the world, developed to the limit of their inner logic, are under the shadow of Golgotha. The contradiction between the eternal, arrow-straight yearning and the closed, circle- and globe-shaped worldliness, is the brand of the cross burned into the world's being. The horizon of the world is the cross itself."

The problem, then, raised by this drama, the problem that will not leave Balthasar, is this: How is it possible to be at once entirely worldly and entirely God's own?

For Bernanos, too, the *locus* of his existence lies where the three-fold counsel of Christ's Sermon on the Mount "intersects with the full existence in the world; the place at which the form and ideals of the two positions, closed toward one another, open themselves each to the other"; it is the place "of the essential transcendence of the Church into the world." Bernanos' concern is the world, and the Church is to him the means and the way for the world's redemption. By sinking himself into the extreme solitude of anguish and death, he also experiences the deepest communion with men, the solidarity of guilt, and vicarious atonement. The deepest human anguish turns into the anguish of grace.

"Bernanos gives the decisive Christian (not existentialist!) answer to the philosophical method of Heidegger and Sartre, who have raised anguish to the pre-eminent means and medium of the experience of existence. He, for whom anguish is not a matter of literary interest but a terrible elementary experience, allows us to see what truth there may be in it; and also what Christian meaning the whole may have, or may assume—the meaning of a complete denuding of all being before God, and immersion of this entirely denuded being into the embracing, in-grace-covering, passion of the Son of God."

In 1953 Balthasar also presents a theological study of the problem, under the title *The Christian and Anguish* (*Der Christ und die Angst*). He first turns to scripture. The Old Testament knows the general anguish of existence, the anguish of the sinners who from the luminous presence of God go out into the darkness that separates and renders solitary, and the anguish of the just who forever tremble for their tie with God. In the New Testament we encounter again the same forms of anguish, more often even heightened. But what is decisively new is the anguish of the Redeemer.

The new eon is born in anguish upon the cross. Balthasar formulates three laws of Christian anguish:

"First: Christianity intends and is able to deliver man from the anguish of sin, if man will open himself to redemption and its conditions; Christianity freely gives to man, in place of the anguish of sin, the fearless access to God in faith, love, and hope; but these, themselves stemming from the cross, may bring forth a new, grace-inspired, atoning form of anguish which stems from Catholic solidarity.

"Second: Inasmuch as we are sinners, and even as believers may ever again become sinners, the objective act of redemption upon the cross does not simply relieve us of the anguish of sin; rather, this anguish confronts us also in the New Testament. We may leave it behind to the extent that we appropriate in truth the faith offered to us from the cross, that is, the faith that works in our life; but even in the grace of the anguish of the cross that is bestowed on us, the distance between the original redeeming sufferer and us who suffer with Him is fully retained and is present to the anguished mind.

"Third: God does not bestow the (mystical or merely ordinary) participation in the anguish of His Son upon the cross on any believer to whom He has not first given the gift of the full force of the Christian mission, and of the joy in the full light of faith, love, and hope—whom He has not first relieved of the anguish of sin. To think a 'synthesis' of the two possible, or even desirable, is not in keeping with healthy Christian doctrine."

The question how a Christian of today may respond most deeply to the anguish of the world, the anguish of sin and of the cross, and help to bear it: this is the question also of what the Church must be like today to fulfill her mission in the world. What is needed here, Balthasar says in *The Razing of the Ramparts* (*Die Schleifung der Bastionen*) of 1952, is the breaking down of the encapsuled and hardened attitudes that have grown through history. After listing the most important issues for the Church's self-appraisal, he names two axioms that call for radical re-thinking: the ancient tenet,

"There is no salvation outside the Church," and Christ's imperative statement, "You are the light of the world." Both are focused on the idea of the common fate that is the mark of our time. To realize this idea, an ever deeper and more resolute incarnation of the Church in the world is needed. The more the Church comes out of its isolation, the more it steps forth from behind its ramparts in order to re-establish contact with the sorrows and hopes of mankind, the more the individual Christian must think of himself, with the Church, as himself the Church.

We thus return once again to the point which for Balthasar marks the intersection between the eternal, arrow-straight yearning and the closed, circled worldliness. It is both the starting point and terminal point of Christian existence, especially of that existence which intends to be both all worldly and all God's own, in the midst of the world but not of the world.

A form of the Church's radiation into the life of the world which is particularly in keeping with our times is, in Balthasar's view, the secular institutes. Even in those early years, 1940 to 1948, when he was student chaplain at the University of Basle, he worked intensively for this new form of Church life, both among young academicians and far beyond their circle. In 1950, after consultation with the General of the Order, he left the Society of Jesus in order to devote himself fully to the secular institutes, and to his own writing.

A book of 1948, *The Layman and the Orders* (*Der Laie und der Ordensstand*), as well as an essay of 1956, sketch the theology of the orders and, in particular, of the secular institutes.

All theological understanding of the orders of the Church, Balthasar says, must start with the fact that the Church, as the body, the bride and the fullness of Christ, is a mystery. Therefore, the vital forms of the existence of the Church, too, are related to each other in a mysterious dialectic.

Balthasar sees a first field of tension in the relation between eschatology and incarnation. The state of those who follow the counsels of perfection, and live in chastity, poverty and obedience, is the acceptance in all earnest of the fact that the Christian has been called out of the old eon. In this light, the secular state is and re-

mains a sort of "concession" to the old eon. An eschatological existence, on the other hand, oriented toward the end—the Return of
the Lord—does not mean detachment, spiritualization, a turning
away from history but, on the contrary, is the starting point of the
Christian mission to the world. The Resurrection does not contradict the Incarnation: it represents its perfection.

The second field of tension is that between general and special
vocation. To follow closely the counsels of perfection is somehow
exclusive, single-minded; the secular state, by contrast, seems characterized by "division" and the "care of the world." These "degrees," found unmistakably in the teachings of Christ, of Paul and
of the Church, can, however, be explained in terms of ethics only
if seen in context with the special vocation which, after all, is not
simply a personal choice.

Now since all Christians are, in a general sense, "called," the state
of those who follow the counsels of perfection is merely the radical
form of the Christian state as such.

At this point Balthasar asks: Why should not this radical form
lay stress at one time on the "eschatological," at another time on
the "incarnational" dimension?

"Just as it is impossible to indicate with precision Christ's position in relation to the world, just so it is impossible to fix with precision the position of him who follows Christ (radically)—and that
impossibility is merely a reflection of the general condition of sus-
pense of the Christian 'in the world but not of the world.' By
following the counsels of perfection, man *can* and may assume the
eschatological position, with its emphasis on distance toward the
world. But just as surely—and this is what happens in the secular
institutes—he may choose a position in the world, among the
Christians of the secular state and the men outside the Church.
Christ Himself did just that, as a laborer no less than as a teacher
and miracle-worker."

More difficult to explain is the tension between general and
special vocation. There is no denying that the Lord, in the Gospels,
calls His disciples to an exclusivity for Himself, for His person.
He who follows Him must leave all earthly things behind. But he
who "chooses" God in Christ cannot exclude the world, because

God has let all creation share in the eternal procreation of the Son. "Just as in Christ exclusivity appears only at the point where the Word becomes flesh, just so the exclusivity of followership comes to the fore only in the bodily sphere"—which means: "In the bodily sphere the states part company." For Paul, the criterion for distinguishing the states is virginity. Poverty and obedience follow from the bridal relation to Christ. And in Mary, archetype of the bridal Church, in her who is virgin so that she may become mother, there also radiates the mystery of the imitation of Christ in the Church: this imitation "precisely by choosing virginity leads toward that total motherhood of the Church which embraces both states, both ways of life."

The whole tradition of the Church has held fast to the radical imitation of Christ as a specific state of life. Balthasar can show that the charismatic idea of the early Church lives also at the very heart of scholasticism. St. Thomas sees in the counsels of perfection both the way to personal sanctification and sanctity as a mission which is effected ever anew by the Holy Spirit.

In this way Balthasar, out of the tension of Christian existence in general, and out of the tension of the orders within the Church, evolves the justification of Christian life under the counsels of perfection within the world, the life which is the goal of the secular institutes.

The tension between eschatology and incarnation; the mysterious unity of Christ the Logos become flesh, in whom the cosmos is created and redeemed; the fruitful tension of Christian existence, which is at once responsible to the world and a call to absolute surrender to the Lord—these are the polarities that give their impulse to Balthasar's theological reflections and activities. In opening up, interpreting and translating in the many senses of the term, he offers us a new understanding of Christian theology: a new understanding of the patristic texts, of Protestant and Jewish theology, of sanctified existence and of mission, and of the fusion of being and being a Christian—the phenomena of our time.

YVES CONGAR

BY

Jakob Laubach

As soon as one begins to look about for new interpretations of Christian theology, the names of French theologians at once arise. Their well-known gift of logic and their much under-rated gift of mysticism; their zest for discussion and precise formulation; but above all their salutary awareness that they are living in *terra missionis* and, therefore, must rethink and proclaim anew the Christian message—these are some of the internal and external conditions that have combined to give to French Catholicism of the last half-century its vigorous energy.

The work of Yves Congar affords perhaps the clearest reflection of the liveliness of French theology today. Clearer than most, it shows how a theologian responds to the urges, the questions, even the cries of agony of our age—how he analyzes them in the light of scripture and Church tradition and tries to find the answers that are apt to serve the Gospel in this age.

Yves Congar was born in 1904. The misery of the prisoners of war he saw during his childhood in his native Sedan so deeply touched his heart that he conceived there and then the idea of becoming a priest. He went to school in Sedan and in Rheims, and then for three years studied philosophy at the *Institut Catholique* in Paris. Jacques Maritain introduced him to Thomistic doctrine. To this day Congar has remained a Thomist. But to him Thomism does not mean the strict adherence to the letter of Aquinas, as though no new thought had been conceived since 1274. For Congar loyalty to St. Thomas means loyalty to his spirit, his philosophy of the real; it means a mind open to reality.

In 1925, Congar entered the novitiate of the Dominicans, the Order of Preachers, and Père Chénu became one of his especially revered teachers.

After ordination, from 1931 to the outbreak of the Second World War, he taught fundamental theology at the seminary of the order, "Le Saulchoir," which had been transferred to Belgium in 1905 when the Dominicans had been expelled from France. In July 1939 he was drafted into the army; in 1940, on Armistice Day, he was captured by the Germans and until the end of the war remained a prisoner in various camps.

From 1945 to 1954, Congar again taught at "Le Saulchoir," which is now situated not far from Paris. The measures taken by the French hierarchy against the so-called left-wing Catholics did not spare him: he had to give up teaching. He spent some time abroad —in Jerusalem, Rome, and Cambridge—until 1956 when he joined the Dominican monastery in Strasbourg.

The story goes that Congar, accused one day of avant-gardism by one of his superiors, replied: "Avant-gardism? When I look at the present situation and problems of the world, I seem to myself far behind the times—far behind the front-line one ought to hold."

Even during his novitiate, while he was reading and meditating on the Gospel of John—especially the seventeenth chapter—Congar had an experience which he later called his "ecumenical vocation." His doctoral dissertation had dealt with "The Unity of the Church in Thomas of Aquinas." Nor does he ever stop reflecting on the Church. The right concept of Catholicity; the mystery of the Church as institution and as community; the church concept of his orthodox and Protestant brothers; the causes of the disastrous division; true and false Church reform; the layman's place in the Church; the problems of a living missionary Church in France: these are the issues around which his thinking moves as if in concentric circles.

Such reflections often lead Congar to a close critical study of the Reformers, and of the Protestant, and at times also, Catholic, theologians. He proceeds with the passion of a Christian whose heart is torn by the scandal of separation—and by the responsibility for it. But he does not seek polemics for the sake of polemics. In the same spirit we shall present his thought.

In January of 1936, on the occasion of the Week of Prayer for the Reunion of Christians into One Church, Congar delivered a series of lectures out of which grew his book *Divided Christendom*, first published in 1937. He starts from the position that the Catholic Church is not just one church among many. It has preserved its substance since the days of the apostles. But it has also evolved— evolved away from the divided churches. In many respects, and in many of its external forms, it appears to live out only a part of its inheritance; it appears to give just cause for the separated divisions and to furnish material for new accusations. To quote:

"In face of these one-sided deformations of truth, the Church affirms indeed not only the particular truth which is perverted, but the whole corpus of truth which is above all partial statements; yet, at the particular moment, it is inevitable that emphasis should be laid on the aspect denied or distorted by the heresy. It is quite impossible that apologists should not seek to re-establish the partially misunderstood truths, and that theologians should not devote themselves to more precise and detailed development of the doctrine. For orthodox theology, heresy therefore is at once an opportunity for progress and a danger of one-sidedness. Whenever an erroneous emphasis or statement is made, the organism of the Church stiffens into concentrated resistance, with the result that since error is always partial, dogmatic truth runs the risk of appearing partial as well."

A true reunion of divided Christendom, then, means the integration of all the dispersed values into the oneness of the *Ecclesia Catholica*. What is the essential nature of that oneness?

For Congar, the oneness of the Church is a communication and extension of the oneness of God Himself, of the Godhead of the Three Persons of the Blessed Trinity—and more: God is the Uncreated Soul of the Church; all this, to be sure, in Christ and only in Christ. But by the incarnation of Christ, the Church is also the Church of mankind, the visible oneness of God's people, brotherhood, community.

The oneness of the Church takes concrete form on a twofold plane: It is a divine unity, an organism with its members, a hierarchy of holiness, the union with Christ in living faith through charity—and it is a social unity, an organization, with a graded social hierarchy, with functions, powers, and valid sacramental acts; it is spirit, Christ is its only Head, is the Mystical Christ, exists eternally—*and* it is commission, has of right the sovereign powers necessary to its life, and a Vicar of Christ, a corporate body that exists on earth and in time, is itself corporeal.

Yet this twofold plane and unity does not mean that there are two Churches. The eternal life and the temporal commission of the Church are related in an inner dialectic; the Church is an organic unity analogous to that of body and soul. Just as the soul, in the terminology of Thomism, is the "first act" of the body, and as the body may be said to "localize" the soul and is its instrument and manifestation, so the eternal life and corporeal commission, the spiritual and corporeal elements, compose the one Church in its unity. The Church is the great sacrament—inner grace and outward sign.

The Catholicity of the Church Congar conceives as the law which governs the relation of what is divers and multiple to unity. The Catholicity of the Church has long been interpreted in an exclusively geographical or, at any rate, quantitative sense. But the Fathers recognized, beyond that, a qualitative Catholicity, counting among its elements the universality of truth, universality of redemption, and healing for humanity, from the Old Covenant to Judgment Day and even beyond. It is of the essence of the Church to adapt itself to all the divers human material which it has to incorporate in order to incorporate it into Christ in unity. On the one hand, then, Catholicity hallows human diversity—cultures, religious experiences, theologies, national temperaments—for these are its "material." On the other hand, the Church unites the diversities, subordinates to the highest law of its unity all it incorporates.

After a short sketch of the history of the ecumenical movement, and of the Anglican and orthodox doctrine, Congar goes on to raise the question as to how the Church—theologically speaking, to be sure—looks upon the separated Christians and the "good heathen."

First of all, he maintains, we must keep in mind that Christendom is more extensive than the visible reality of the Church. There are multitudes of the baptized and countless spiritual and holy souls in other Christian communions, and among the heathen there are members of the Mystical Body, predestined to eternal life. The principle *Extra Ecclesiam, nulla salus* is valid, to be sure, but it does not deny that souls that are justified and saved, though they may not visibly belong to the Church, are incorporated in Christ. Since the Church is *by definition* the Body of Christ, these souls must in some fashion belong to the Church.

Theological tradition here knows a distinction of the manner in which a soul belongs to the Church. Congar formulates two truths:

First: Directly a soul is in any degree united to Christ it belongs by that very fact to the Church; or to put it another way, in it, by that very fact, the Church is realized, for the Church is nothing else than humanity reconciled with God in Christ.

Second: The Church is not a simple substance of which one can say, as of an individual, that it is entirely present or entirely absent. The Church has within itself the fullness, and derives from Christ the principles capable of reconciling with God every man and all humanity. These principles can to some extent be realized in separation, not indeed in the Church as such but in its members who may be unequally inspired, and whose membership in the Church may thus be, theologically speaking, more or less perfect.

But Congar goes one step further to pose this question: Why is

Christendom or the Mystical Body not coterminous with the visible reality of the Church? His answer:

"The reason for it would seem to be that the Church is the Body of Christ *crucified*. The disproportion that we see is the extension and manifestation of a disproportion in the exercise by Christ Himself of the two prerogatives of His Priesthood and His Kingship. Christ the Savior is indeed Christ the King, but the kingly prerogatives are, as it were, obscured, and to all appearance very nearly in abeyance for the benefit of His priestly work of salvation by the cross. Though He had the right to the adoration of mankind and to the obedience even of natural forces, He came not to be ministered unto but to minister, in the form of a servant and not of a conqueror. He who could have asked of His Father twelve legions of angels bade Peter put back his sword into its sheath. Here on earth the Christ saves rather than reigns, and where He does reign it is not in a Kingdom manifest in its perfection, but in an interior Kingdom, hidden, crucified and crucifying—the economy of salvation by the cross and not of triumphant Kingship.

"The disunion of Christians is verily a rending of Christ and a continuance of His passion. But it also testifies, with the multitude of the saved to some of whom He is not even a name, that He is a saving Victim, and that He came into the world to save it rather than to dominate it. This is the reason, as it seems to us, why His saving work reaches beyond the visible ark of salvation, the Catholic Church, and why the reality of His mercy as Savior surpasses the visible realm of His Kingship; why the Church, too, saves to a greater extent than it rules, and secretly incorporates more members than it can claim as subjects. From beginning to end the work of God in saving mankind follows the same law. Through all the course of history He has made Himself lowly, and if one can say so, strangely put Himself at our mercy. He will come again as Lord, for the perfect establishing of His Kingdom, but now He comes above all as Savior, and knows for His own far more souls than the leaders of His Church can enumerate in their official returns."

Many dissident Christians, then, and many unbaptized but justified souls belong to the One Church in varying degrees. But what

about the dissident bodies themselves, regarded as separated ecclesiastical communities? Congar describes them as "in some fashion *elements* of the Church" in varying degrees, because they
possess the elements of the One Church: sacraments, a creed, functions. The unity of Christians can therefore not be understood as
nothing more than the return of individual men into the fullness,
but must be understood also as a reincorporation of these elements
of the Church into the One Church, the perfection of these "elementary" Churches into the complete Church.

Congar's view of the theological significance of reunion may be
summed up as follows:

The starting point, the state of divided Christendom, is a state
of things wherein values and realities, destined of their nature to
develop in unity, are kept unduly apart, isolated and therefore always incomplete and imperfect. The result is a breach in the heritage of our Lord Himself. The goal of a reunion movement must
be Catholic unity or unity in the fullness of the mystical Christ.
This unity, the one Catholic Church of Christ, is a present reality.
But the Catholicity of the Church is not fully actualized, and in a
sense we may truly say that the Church realizes that Catholicity
only in an imperfect degree, the divisions of Christendom being an
important factor in this imperfect realization of Catholicity. That
of which the separation of our brethren has deprived the Church
is a loss to the outward actualization of its own Catholic capacities.

The reunion movement, then, is not a matter of renouncing real
and positive religious values, but only of renouncing those particu-
larist and sectarian sentiments which inhibit full communion. Reunion, therefore, is a perfection in the fullness of communion and
of Christ's inheritance.

The greatest contribution Catholicism can make to the reunion
of divided Christendom, according to Congar, is the return, rightly
understood, to the sources and to the deepest life of the Church.
The best way to serve a reincorporation into Catholicity is to explain errors in critical analysis inspired by love, to show the

Church's own position in all its fullness and scope, to actualize the Church's capacity for assimilation, and to continue resolutely the Church reform as it began under Pius X. The true and the false reform of the Church—*Vraie et fausse réforme dans l'Église,* as he entitled a large volume published in 1950—is at the very heart of Congar's theological endeavor.

Reform is a permanent fact in the life of the Church—Church history shows a steady rhythm of reform movements. In order to distinguish the holiness of the Church from its fallibility, that is, from its need and capacity to reform, Congar studies the Church as an institution that mediates salvation, as the community of the faithful, and as hierarchy.

The means to salvation established by Christ—faith, sacraments, apostolic functions—which the Church *qua* institution passes on through time are infallible and unreformable.

The Church as community embraces all sinners, but the community itself is holy because it cannot be separated from God, from the Holy Spirit. Yet the true face of the Church is often more distorted and concealed by the so-called Christian setting than by the sins of individual Christians.

The teaching and pastoral function of the Church is under the guidance of the Holy Spirit, and is infallible in its definitions which, however, are valid only on certain specific conditions. But individual bishops, Fathers, theologians, and schools of theology may err—as history proves.

That which is perishable in the Church and in need of reform, says Congar, arises from a twofold temptation: the temptation of phariseeism, and the temptation of becoming a synagogue. The term "synagogue" is used here in the context of the history of salvation, to describe the community of believers that rejected the Messiah. The pharisee is he who substitutes the means for the end—he forgets that the truth of religion resides in man alone, and not in objects, institutions and works. The synagogue, on the other hand, clings to forms that have become established, and refuses to adapt them to new situations. The concern of every reformer must be, therefore, that the form retain the spirit instead of displacing it.

There are four conditions that must be met first of all, according to Congar, in order that the "contrast" which is part of the fullness of the living Church may not, in Adam Möhler's terms, turn into a "conflict" that tears unity apart. They are: first, the primacy of love and of ministry over the spirit of the system; second, continued membership in the community of the whole; third, a patience that eschews unconditional demands; and fourth, a recurrence to principle and tradition.

Love and the ministry of the faithful under one's care are a great school of truth. To lose contact with the living proclamation means to be in danger of systematizing and sectarianism. Congar here recalls the words that Lacordaire applied to Petrus Waldes—"He thought it impossible to save the Church by the Church"—and goes on:

"It is impossible to express more clearly the obligation of the reformer: he cannot start with a self-prepared concept of the Church; he must start with the Church as it exists, as concrete fact. True, that is not a simple matter, because it is precisely this concrete Church that calls for reform in this or that aspect. He must both accept the Church and not accept it as it is. Not to accept it is to set up another Church—unless indeed the whole thing is a miserable failure which sets up nothing at all—and not to reform this Church. To accept it is to change nothing in it, now or ever. The Church must not be changed, and something in it must be changed. There must be no setting up of a *different church*, and the Church must to some degree be made *different*."

Equally important, and equally difficult, is the second condition of reform: continued membership. The prophet and reformer is of necessity one-sided. But if he remains in communion with the hierarchy and the Church as a whole his theses will undergo constant clarification and completion.

In this context Congar notes that nearly every initiative and every movement of reform in the history of the Church start from the periphery. They do, of course, become truly effective only when the ecclesiastical authorities, the center, take up and approve the initiatives from the periphery.

Patience is the third condition of true reform because every reform is in a way "an anticipation of the Kingdom at the end of time, of its justice and purity."

Here, too, we see how fine a line the reformer must toe within the Church. The Church has no liking for the *via facti*, the creation of accomplished facts, and yet it is really in this way that many of the Church institutions have become first custom and then law. But true reform realizes the new without exalting it at once into a theory; and everything that grows out of the inner life by the promptings of pastoral care does in the end find the approval of the hierarchy. Congar recalls the words of Gregory VII: "Christ did not say 'I am the custom,' He said 'I am the truth.' Custom, however venerable and however familiar, must give way to truth."

True renewal, the fourth condition of reform, can be accomplished only by a recurrence to tradition, a "revivification of the sources" (scripture, the apostolic tradition, the patristic texts), and not by the introduction of "novelties" or by mechanical adaptation.

After this general clarification, Congar proceeds to study the theological problems of the sixteenth-century Reformation in the full light of the available historical source materials.

The church concept of the reformers, of special interest in this context, has several roots. First of all, it takes up again an undeniable dualism in St. Augustine, which places the deeply spiritual and eschatological reality of the saving Church in a certain opposition to the social and corporal means of salvation that are at the church's disposal. That dualism appears again in the spiritualistic and nominalistic currents of the twelfth century. Other ideas entering into the picture are that of the conciliar movement since the Council of Vienne, and the growth of national churches.

The Reformers hold that redemption is accomplished independent of man, exclusively by the risen Christ and the Holy Spirit. The Church as an institution has no efficient part in the redemption—the Church is merely the result of Christ's action in the souls of men. Instead of the sequence, Christ, the Word become flesh which founded the institution of the Church and lives in the Church as a community, the Reformers set up another sequence:

the risen Christ works the salvation of the Christians who form the Church. This gives rise to the distinction between the—invisible—"Church," and the purely empirical, corporal "churches," which are the ecclesiastical establishments of the various confessions. But the unity of the spiritual reality of the Church with the visible Church organism is lost in the process.

In their desire not to deliver the Church into the hands of man, the Reformers also misunderstood the very real bond of the historical Church with the Word become flesh. Congar places the blame on the "Galatism" of the Reformers, and especially of Luther, which interprets with greater one-sidedness Paul's already somewhat one-sided theology that must be understood as a defense against certain attitudes of the Galatians:

"No doubt the Church lives only by Jesus Christ—but it lives by the Christ who was born, who spoke and acted and finally suffered, and it lives by the Christ who, transfigured, sends His Spirit. The error of an exaggerated and one-sided Galatism, of an exclusivity which Paul did not intend, lies in cutting the Church off in an effort to make it dependent upon God alone, to leave nothing of its life in the hands of man—cutting the Church off even from the Son of Man, tracing its life back exclusively to the risen Lord, and so failing to see how the Church through the apostolic succession lives by what Christ, who was made flesh and lives among His own, has done for the Church and left in its possession."

Congar's "ecumenical vocation" constantly drives him on to discover and expound the full Catholicity of the Church in reality. His "sketch of a theology of the laity" of 1952, published under the title *Lay People in the Church*, is part of this endeavor. The intellectual currents in and outside the Church, and not least his close connection with the *Jeunesse Ouvrière Catholique*—The Young Catholic Workers—and with Catholic Action, which in France is organized by professions, compelled him to define the layman's position in the Church.

Congar defines the laity as follows:

"As members of the people of God, lay persons are, like clerics and monks, by their state and directly, ordered to heavenly things. All of them have been made fit 'for our portion of the inheritance of the saints in light.'

"But lay people do not live exclusively for heavenly things; that is, so far as present circumstances allow, the condition of monks.
. . .

"Lay people are Christians in the world, there to do God's work *in so far as it must be done in and through the work of the world.* . . . For the fullness of its work in accordance with the purpose of the living God, the Church has to have laity, faithful who do the work of the world and reach their last end in dedication to the work. . . .

"The layman is one for whom, through the very work God has entrusted to him, the substance of things in themselves is real and interesting."

To determine, then, the position of the Christian laity in the Church and in the world, one must keep in mind God's design for mankind. God—this is the meaning of His revelation—wills to lead the mankind He created into living communion with Himself. In this design, Jesus Christ, the Son of God become man, plays the decisive role: Christ is head of the Church, but also the head of all creation; He is the cause of salvation; He also has a cosmic sovereignty which extends to the whole of creation, seen and unseen. But Christ's dominance shall be unfolded in two times or stages: the first when the cause of universal salvation is present but does not produce all its effects—this is the time of 'space-between,' the time of the Church, from His ascension to His return in glory; and the other time—when the fullness of His power and Kingdom break forth, into all eternity.

During the time of "space-between" there is a duality of Church and world. Each of the two realities has its own relation to the final consummation of the Kingdom

The constitution proper to the Church lies in this, that it has already within itself the decisive causes of that renewal of which the Kingdom will be the consummation: the kingly, priestly, and prophetical power of Christ, and the Holy Spirit.

The meaning of history or of the world is the quest for the triumph of good over evil, truth over falsehood, justice over injustice, life over death.

Next Congar turns to the question, in what sense and to what extent the laity shares in the priestly, kingly, and prophetical function of Christ and His Church.

Priesthood is above all else a sacrificial service. The laity belonging to the priesthood of the lay faithful—as distinguished from the hierarchical priesthood, the priesthood of holy orders—may take part in this service in a number of ways. Congar mentions "spiritual sacrifice," by which man lives wholly in the Divine Spirit; the "spiritual" priesthood of martyrdom, of virginity, of marriage, and of sickness offered up to God—an example stressed by Robert Grosche; participation in Holy Communion, where Church and Christ together are one single sacrificial body, while the ordained priest performs his office merely as a servant of Christ; and finally the power to celebrate and give the sacraments of baptism and marriage.

But there is not only a spiritual-real priesthood of the lay faithful, there is also a spiritual kingship that is related to the Kingship of Christ. This kingship, Congar states, signifies first of all the Christian's kingship over himself and over the world—however, in time, the time of "space-between," only under the sign of the cross. Does the layman have kingly powers even in the ordering of the Church? History tells us of laymen participating in the election of bishops; of the not always fortunate role of princes; of lay advisors at Church councils; and of a certain share in the administration of Church property. Still, it is in respect to the kingly function that the hierarchical structure of the Church manifests itself most clearly.

The prophetical function of the Church includes the more specific one of teaching. The revealed sources say both that all are illumined, and that the teaching authority in the Church belongs to some only. Congar leaves no doubt that in fact there has always been a Church that is "teaching" and a Church that is "taught."

"If the Church be regarded only as reality and fellowship of grace, then there is no difference between the members beyond their varying degrees of fervour, due to the gifts being received and used in equal measure. But if—as we must—we see the Church also as an institution or aggregate of means of grace, then there are differences of ministry among the members, and these differences affect their position in the social body of the Church. So we have the distinction between the teaching Church and the taught Church: this expression is perhaps recent, but the reality for which its stands is indicated, in somewhat similar terms, in very early times and, in equivalent terms, in the New Testament itself. There is then in the Church a combination of inequality of function with equality of life: as St. Augustine was fond of saying, the same men are shepherds of the faithful in Christ's name and are also, with and among the faithful, sheep beneath Christ's crook."

The Acts of the Apostles, Congar points out, show us the Church less in its institution by Christ than in the upsurge of its life through the power of the Holy Spirit; without any diminution of the hierarchical principle, this book displays the communal principle at work. Congar finds the explanation of this communal, or collegiate, principle in God Himself and in His economy of grace, whereby a principle of help and fulfillment is joined to a principle of authority or hierarchy.

The communal or collegiate principle applies first of all to the "Apostolic College" of the Apostles and their successors. Rightly understood, it may be applied also to a certain "cooperation" of the laity in matters of faith. John Henry Cardinal Newman, in his famous article "On Consulting the Faithful on Matters of Faith" (in *The Rambler,* July 1859), mentions the share of the faithful people in the rejection of Arianism. Congar gives as example the work of lay people in preparing the encyclical *Rerum Novarum*, and the influence of the laity on the definition of Marian doctrine. But these are exceptions.

The laity, in the words of St. John Chrysostom, is the bishop's "priestly *pleroma*." It is the lay people who lend to the bishop's apostolic office the necessary fullness and extension in the world.

The part of the faithful is not the teaching of the apostolic deposit, but the bearing of witness to it by living it. In the closing chapters of *Lay People in the Church* Congar studies the ecclesiological foundations of the layman's mission and, especially, of Catholic Action. He concludes that service in the world and to the world, which is the layman's mission in God's economy of grace, always remains a service under the sign of the cross.

God's plan, and the place of the faithful within it, are magnificently captured in the many-faceted work *The Mystery of the Temple*: "a temple built of living stones," in which Congar deals with the manner of God's presence in the world. The book, published in 1957, may be considered a continuation in depth of Congar's theological work on the reality of the Church.

The presence of God, of the "Temple," is a mystery in a threefold sense: in the theological sense of a truth whose content the created intelligence cannot fathom; in the Pauline and patristic sense of a divine plan unfolding and realizing itself in progressive stages; and finally in the liturgical sense of a real celebration or communication of the great acts of salvation God has accomplished, and with the prospect of their consummation at the Last Day.

The Bible has little to say of God's presence in His creation, yet such is presupposed whenever God establishes a truly personal presence among men. In the days of the patriarchs God intervenes by what may be called momentary contacts or encounters. Then God forms His people, whom He guides and judges. Until the building of the Temple, His presence has an uncertain and changing character. But when the Sacred Presence has become fixed in a given place, the prophets do not cease to preach that God desires to reign, not in a material locale, but in men's hearts.

The Incarnation inaugurates an entirely new stage in the history of God's Presence. There is now only one Temple in which we can validly adore, pray, offer and truly meet God: Christ's body. True, Christ ascended into heaven, and only the eschatological Temple—the new heaven and the new earth—will be the fullness and eternity of the divine-human Temple. But even scripture and tradition know of a mysterious bond between Christ sitting at the right hand of the Father, the Eucharistic body, and the mystical body of Christ:

"These three realities... are reality only in the sense that there is one and the same single mystery accomplished in all three of them, the mystery of the Pasch, of Christ's passing to His Father. This mystery, accomplished in one man, but for the sake of all men, is to become the mystery of all men in one man. And the means by which what was accomplished in the body born of Mary passes to the 'mystical' body (as it is called; we prefer to use the epithet 'community') which we are called to become, is the sacrament of the body of Christ, the memorial of His Pasch celebrated in the bread and the wine. The physical body of our Lord, our food in this sacrament, makes us fully members of Him and forms His 'community' body. In this way, then, the three forms of one and the same mystery are dynamically linked together. Thus the sacred body, which, from the moment of the Annunciation until its death on the cross, was the perfect Temple of God on earth and the perfect realization of the true Religion of the Father, takes to itself, through the combined action of the Spirit and of the sacrament containing its own essential mystery, a 'whole' body of which it is the head and we are the members. The one unique stone expands, in a certain sense, and becomes a temple commensurate with humanity."

Thus Congar traces the great curve of the history of salvation, the history of God's presence in the world, in the mysterious dimensions of the Temple. He says in conclusion:

"The history starts in Paradise and ends in Heaven, and the space of life between is one of suffering. In the beginning we see a sacred world which, as the creation of God and full of the reflection of His glory, is therefore God's Temple, with Adam in its midst as its priest. In the new heaven and on the new earth, the New and glorious Adam will be their priest and once again the whole universe will be the Temple. The priestly power of Christ, when exercised in accordance with His fully royal character, has this characteristic, that it unites the visible and the invisible, the things below and the things on high, nature and grace, under the sovereign ascendancy of the Spirit. The world is blessed and pardoned and becomes once more the Temple of God through the Redemption, whose full effect will only be seen at the general resurrection. Between the Temple of Paradise and the Temple of the world to come, each of which is both cosmic and spiritual, runs the time of our earthly history, when salvation is prophesied, is prepared, and finally becomes a reality in Him who is its determining cause."

Congar's theology, then, is a theology of the Church. With the Dominican's intellectual passion, and with an equally burning love for his separated brothers, he inquires into the theological causes of the division of Christendom; his concern for those who have grown strangers to the Church drives him to study the conditions of Church reform, by which the Church might once again be all things to all men; the awakening of the Church in the laity prompts him to define more clearly the participation of the laity in the kingly, priestly, and prophetic functions of Christ.

All of Congar's work is distinguished by that fruitful interplay of speculation and practice that is so characteristic of French Catholicism today. It is a massive contribution to today's theology, a new interpretation of Christian teaching, because it opens up anew the inexhaustible fullness and scope of the Church, her dimensions in space and in time, the Catholicity of the One Church.

KARL RAHNER

BY

Jakob Laubach

The philosophy of recent centuries has concerned itself ever more resolutely with man as such—the subject, the ego, existence. It is true, of course, that theology has taken notice of the situation, and has consistently and justly opposed philosophy's anthropocentrism with its own theocentrism. But theology has not been sufficiently concerned with man's century-long struggle for self-understanding —that concern which would enable it to see God as the One whose own word became man, so that man once again might discover his selfhood in Him as the great mystery of divine love.

Karl Rahner is one of the very few Catholic theologians who understood that challenge, urgent as well as difficult, and who accepted it. His many essays, papers, and articles in encyclopedias all converge upon his fundamental endeavor, to develop a theological anthropology in the true sense.

He was born in Freiburg-im-Breisgau in 1904. After attending a gymnasium, he entered the Society of Jesus at the age of eighteen. He studied philosophy three years at the seminary of the Order in Pullach near Munich; taught two years at the Jesuit gymnasium in Feldkirch, Austria; and spent four years studying theology at the Jesuit seminary in Valkenburg, Holland. In 1932 he was ordained in Munich. His theological studies ended, and he followed Martin Heidegger's courses at Freiburg for several semesters. In 1937 he began his academic career, which took him to Innsbruck, Vienna and Pullach, and in 1948 back to Innsbruck as professor *ordinarius* of dogmatic theology.

Rahner's first substantial publication, *Spirit in the World (Geist in Welt,* 1939) is an investigation of the metaphysics of finite knowledge in Thomas Aquinas. This work reveals his intellectual background, and his own original turn of mind. Rahner interprets Thomas. He wants to get away from "neo-scholasticism" and back to Thomas himself; in Rahner's view, the essence of a philosopher's thought can be grasped only by "joining him in looking at the thing itself." There is no other way to salvage "the eternal in a philosophy from the irrelevancies of what merely has been."

In Thomistic thought, the proposition of the *conversio intellectus ad phantasma,* the turning of the mind to the data of the senses, is one of the basic unifying principles of all the powers of the human mind.

Rahner is fully aware that his own interpretation of this proposition owes much to Pierre Rousselot, as well as to Joseph Maréchal (1878-1944), the Belgian Jesuit who attempted to interpret Thomas in the light of Kant's philosophy.

The "turning of the mind to the data of the senses" of Thomas Aquinas deals with the same problem as Kant's *synthesis a priori:* all human knowledge is finite and always dependent upon sense perception; and sense perception is the intellect's self-receptivity which the intellect projects. This projection, the intellect's transcendence beyond the object that is to be known, is the condition which makes the knowledge of the object possible. The *a priori* forms of the intellect and the pure perceptions of the senses, in their encounter with the *a posteriori* material of the sense data, give rise to knowledge, to the concept.

In his book, *Hearers of the Word* (*Hörer des Wortes*) of 1941, Rahner applies this metaphysic of knowledge to the problems of fundamental theology, and to the philosophy of religion. He shows how man—man who forever finds himself cast out into the world and who, being spirit, forever strains to reach beyond it—can become the hearer and the *locus* of a possible revelation in history.

But if man is hearer and *locus* of revelation, then theological anthropology, the doctrine of man interpreted by the word of God, assumes a special rank. Rahner is sketching the outlines of such an anthropology in the monumental theological encyclopedia, the *Lexikon für Theologie und Kirche,* which together with Josef Höfer he is preparing in a new edition.

Rahner begins by pointing out that since the incarnation of Christ there is no area that does not formally belong to theological anthropology. Accordingly, every theological proposition of dogmatic may be read as a proposition of theological anthropology. Rahner here stresses, though he does not elaborate, that theology cannot speak of God, the One and triune, without at the same time saying something of man, the recipient of God and His grace. But since man, in relation to God, is essentially eccentric—and only in that way is rightly "present-to-himself"—therefore man's propositions about God should find their place in a theology apart from anthropology proper. This theology, however, must never lose sight of man's "existential" situation.

However, theology and anthropology rightly understood are not opposites. Thus, in his encyclopedia article on "Anthropocentrism" Rahner can say:

"The attempt to leap beyond one's own self in an anti-anthropocentric manner, regardless in which dimension of human existence that attempt is made, would be inhuman and thus against God—God to whom one cannot come closer by diminishing oneself but only in the frank awareness and realization that He Himself has created all things that they might be (Wisdom 1:14). This holds still more in the order of Christ. For by the incarnation of the Word of God, the opposition between anthropocentrism and theocentrism is just that interpretation of human existence of which we are to be delivered; there is no longer a theoretical, no longer a practical theology that would not itself be an anthropology. This, of course, remains true: Man still must find his own essence as something to be realized; he may fall into guilty error concerning his essence, and he finds it ultimately only by sharing in the death and resurrection of the Son of Man."

Concern with man is primary in all of Rahner's theological reflections. It also inspired his "Scheme for a Treatise of Dogmatic Theology" which is included in the first volume of his *Theological Investigations*. In the thirties, Rahner had begun to publish numerous articles on the history of dogma, pastoral theology, and asceticism, with the original intention to write a large dogmatic in cooperation with another theologian. Circumstances compelled him to abandon the project, and since then the results of his theological researches have appeared in short separate essays. After the Second World War he became the editor of the great encyclopedia, *Lexikon für Theologie und Kirche,* and of two well-known periodical collections in dogmatic theology.

The opening division of Rahner's "Scheme" is devoted to "formal and fundamental" theology. It deals with the fundamental relationship between God and creature, the general possibility of revelation to the world, the idea of redemptive revelation, and the idea of theology as a science. His fundamental theology, which includes a phenomenology of religion generally and of Christianity, is not intended to take the place of fundamental theology proper.

The second main division of Rahner's scheme, "Special Dogmatic Theology," shows his anthropological emphasis with special clarity. It first considers man and his world as nature with a supernatural finality, to proceed to the theology of the duality of the sexes and of such states and events of human life as birth, eating and drinking, work, laughter and tears, and death. To the supernatural dimension of human reality belong the doctrines of God and the Trinity, grace as participation in the trinitarian life of God, and the doctrine of the Mediator, the God-man. Next under the heading "Fall and Redemption," follow sin, the Redeemer—His annunciation in history, incarnation, cross and glorification; the Church in its basic structure and its existence in history; the theological anthropology proper of the redeemed; and the doctrine of the last things, the eschatology.

Rahner points out that in reading his scheme we must realize and appreciate the inevitable cooperation and interpenetration of the theologies of essence and existence (theological ontology and historical report), since both are of the nature of theology. It is the business of dogmatic theology to answer the question: "What must I do that I may enter into eternal life?" True, the division into moral and dogmatic theology, which was unknown to the Middle Ages, can no longer be revoked. But to Rahner, "moral theology is always in danger of becoming a peculiar mixture of philosophical ethics, natural law, a positivism based on canon law, and casuistry," and it thus stands in great need of dogmatic foundation.

Among Rahner's methodological preparations is the important essay on "The Development of Dogma." The meaning, the possibility, and the problems of such a "development of dogma" cannot be deduced from general theological considerations alone, but must be arrived at inductively from the actual facts of such a development. But first Rahner states theree conditions that will prevent the rank proliferation of theological speculation which anxious theologians might fear.

First, there are of course certain laws of dogmatic development which may be applied—though certainly with prudence—in order to determine whether they are genuine developments of the faith of the Church or, on the other hand, contain the danger of a wrong turning. They can be applied only in the Church and only *by* the Church.

Next, every advance achieved in this world of the finite always has something final about it and inevitably marks a restriction of future possibilities. The fuller and clearer the truth becomes, the more strict it becomes. Looked at from this point of view, progress in the development of dogmas must in a certain respect become progressively slower.

Third, and this is the decisive point: the Church has the promise of the Spirit, which guides it in safeguarding the truth.

Yet all human statements, even those in which faith expresses God's saving truths, are finite. Says Rahner:

"The statements which we make about them, relying on the Word of God which itself became 'flesh' in human words, can never express them once and for all in an entirely adequate form. But they are not for this reason false. They are an 'adaequatio intellectus et rei,' in so far as they state absolutely nothing which is false.... But because our statements about the infinite realities are finite and hence in this sense inadequate—that is, while actually corresponding to reality, yet not simply congruent with it—so, every formula in which the faith is expressed can in principle be surpassed while still retaining its truth. That is to say, in principle at least, it can be replaced by another which states the same thing, and, what is more, states it not only without excluding more extensive, more delicately nuanced prospects, but positively opens them up: from prospects onward to facts, realities and truths which had not been seen explicitly in the earlier formulation and which make it possible to see the same reality from a new point of view, in a fresh perspective."

The development of dogma, it is true, is not limited to the logical explication of propositions and the avoidance of wrong turnings, but contributes to the inner development of the deposit of faith. Rahner shows in detail how the development of dogma can be understood as explication which turns implicit into explicit knowledge. Love serves him as example. The lover knows of his love: this knowledge is infinitely richer, simpler and more complete than that of a body of propositions about the love. The progress of love is a living growth out of the original (the originally conscious) love *and* out of exactly that which the love itself has become through a reflexive experience of itself. Original, non-propositional, unreflexive yet conscious possession, on the one hand, and the reflexive, articulated knowledge of this original consciousness are not, however, competing opposites but are reciprocally interacting factors of a single experience necessarily unfolding in historical succession.

The Apostles, too, did not merely bequeathe propositions about their experience, but also their Spirit, the Holy Spirit of God. The apostolic succession hands down not only a body of propositions but the living experience as well. Thus more is communicated, as it can be in normal human propositions, and more is intimated in overtones, than what has been explicitly stated. And that communication can be developed.

It is no surprise that the dogmatist Karl Rahner should also turn his hand to methodical reflections on scripture. For scripture is in practice always the starting point of new theological work in any matter not already "established by the magisterium of the Church and explained and expanded in scholastic theology."

In an essay on *Inspiration in the Bible,* Rahner shows that the traditional concept of inspiration has a certain formal abstractness. There are two questions in particular that arise in explaining the inspiration of scripture: first, in what sense to understand the divine and the human authorship of scripture; and second, what is the point of an infallible teaching authority if there is an infallible Bible?—or conversely, what is the point of an infallible Bible if there is an infallible authority?

To answer these questions, Rahner proposes a thesis that rests upon several theological statements about the Church. God wills the Church; it is the ultimate and irrevocable economy of salvation. The Apostolic Church, in a qualitatively unique manner, is subject to divine intervention. The Bible, too, belongs to the constitutive elements of this Apostolic Church as the qualitatively unique work of God and the permanent "canonical" origin for the later Church. The scriptures are as much God's word to man as they are a self-expression of the faith of the Church, a written embodiment of that which the primitive Church believed. His thesis follows:

"In creating through His absolute will the Apostolic Church and its constitutive elements, God wills and creates the scriptures in such a way that He becomes their inspiring originator, their author. Let it be noted that we say 'creating,' for we wish to stress that the scriptures originate not only on the occasion, or in the course of the institution of the Apostolic Church, but that the active, inspiring authorship of God is an intrinsic element in the formation of the primitive Church becoming Church, and derives it marks from being this. God wills the scriptures and Himself as their originator. He achieves both because and insofar as He wills Himself as the acting and efficient author of the Church. The inspiration of the scriptures is but simply the causality of God in regard to the Church, inasmuch as it refers to that constitutive element of the Apostolic Church, which is the Bible."

This conception is more likely than others to solve certain questions, such as how God and man can both be authors of the same scriptures; whether or not inspiration could be an unconscious process; how the Church recognizes the inspiredness of the Bible. But most important are its consequences for the relationship of inspired writings and teaching authority. There is no clash of two infallibilities.

"The infallible teaching authority of the early Church ... is the capacity for creating the scriptures. The infallible teaching office of the Church *after* the early Church is the authoritative interpretation of the Bible.... The Church possesses the scripture, not only as a book, approaching it as it were from the outside like an unbelieving historian or exegete, in order to investigate what can be used out of it in regard to this or that question. The Church possesses the scripture as something written and always read and accomplished in its own life. The reference to this earlier reading of the Bible is also part of the 'oral tradition.'"

189

Having discussed Rahner's basic concern with anthropology, and his methodological investigations, we may now turn to what he was to say on the central realities of faith.

An essay of 1950 on the concept of God, "Theos in the New Testament," furnishes ample proof of how intensively he, a dogmatist, works in biblical theology. He starts with the question as to who is meant when the New Testament speaks of *o theos*. Excepting only six passages in which Christ is called *o theos,* the overwhelming majority of passages refers to God the Father, first person of the Trinity. Thus it is clear that the New Testament, when it refers to God, has in view the concrete, individual, unexchangeable person of the Father. Rahner sees this fact as a confirmation of the so-called Greek conception of God. This conception starts with the three divine persons—Father, Son, Spirit—while the Latin or scholastic conception takes as the starting point of its speculation the oneness of the divine essence.

This doctrine of the Trinity, based on the New Testament and developed by the Greek Church Fathers, yields important consequences for the relation of man to each of the three divine persons. Karl Rahner studies these relations in greater detail in a contribution to the *Festschrift* 'Universitas' in honor of Dr. Stohr, bishop of Mainz.

With all their belief in the Trinity, Christians are in practice "monotheists," Rahner states in that essay, entitled "Remarks on the Dogmatic Treatise *De Trinitate*" ("Bemerkungen zum dogmatischen Traktat *De Trinitate*"). But the Trinity is a mystery of salvation, else it would not have been revealed. This calls in turn for a clarification of the relation between the Trinity of the "economy of salvation" which is concerned with the salvation, the redemption of man, and the "immanent" Trinity which is concerned with the internal divine life of the three persons. Rahner's basic thesis, traces of which may already be found in Scheeben, runs thus: The "economic" Trinity is always the immanent Trinity, and vice versa. Therefore, it is not possible to say that any statement on the history of salvation could be made of the triune God as well as of each person of the Trinity, singly. Equally false is the assertion that a doctrine of the Trinity is limited to statements about the divine inner life within the Trinity. But it is correct to say that the doctrine of the Trinity and the doctrine of salvation cannot be adequately distinguished. In Christ, the Logos with God and the Logos among us, the immanent and the economic Logos are strictly one and the same.

Rahner draws the conclusion:

"Each of the three divine persons communicates Himself to man in freely given grace, as Himself in His personal selfhood and uniqueness. This trinitarian communication (the 'indwelling' of God, the 'uncreated grace,' understood not only as communication of divine 'nature' but, since it takes place in the spiritually free, personal act, that is, from person to person, understood also and even primarily as communication of the 'persons') is the real-ontological ground of the life of grace in man and (other conditions being present) of the immediate vision of the divine persons in perfection. It goes without saying that this self-communication of the divine persons occurs in accordance with their personal selfhood, which means also according to and on the strength of their relatedness to one another. If one of the divine persons were to communicate Himself in a way other than in and through His relatedness to the other persons, in order to establish a relation of His own to the redeemed (and *vice versa*), this would in fact establish and assume that each of the three persons (as such and precisely in His intellectual differentiation from the One and same Essence) is something absolute, and not merely relative: the true basis of the doctrine of the Trinity would have been relinquished. And that means in turn: these three self-communications are the self-communication of the one God in the threefold relative way in which God subsists. Thus the Father gives Himself to us, too, as *Father*— that is, precisely by expressing Himself as and in being Himself (essential) and present-to-Himself; thus He communicates the Son as His own, personified self-revelation; He gives Himself to us in that the Father and the Son (receiving from the Father), in the affirmation of *love* tending toward Himself and arriving at Himself and *thus* received in love, communicates Himself as the Holy

Spirit. God's relation to us is threefold, and precisely this threefold, free and freely granted attitude toward us *is* not merely an image or an analogy of the inner Trinity—it is *the* Trinity itself, though communicated freely and as an act of grace.

"The Trinity is not a reality which can be stated only as doctrine. It occurs among ourselves, and is not merely as such established for us by the fact that revelation *contains* statements about it. Rather, those statements have been made to us simply because the reality of which they treat has itself been stated to us. They are made to us, not to test our faith in something to which we have no real relation, but because our own sanctifying grace and glorification cannot be fully unveiled to us in any other way than by giving word to this mystery; so that both mysteries, that of our grace and that of God within Himself, are one and the same unfathomable mystery."

The Trinity, then, is to Karl Rahner the structure of man's sanctifying grace. What must man be like so that he may be able to receive Love, God Himself?

Man is essentially "spirit in world," and as such, in his forward reach he is radically open to God; "man is he who grasps and apprehends by and through his forward reach beyond all that can be grasped and apprehended, all that can be said and defined, outward and into the darkness of the incomprehensible, of the mystery," as Rahner once phrased it, in a lecture on the *mysterium* which he gave at Heidelberg. And man is the "hearer of the word," of a possible message from God.

In his essay of 1950 "Concerning the Relationship between Nature and Grace," Rahner shows that the average textbook theology of the most recent centuries presupposes a human "nature" that is one-sidedly oriented to the nature of less than human things. It is tacitly or explicitly presupposed that whatever man comes to know by himself, independently of Revelation, about himself or in himself, belongs to his nature. This view, however, involves many problems. Rahner himself says about the relationship between nature and grace:

"God wishes to communicate Himself, to pour forth the love

which He Himself is. That is the first and the last of His real plans and hence of His real world too. Everything else exists so that this one thing might be: the eternal miracle of infinite Love. And so God makes a creature whom He can love: He creates man. He creates him in such a way that he *can* receive this love which is God Himself, and that he can and must at the same time accept it for what it is: the ever astounding wonder, the unexpected, unexacted gift. And let us not forget here that ultimately we only know what 'unexacted' means when we know what personal love is, and *vice versa*: we do not understand what love is by knowing the meaning of 'unexacted.' Thus in this second respect God must so create man that love not only pours forth free and unexacted but, also, so that man as real partner, as one who can accept or reject it, can experience and accept it *as* the unexacted event and wonder not owed to *him,* the real man. As unexacted, not only because he does not deserve it as *sinner,* but further because he can also embrace it as unexacted when, already blessed in this love, he is allowed to forget that he was a sinner once."

Man, who is to receive this love must, therefore, first have a congeniality for it, a real "potency" for it, the *potentia oboedientialis* or "power of obedience." It is not a power like so many others, but is the central and abiding existential of man as he really is.

Real man should, secondly, be able to receive this Love as what it necessarily is: a free gift. But this means that this central, abiding existential, consisting in the ordination to the threefold God of grace and eternal life, is itself to be characterized as unexacted, as "supernatural."

The man who receives this Love, in the Holy Spirit and by way of the word of the Gospel, will, thirdly, know how to distinguish and delimit what he always is (his concrete, indissoluble "quiddity") from what this unexacted real receptivity is, the supernatural existential, and what is left over as remainder when this inmost center is subtracted from the substance of his concrete quiddity, his "nature." Nature in this sense is a remainder concept, a possible abstraction whose exact content, however, cannot be experienced, nor described, in a pure state.

However much ontological precision is desirable, Rahner continues, we must not forget that scripture understands grace as communication of the Spirit, the divine *pneuma*. Scripture speaks of "life," "unction," "comfort," "light." But this means that sanctifying grace is more than an existential "exaltation" of moral acts which, remaining existentially unchanged in man's consciousness, are altered only in faith. "Faith overarches and reforms our conscious life as well, not only our essence but also our existence." On various occasions, Rahner speaks of a "capability of experiencing" supernatural grace—and that applies not only to mystics.

If grace overarches and suffuses our existence, we must ask further what theology has to say about the innermost relation of the order of creation and the order of grace. This brings us to the Incarnation.

In other essays, Rahner deals further with the relation between the order of grace and the Incarnation. The Incarnation throws the radical Christological character of grace into clear relief.

Both grace and the Incarnation stem from a free, loving act of God. But does it necessarily follow that they are two different acts of God? In Rahner's view it can be held—and the old Logos theology of Nicaea and pre-Augustinian days contains many a hint—that the possibility of creation rests upon the possibility of the Incarnation. It is true, of course, that the *reality* of creation—as nature—does not of necessity include the realization of God's self-surrender in the Incarnation. It follows that the incarnated Logos is not merely in fact the mediator of grace by virtue of His merit, but is He who by His freely given incarnation creates the world's order of nature and order of grace.

Karl Rahner's work on the Incarnation, Logos become man, and on the Christological and anthropological problems connected with it, are beyond doubt the very heart of his theology. In his encyclopedia article on "Anthropology" Rahner's understanding of the Incarnation is formulated with particular intensity. He writes:

"The Incarnation is rightly received and understood only if Christ's humanity is not merely the—in the last analysis—external instrument through which a God who remains invisible makes Himself known, but is exactly the same as what God Himself—while remaining God—becomes when He gives Himself over into the dimension of the other-than-Himself, the nondivine. . . . But then, man is in original definition: the possible being-other-than-himself of God's self-surrender and the possible brother of Christ."

From this definition of man, Rahner can move on to say: "Whoever accepts completely his own humanity has accepted the Son of Man, because in Him God accepts man."

In an essay on nature and grace, Rahner draws out some of the consequences of this situation:

There is, he writes, a saving grace outside the Church and the sacraments; every morally good human act is in fact also an act of supernatural saving grace; all of man's spiritual life is constantly overarched and formed by grace; the history of religion, even that which lies outside the official history of revelation, is the result not merely of natural reason and sin, but the result also of natural spirit, grace, and sin.

The Incarnation of the Logos understood in this way poses new questions for Christology. Rahner touches upon the most important ones in his essay on "Problems of Christology Today," which first appeared in the collection, *The Council of Chalcedon*. We can deal here with only one of those problems, which is of special concern to us, and which finds its ultimate answer only in Christ becoming man: the problem of death.

In the series *Quaestiones Disputatae*, Rahner in 1958 published an essay, "On the Theology of Death." Even more clearly than most of his other works, it shows how Rahner practices theology not only *from* man as his point of departure, but also *for* and *toward* man—to man's spiritual comfort in the fullest sense. It shows further that Rahner, more than most theologians, is keenly aware of his responsibility toward the spirit of our age, the problems raised by physical science and its cosmology; and that he feels bound to define life as a being-toward-death.

He begins by recalling the sure, clear statements of the Christian faith concerning death. Death as accepted through divine revelation is not based on any biological necessity, but something proper to man's relationship to God. All men are sinners; therefore, all men must die.

The theological description of death, now a classic, and again a statement of the Christian faith, is that death is the separation of body and soul. But this, says Rahner, is not an essential definition of death. We must ask further: Does the soul, in death, become strictly "out of this world" or does it rather, by virtue of the fact that it is no longer bound to an individual bodily structure, enter into a much closer, more intimate relationship to the universe as a whole, that basic oneness of the world? For Christian metaphysics, here under the persistent influence of a Neoplatonic mentality, this way of presenting the question is at first unfamiliar. But even the older scholastic doctrine conceived the relationship as the soul informing the body—the soul, so to speak, grafted upon the material reality.

The modern doctrine of "life-entelechies" of subhuman beings and their relationship to matter might give a further indication. Death in the subhuman realm here appears as the surrender of the entelechical relation at a certain space-time conformation of the world, while the entelechical powers remain solidly implanted in the universe.

On the analogy of those subhuman entelechies, it becomes permissible to suppose that the human spiritual soul, on man's death, will become not a-cosmic but "all-cosmic." Thus becoming open towards the "all," the soul might in some way become a co-determining factor of the universe. We know as a doctrine of faith that the moral quality of each individual life, when consummated before God, becomes "co-responsible" for His attitude towards the world and towards all other individuals; similarly, the individual person, once rendered all-cosmic through death, might come to have a real influence on the whole of the universe.

The third proposition of faith affirms: with bodily death, man's state of pilgrimage comes to a definite end, rendering his decision for or against God, reached during the time of his bodily life, final and unalterable. Even the total, created reality of the world grows in and through persons having body and spirit, and the world is, in a certain sense, the body of those persons. Their death slowly brings the universe to its final stage.

And now, Rahner poses the decisive question: Does God turn

death into judgment because man himself determines in and through his death his own final constitution; or does judgment follow death, because God has so ordained that this judgment, different in itself as it is from death, brings about the finality of the personal attitude which death by itself could not impose? Rahner, in agreement with Thomas Aquinas, replies: The finality of the personal life-decision is intrinsic to death itself, since it is a spiritual-personal act of man. This presupposes, however, that death is not an experience which is suffered passively, but must be understood as a human act, as a deed of man, originating within— in the sense that in death the soul achieves the consummation of her own personal self-affirmation.

"Death must be both of these. As the end of man, who is a spiritual person, it is an active consummation from within brought about by the person himself. It is a growing up, the result of what man has made of himself during this life, the achievement of total self-possession. It is the real self-creation, the fullness of his freely exercised personal reality. At the same time, death is at the end of the biological life. It strikes men with one blow which cannot be resolved into a number of partial causes; it strikes him in his totality, breaking him up from without. It is destruction, an event overcoming man from without, unexpectedly. Under this aspect, a man's own death, from within, through the act of the person, is an event of the most radical unmastering of man, activity and passivity at once. If the substantial unity of man is taken in its full significance, it will be impossible to parcel out these two dimensions of human death, one to the body and one to the soul, thereby dissolving its very essence."

Having thus developed the dialectical unity of death, Rahner studies it under the aspect of a consequence of sin. Catholic theology still holds, as against the Protestant reformers and the Jansenists, on theological grounds, that death has also a natural essence. Death is never merely a natural process, though it must also be a natural process, for otherwise it could not be an event of salvation or damnation; there could be no participation by faith in the destiny of Christ.

Within the natural essence of death as fate is "hidden" its personal essence as fact. No human experience will ever be able to reveal whether death is truly a pure perfection or a pure act of the man who died.

But how can the darkness, the hidden character of death be experienced as a penalty for sin, since it belongs to the spiritual-bodily, the natural essence of man? That is possible, Rahner states, because even after Adam's fall man is never a pure nature. He still retains the supernatural existential element as a real determinant of his nature. When man, endowed with this supernatural, existential quality suffers death in darkness, then he dies a death which even now ought not to be.

"Man is, rightly, afraid of death. Actually, he should not die, for he still possesses within himself, if not the reality, then the due demand, at least, for that vitality of divine life, which if it could assert itself, pure and unveiled, in this earthly life would completely eliminate death.

"That man dies, and does not simply consummate his life, is a consequence of the sin which lies at the beginning of human history, and of all the sins through which every man makes his own the sin of his first parents. . . . The emptiness, the finality, the hollowness, the insoluble tangle of determination and indetermination, of noblest action and most humiliating subjection, all these peculiarities of the death which we must actually die are nothing but the appearances or manifestations of sin. . . . Because a creature belongs to God, it shrinks back, by a movement of its innermost essence, before this last mystery of emptiness, of finality, of nothingness, before, in a word, the mystery of iniquity. Because this same creature, be he holy or sinful, so long as he lives is driven by the power of the divine life which calls him and works in him, he will, therefore, always experience a mysterious horror of death, which can never be explained by himself, or on the basis merely of what he can observe in himself. In this horror which he experiences before death, there arises before him the vision, emerging on the surface of visible existence, of the eternal, of the only proper death.

"Should man try to deny the reality of this horror, by misrepresenting death as a merely natural process, by taking refuge either in frivolity, despair or a tragic heroism, then by this very act he pursues that which he most dreads, that is, a beginning of eternal death. Death, undiluted, unquenched, remaining in its full reality, together with the attitude of man towards it (which is, after all, a part of death's own nature) will be transformed only when it shall be viewed in the light and with the strength of Jesus Christ who died and rose again. Then death will become what it can be, the dark night of the cross in which the eternal life, dying, penetrated this world to its foundations, in order to make it live again."

It follows that, in a real death, Christ died our death. And it is by His *death* that He redeemed us. The so-called theory of satisfaction, hardly elaborated further since it was worked out in the early Middle Ages, has according to Rahner failed to consider this fact adequately. Christ enacted and suffered death, as death is the expression, the manifestation and the revelation of sin in the world. But through His death, death becomes, first, and at least for him, something absolutely different.

And now Rahner applies his thesis mentioned earlier—that through his death man in some way introduces the result of his life into the basic, real oneness of the world—to the death of Christ: through Christ's death, His spiritual reality becomes open to the whole world and is inserted into this world as a permanent destiny. And thereby the world as a whole and as the ground for human actions becomes very different from that which it might have been had Christ not died.

"The thought that Christ, in the whole reality of His life and death, belongs to the innermost reality of the world, would be less alien to us if we were not so prone to identify the world with the handful of crude and superficial data gathered daily through sense-experience, or if we were better able to realize how profound, mysterious and filled with spiritual realities this world truly is, and how every part of it draws life from the whole universe, sending its roots into measureless depths. When the vessel of His body was shattered in death, Christ was poured out over all the world; He became actually, in His humanity, what He had always been according to His dignity, the heart of the world, the innermost center of creation. Realizing this, we might better grasp the fact that we, in our spiritual lives as human persons, willingly or unwillingly, whether we accept or deny it, are always face to face with this ultimate depth of the world which was conquered by Christ when, in death, He descended into the infernal regions."

Since Christ's descent into the lower depths, the Christian in a state of grace dies a different death from the sinner. Death itself is for him a saving event. What takes place "sacramentally" in baptism and in the Eucharist—high points of the sacramental life of the Christian—takes place "really" in the death of the redeemed: participation in the death of the Lord. The lowest and the highest extreme of Christ's death are expressed in the two words: "My God, my God, why hast thou forsaken me"—and "Father, into thy hands I commend my spirit."

Unceasingly, Karl Rahner the theologian inquires into the Word, the Revelation of the triune God embodied in the faith of the Church and become flesh in Jesus Christ. Although we could suggest here only the starting point of his theological work—the relation between man and God—space limitations have kept us from relating how the realities of the Incarnation and Revelation are shown in Rahner's work in their unfolding in the historical and social dimensions. We must also pass over a large number of Rahner's further contributions to dogmatic and pastoral theology, as well as his writings on the dynamism, the freedom, and the place of the laity in the Church.

At first encounter, Rahner's opus tends to confuse by the multitude and variety of the problems it takes up, and by its ever renewed, ever more profound searching into the infinite realm of divine revelation. But on closer study there emerges a basic structure that unifies all his labors: Rahner's radical concern is man—to understand man, and through him the God-man.

This structure arises from the very nature of all human understanding, in which the spirit forever implies the openness of all that has being—that openness which to Rahner is the condition even for the possibility of sense-perception. This openness is, in the concrete order of things, determined by that supernatural existential which is the condition for the possibility of sanctifying grace, the communication of the love of God. Pure openness, by which transcendence becomes man's own theme, is ultimately also the condition for the Incarnation, the embodiment of the Logos in the flesh and in the world—for man's being the "possible being-other-than-himself of God's self-surrender," for man's sanctifying grace as participation in the inner life of the Trinity.

By means of this consistent structure Rahner can clarify, in the strictest conceptualization, something of the inconceivable relatedness and interpenetration of the orders of creation and of grace; he can present dogmatics as a theological anthropology. As a meticulous hearer of the word of God and thoughtful student of theological tradition, and healthily stirred up by the problems raised by philosophers from Kant to Heidegger, Rahner can give us a truly new interpretation of Christian theology.

There will be those who ask why a theology of this kind must talk so much of man. But every time a Catholic takes part in the sacrament of Holy Communion he prays to "God by whom the dignity of human nature was wondrously established and yet more wondrously restored." And Karl Rahner says somewhere that God does not grow smaller if man grows larger. This thought, of course, should not go to our heads, but to our grateful hearts. . . .

Bibliography (up to 1964)

I. *Works Cited in the Text*

KARL ADAM

The Christ of Faith: The Christology of the Church. New York: Pantheon, 1957; London: Burns & Oates, 1957; New York: New American Library (Mentor), 1962.

The Spirit of Catholicism. London: Sheed & Ward, 1929; New York: Macmillan, 1929, 1935, 1937, 1952 (revised edition); New York: Doubleday (Image), 1959.

PAUL ALTHAUS

Fact and Faith in the Kerygma of Today. Philadelphia: Muhlenberg Press, 1959; Philadelphia: Fortress, 1960.

Not Translated:

Die Christliche Wahrheit / The Christian Truth /, Vol. I/II, 1947/ 1948.

Grundriss der Dogmatik / Outline of Dogmatics /, Vol. I/II, 1929/
1932 (Published together, 1958).

Die letzen Dinge / Eschatology /, 1922, 1956.

Die Lutherische Rechtfertigungslehre und ihre heutigen Kritiker /
Luther's Doctrine of Justification and its Present Critics.

Luther's Lehre von den beiden Reichen im Feuer der Kritik / Luther's
Doctrine of the Two Kingdoms Under Attack.

Grundriss der Ethik / Outline of Ethics /, 1953.

Paulus and Luther über den Menschen / Paul and Luther on Man /,
1958.

HANS URS VON BALTHASAR

*Martin Buber and Christianity: A Dialogue Between Israel and the
Church.* New York: Macmillan, 1961; London: Harvill Press,
1961.

A Theology of History. New York: Sheed & Ward, 1963.

Epilogue to translation of Paul Claudel's *Satin Slipper,* 1959.

Not Translated:

Fragen der Theologie heute / Current Problems of Theology /
(article) 1958.

Das Herz der Welt / The Heart of the World / 1945.

Der Christ und die Angst / The Christian and Anguish.

Menschen der Kirche in Zeugnis und Urkunde / Men of the Church
in Witness and Document, 1954.

KARL BARTH

Church Dogmatics. I/1-IV/3, 12 Vols., New York: Scribner's Sons;
Edinburgh: T. & T. Clark, 1936-1962. *The Doctrine of Creation*
(Vol. III, Pt. 1, Pt. 2), Edinburgh: T. & T. Clark, 1958/1960.

The Teaching of the Church Regarding Baptism. Naperville, Ill.:
Allenson, 1956; Edinburgh: Oliver & Boyd, 1963; London: Student Christian Movement Press, 1954, 1959.

Theological Existence Today! A Plea for Theological Freedom. London: Hodder and Stoughton, 1933; Lexington, Kentucky: The
American Theological Library Association Committee on Reprinting, 1962 (facsimile reprint).

Not Translated:

Christengemeinde und Bürgergemeinde / Christian Community and
    Civic Community /, 1946.
Rechfertigung und Recht / Justification and Justice /, 1938.

HEINRICH EMIL BRUNNER

The Divine-Human Encounter. Philadelphia: Westminster Press, 1943.
The Divine Imperative, A Study in Christian Ethics. New York:
    Macmillan, 1938; London: Lutterworth, 1937; Philadelphia:
    Westminster Press, 1947.
Justice and the Social Order. New York and London: Harper & Bros.,
    1945; London: Lutterworth Press, 1945.
Man in Revolt—A Christian Anthropology. London: Lutterworth
    Press, ·1934; New York: Scribner's Sons, 1939; Philadelphia:
    Westminster Press, 1947.
The Mediator, A Study of the Central Doctrine of the Christian Faith.
    London: Lutterworth Press, 1934, 1942, 1952; New York:
    Macmillan, 1934; Philadelphia: Westminster Press, 1947.
The Misunderstanding of the Church. London: Lutterworth Press,
    1952; Philadelphia: Westminster Press, 1953.
"Nature and Grace" in *Natural Theology.* London: Geoffrey Bles
    (Centenary Press), 1946 (with Karl Barth's essay: "No!").
*Revelation and Reason, The Christian Doctrine of Faith and Knowl-
    edge.* London: Student Christian Movement Press, 1946; Phila-
    delphia: Westminster Press, 1946.

Not Translated:

Die Mystik und das Wort / Mysticism and the Word /, 1948.

RUDOLF BULTMANN

Essays Philosophical and Theological. New York: Macmillan, 1955;
    London: Student Christian Movement Press, 1955.
"The Study of the Synoptic Gospels," R. Bultmann and K. Kundsin,
    in *Form Criticism, Two Essays on New Testament Research.*
    Gloucester, Mass.: Peter Smith Co.; New York: Harper & Row
    (Torchbooks), 1962.
Jesus and the Word. New York: Scribner's Sons, 1934 (paper, 1958);

London: Nicholson & Watson, 1935; London: Collins (Fontana), 1962.

The History of the Synoptic Tradition. New York: Harper & Row, 1963; London: Blackwell, 1962.

Kerygma and Myth (with others). Ed. by Hans W. Bartsch. London: S.P.C.K., 1953; Vol. II, 1962. New York: Harper & Row (Torchbooks), 1962 (Essay titled: "The New Testament and Mythology.").

Theology of the New Testament. London: Student Christian Movement Press, Vol. I, 1958; Vol. II, 1959. New York: Scribner's Sons, Vol. I, 1951; Vol. II, 1955.

Not Translated:

"The New Testament and Mythology," in *Offenbarung und Heilsgeschehen* / Revelation and the Event of Salvation /, 1941.

YVES (JOSEPH MARIE) CONGAR

Divided Christendom, A Catholic Study of the Problem of Reunion. London: Geoffrey Bles (Centenary Press), 1939.

Lay People in the Church, A Study for a Theology of the Laity. London: Bloomsbury Pub. Co., 1957; London: G. Chapman, 1959; Westminster, Maryland: Newman Press, 1957, 1959.

The Mystery of the Temple. London: Burns & Oates, 1962; Westminster, Maryland: Newman Press, 1962.

ROMANO GUARDINI

The End of the Modern World, A Search for Orientation. New York: Sheed & Ward, 1956; London: Sheed & Ward, 1957.

Freedom, Grace and Destiny. London: Harvill Press, 1961; New York: Pantheon, 1961.

The Humanity of Christ, Contributions to a Psychology of Jesus. New York: Pantheon, 1964.

The Life of Faith. Vols. I/II. London: Burns & Oates, 1961; Westminster, Maryland: Newman Press, 1961; Glen Rock, New Jersey: The Paulist Press, 1963.

The Lord. Chicago: Regnery, 1954; London, New York: Longmans, Green & Co., 1956.

Mary, Mother of the Lord, Theological Meditations. New York: Herder & Herder, 1963.

Not Translated:

Der Gegensatz / The Antithesis /, 1914.
Das Wesen des Christentums / The Essence of Christianity /, 1958.
Vom Sinn der Kirche / On the Meaning of the Church /, 1933.
Religion und Offenbarung / Religion and Revelation /, 1950.
"Thule und Hellas," (essay), 1928.

REINHOLD NIEBUHR

Faith and History. New York: Scribner's Sons, 1949; London: Nisbet & Co., 1949.
Moral Man and Immoral Society. New York: Scribner's Sons, 1932, 1960; London: Student Christian Movement Press, 1963.
The Nature and Destiny of Man, A Christian Interpretation. 2 Vols. New York: Scribner's Sons, Vol. I, 1941; Vol. II, 1943; One Vol. edition, 1949. London: Nisbet & Co., Vol. I, 1941; Vol. II, 1943.
(*About* Niebuhr, with him as a contributor). *Reinhold Niebuhr, His Religious, Social, and Political Thought*. Edited by Charles W. Kegley and Robert W. Bretall. New York, London: Macmillan (Library of Living Theology, Vol. 2), 1956, 1961.

KARL RAHNER

Inspiration in the Bible. Freiburg: Herder, 1961; London: Nelson, 1961; New York: Herder & Herder, 1961.
On the Theology of Death. London: Nelson, 1961; New York: Herder & Herder, 1961.
Theological Investigations. Vol. I, *God, Christ, Mary and Grace*. Baltimore: Helicon Press, 1961; London: Darton, Longman, and Todd, 1961.
Theological Investigations. Vol. II, *Man in the Church*. London: Darton, Longman, and Todd, 1964.

Not Translated:

Hörer des Wortes / Hearers of the Word /, 1941.

HEINRICH SCHLIER

Not Translated:

Der Brief an die Ephesier, Kommentar, / The Epistle to the Ephesians, A Commentary / Excerpt: "Christ and the Church in the Letter to the Ephesians," 1930, 1957.

Die Verkündigung im Gottesdienst der Kirche / The Proclamation in the Divine Service of the Church /, 1953.
Die Zeit der Kirche / The Age of the Church /, 1958.
Das Wort Gottes, eine neu testamentliche Besinnung / The Word of God: A Meditation on the New Testament /, 1958.

PAUL J. TILLICH

The Protestant Era. Chicago: University of Chicago Press, 1948 (abridged Phoenix Paperback, 1957).
Systematic Theology. 3 Volumes. London: Nisbet & Co.; Chicago: University of Chicago Press, Vol. I, 1951; Vol. II, 1957; Vol. III, 1963.

II. *All Works Published in English, with All Editions:*

KARL ADAM

Books:

The Christ of Faith, The Christology of the Church. London: Burns & Oates, 1957; New York: Pantheon, 1957; New York: New American Library (Mentor), 1962.
Christ Our Brother. London: Sheed & Ward, 1931; New York: Macmillan, 1931; New York: Collier, 1962.
Holy Marriage. Collegeville, Minnesota: The Liturgical Press, 1956.
Moral Re-Armament and Christianity in the West. 4 Hays Mews, M.R.A., n.d.
One and Holy / *Roots of the Reformation* /. New York, London: Sheed & Ward, 1951; (latter title) New York: Sheed & Ward, 1957.
Saint Augustine, The Odyssey of His Soul. London: Sheed & Ward, 1932; New York: Macmillan, 1932.
The Son of God. London: Sheed & Ward, 1929; New York: Sheed & Ward, 1934, 1940; New York: Doubleday (Image).
The Spirit of Catholicism. New York: Macmillan, 1929, 1930, 1935, 1937, 1952 (revised edition); New York: Doubleday (Image), 1959.
Two Essays by Karl Adam: Christ and the Western Mind; Love and Belief. New York: Macmillan, 1930.

Essays:

"An Act of Faith," *Worship* 31:120-25 1957.
"Dogmatic Bases of the Liturgy," *Orate Fratres* 11:481-7, 529-36; 12:8-14, 56-59, 97-104, 145-51; Oct. 3, 1937-Feb. 1938.
"Easter Sermon," *Worship* 27: 254-6 April 1953.
"In the Jubilee Year," *Commonweal* 20:361-3 Aug. 10, 1934.
"Notes and Gleanings," *Fortnightly Review* 39:235 Oct. 1932.
"Pentecost and Baptism," *Worship* 28:281-3 May 1954.
"St John and Christ," *Jubilee* 6:18-23 June 1958.
"Sanctification of Marriage," *Orate Fratres* 9:171-6, 218-25; Feb.-Mar. 1935.

PAUL ALTHAUS

Books:

Fact and Faith in the Kerygma of Today. Philadelphia: Muhlenberg Press, 1959; Philadelphia: Fortress, 1960.
Mystic Lyrics From the Indian Middle Ages. London: G. Allen & Unwin, 1928.
The So-Called Kerygma and the Historical Jesus / The So-called Kerygma and the Chronological Jesus /. Edinburgh: Oliver & Boyd, 1959; (latter title) Syracuse: Syracuse University Press, 1959.

Essay:

"Evangelical Faith and Anthroposophy," *Lutheran Quarterly* 14:3-20 Feb. 1962.

HANS URS VON BALTHASAR

Books:

Elizabeth of Dijon. London: Harvill Press, 1956; New York: Pantheon, 1956.
Martin Buber and Christianity, A Dialogue Between Israel and the Church. London: Harvill Press, 1961; New York: Macmillan, 1961.
Prayer. London: G. Chapman, 1961; New York: Sheed & Ward, 1961.
Science, Religion and Christianity. London: Burns & Oates, 1958; Westminster, Maryland: Newman Press, 1958.
Theology of History. New York: Sheed & Ward, 1963.

Therese of Lisieux, The Story of a Mission. London, New York: Sheed & Ward, 1954.

Essays:

"Beauty and Revelation," *Philosophy Today* 3:231-42 Winter 1959.

"Science and Religion: A Path to Religious Anthropology," *Philosophy Today* 1:230-37 Winter 1957.

"Scripture as the Word of God," *Downside Review* 68:1-20 Winter 1949.

"What Should Theology Be Doing?" *Cross Currents* 4:349-56 Fall 1954.

KARL BARTH

Books—as Sole Author:

Against the Stream; Shorter Post-War Writings 1946-1952. Ed. by R. G. Smith. London: Student Christian Movement Press, 1954; New York: Philosophical Library, 1954.

Anselm: Fides Quaerens Intellectum. London: Student Christian Movement Press, 1960; Richmond, Va.: John Knox, 1960.

Community, State, and Church. Gloucester, Mass: Peter Smith; New York: Doubleday (Anchor), 1960.

Christ and Adam: Man and Humanity in Romans 5. New York. Collier Books, 1962; New York: Harper & Brothers, 1957; Edinburgh: Oliver & Boyd, 1956.

Christmas. Naperville, Illinois: Allenson, 1959; Edinburgh: Oliver & Boyd, 1959.

The Christian Life. London: Student Christian Movement Press, 1930; Lexington, Kentucky: American Theological Library Association Committee on Reprinting, 1962 (facsimile reprint).

Christianity Divided. London: Sheed & Ward, 1962.

Church and State. London: Student Christian Movement Press, 1939.

The Church and the Political Problems of Our Day. London: Hodder & Stoughton, 1939; New York: Scribner's Sons, 1939.

The Church and the War. New York: Macmillan, 1944.

Church Dogmatics. 12 Volumes—Divided into four "volumes" and "parts." Vol. I, pts. 1-2, *The Doctrine of the Word of God (Prolegomena to Church Dogmatics)*, Edinburgh: T. & T. Clark, 1936 (2 vols.).

Vol. II, pts. 1-2, *The Doctrine of God,* Edinburgh: T. & T. Clark,

1957; New York: Scribner's Sons, 1957 (pt. 1), (2 vols.). Pts. 3-4, Edinburgh: T. & T. Clark, 1961; New York: Scribner's Sons, 1961 (2 vols.).

Vol. III, pts. 1-2, *The Doctrine of Creation,* Edinburgh: T. & T. Clark, 1958 (pt. 1); 1960 (pt. 2), (2 vols.).

Vol. IV, pts. 1-2, *The Doctrine of Reconciliation,* New York: Scribner's Sons, (pt. 1) 1956. Edinburgh: T. & T. Clark, (pt. 1) 1956; (pt. 2) 1958 (2 vols.).

Pt. 3—First Half; pt. 3—Second Half, Edinburgh: T. & T. Clark, 1962 (2 vols).

Church Dogmatics: A Selection. Gloucester, Mass: Peter Smith.

Church Dogmatics: A Selection. Edinburgh: T. & T. Clark, 1961; New York: Harper & Row (Torchbooks), 1962.

Credo, A Presentation of the Chief Problems of Dogmatics with Reference to the Apostles' Creed. New York: Scribner's Sons, 1936.

Deliverance to the Captives. New York: Harper & Row, 1961; London: Student Christian Movement Press, 1961.

Dogmatics in Outline. New York: Harper & Row, 1959; London: Student Christian Movement Press, 1957.

Dogmatics in Outline. New York: Philosophical Library, 1947.

Epistle to the Philippians. Richmond, Va.: John Knox, 1962; London: Student Christian Movement Press, 1962.

Epistle to the Romans. Oxford: Oxford University Press, 1933, 1953, 1957.

Evangelical Theology: An Introduction. New York: Holt, Rinehart & Winston, 1963; London: Weidenfeld & N., 1963.

The Faith of the Church: A Commentary on the Apostles' Creed According to Calvin's Catechism. Edinburgh: Oliver & Boyd, 1959; London: Collins, 1960; New York: World (Meridian), 1958.

The Germans and Ourselves. London: Nisbet & Co., 1945.

God, Grace, and Gospel. Naperville, Illinois: Allenson, 1959.

God in Action. New York: Round Table Press, 1936, 1963; Edinburgh: T. & T. Clark, 1936.

The Great Promise. New York: The Philosophical Library, 1963.

The Holy Ghost and the Christian Life. London: F. Muller, Ltd., 1938.

The Humanity of God. Richmond, Va.: John Knox, 1960; London: Collins, 1961.

Karl Barth's Church Dogmatics, An Introductory Report. Ed. by O.

Weber (Digest of first 8 volumes of *Church Dogmatics*). Philadelphia: Westminster, 1954.

Karl Barth's Table Talk / Table Talk: Discussions for English-Speaking Students /. Ed. by John D. Godsey. Richmond, Va.: John Knox, 1963; Naperville, Illinois: Allenson, 1963; Edinburgh: Oliver & Boyd, 1963.

The Knowledge of God and the Service of God. Naperville, Illinois: Allenson, 1955; London: Hodder & Stoughton, 1938.

The Only Way. How Can the Germans be Cured? New York: Philisophical Library, 1947.

Prayer According to the Catechisms of the Reformation. Philadelphia: Westminster Press, 1952.

Preaching of the Gospel. Philadelphia: Westminster Press, 1963.

Protestant Thought: From Rousseau to Ritschl, / From Rousseau to Ritschl, Being the Translation of 11 Chapters of *Die Protestantische Theologie in 19. Jahrhundert* /. London: Student Christian Movement Press, 1959; New York: Harper & Bros., 1959.

Questions to Christendom; or, Christendom's Present-day Problems. London: Lutterworth Press, 1932.

The Resurrection of the Dead. New York: Fleming H. Revell Co., 1933; London: Hodder and Stoughton, 1933.

Shorter Commentary on Romans. Richmond, Va.: John Knox, 1959; London: Student Christian Movement Press, 1963.

The Teaching of the Church Regarding Baptism. Naperville, Illinois: Allenson, 1956; London: Student Christian Movement Press, 1948, 1954, 1959.

Theological Existence Today! A Plea for Theological Freedom. London: Hodder & Stoughton, 1933. Lexington, Kentucky: American Theological Library Association Committee on Reprinting, 1962 (facsimile reprint).

Theology and Church; Shorter Writings, 1920-1928. London: Student Christian Movement Press, n.d.; New York: Harper & Row, 1962.

Trouble and Promise in the Struggle of the Church in Germany. Oxford: The Clarendon Press, 1938.

The Word of God and Man. Gloucester, Mass.: Peter Smith, 1958. *The Word of God and the Word of Man.* Chicago, Boston: Pilgrim Press, 1928; London: Hodder & Stoughton, 1935; New York: Harper & Bros. (Torchbooks), 1957.

Books—Pamphlets:

The Church and the Churches—A Message to the World Conference on Faith and Order. Grand Rapids, Michigan: Wm. B. Eerdmans Publishing Co., 1936; London: J. Clarke, 1937.

A Letter to Great Britain from Switzerland. London: Sheldon Press, 1941; New York: Macmillan, 1941, "This Christian Cause."

Books—as Contributing Essayist:

"The Church—The Living Congregation of the Living Lord Jesus Christ," in *Man's Disorder and God's Design.* The Amsterdam Assembly Series. New York: Harper & Bros., n.d.

Come, Holy Spirit; Sermons by K. Barth and E. Thurneysen. New York: Round Table Press, 1933; Edinburgh: T. & T. Clark, 1934.

God's Search For Man; Sermons, with E. Thurneysen. New York: Round Table Press, 1935; Edinburgh: T. & T. Clark, 1935.

How to Serve God in a Marxist Land (with Johannes Hamel). New York: Association Press, 1959.

Kerygma and Myth (with others). Ed. by Hans W. Bartsch. London: S.P.C.K., 1953; Vol. II, 1962. New York: Harper & Row (Torchbooks), 1962.

Revelation (with Gustaf Aulen, *et al.*). New York: Macmillan, 1937.

As Essayist in Journals:

"All; A Sermon," *Interpretation* 14:64-9 Jan. 1960.

"Barth to Bereczky: A Letter," *Christian Century* July 30, 1952.

"The Church Between East and West," *Cross Currents* 1:64-77 Winter 1951.

"Church or Group Movement?" *London Quarterly Review* 162:1-10 Jan. 1937.

"Continental vs. Anglo-Saxon Theology," *Christian Century* Feb. 16. 1949.

"The Fear of the Lord is the Beginning of Wisdom: A Sermon," *Interpretation* 14:433-9 Oct. 1960.

"The Great Dispensation: A Sermon" (preprint), *Interpretation* 14: 310-14 July 1960.

"How My Mind Has Changed, 1938-1948," *Christian Century* Mar. 9-16, 1949.

"How My Mind Has Changed in This Decade," *Christian Century* Sept. 13-20, 1939.

"The Humanity of God," *Cross Currents* 10:70-79 Winter 1960.

"A Letter to American Christians," *Christendom* 8 No. 4:442-58 1943.

"The Lord's Prayer" (Excerpt), *Theology Today* 13:298-9 Oct. 1956.

"No Christian Marshall Plan," *Christian Century* Dec. 8, 1948.

"On Systematic Theology" (Autobiographical), reprint, *Scottish Journal of Theology* 14:225-8 Sept. 1961.

"The Protestant Churches in Europe," *Foreign Affairs* July 1943.

"Protestantism and Architecture," *Theology Today* 19:272 July 1962.

"Teach us to Consider . . . ! A Sermon," *Interpretation* 14:161-6 April 1960.

"Theological Dialogue," *Theology Today* 19:171-7 July 1962.

"Thoughts on the Second Vatican Council," *Ecumenical Review* 15:357-67 July 1963.

"Views on the New Oecumenical Climate," excerpts from a *Réalités* interview. *Tablet* 217:36 March 2, 1963.

HEINRICH EMIL BRUNNER

Books—as Sole Author:

Christianity and Civilisation. London: Nisbet & Co., pt. I 1942; pt. II 1948, 1955. New York: Scribner's Sons, 1948.

The Church and the Oxford Group. London: Hodder & Stoughton, 1937.

The Church in the New Social Order: An Address Delivered to the National Congress of the Free Church, Federal Council, Cardiff, on 26th March, 1952. London: Student Christian Movement Press, 1952.

The Divine-Human Encounter. Philadelphia: Westminster Press, 1943; Toronto: Ambassador Books, Ltd., 1943; London: Student Christian Movement Press, 1944.

The Divine Imperative, A Study in Christian Ethics. London: Lutterworth Press, 1937; New York: Macmillan, 1937; Philadelphia: Westminster Press, 1947.

Dogmatics, 3 Vols.,

   Vol. I—*The Christian Doctrine of God.* Philadelphia: Westminster Press, 1950; London: Lutterworth Press, 1949.

   Vol. II—*The Christian Doctrine of Creation and Redemption.* Philadelphia: Westminster Press, 1952; London: Lutterworth Press, 1954.

Vol. III—*The Christian Doctrine of the Church, Faith, and the Consummation.* Philadelphia: Westminster Press, 1961; London: Lutterworth Press, 1962.

Eternal Hope. Philadelphia: Westminster Press, 1954; London: Lutterworth Press, 1954.

Europe and America: A Contribution to Mutual Understanding. Zürich: Swiss-American Society for Cultural Relations, 1952.

Faith, Hope and Love. Philadelphia: Westminster Press, 1956; London: Lutterworth Press, 1957.

Law and the Orders: Outline of a Protestant Theology of Ethics / Das Gebot und die Ordnungen. Entwurf einer protestantisch-theologischen Ethik. / XII, 696 S. Tübingen, Mohr, 1932. 3, unveränd. Aufl., Zürich, Zwingli-Verlag, 1939. Trans. London: Religious Tract Society, 1934; London: Lutterworth, 1947; Philadelphia, Westminster Press, 1947.

God and Man, Four Essays on the Nature of Personality. London: Student Christian Movement Press, 1936.

The Great Invitation and Other Sermons. Philadelphia: Westminster Press, 1955; London: Lutterworth Press, 1955.

I Believe in the Living God: Sermons on the Apostles' Creed. Philadelphia: Westminster Press, 1960; London: Lutterworth Press, 1961.

Justice and Freedom in Society, record of lectures at Seiko Gakuin, Shinjuku, Tokyo, Oct. 1954-Feb. 1955. The Institute of Educational Research and Service, International Christian University, 1955.

Justice and the Social Order. London: Lutterworth Press, 1945; New York and London: Harper & Bros., 1945.

Letter to the Romans: A Commentary (rev. ed.). Philadelphia: Westminster Press, 1959; London: Lutterworth Press, 1959.

Man in Revolt, A Christian Anthropology. New York: Scribner's Sons, 1939; London: Lutterworth Press, 1939; Philadelphia: Westminster Press, 1947.

The Mediator; A Study of the Central Doctrine of the Christian Faith. London: Lutterworth Press, 1934, 1942, 1952; New York: Macmillan, 1934; Philadelphia: Westminster Press, 1947.

The Misunderstanding of the Church. London: Lutterworth Press, 1952; Philadelphia: Westminster Press, 1953.

Our Faith. New York: Scribner's Sons, 1936, 1954.

215

The Philosophy of Religion From the Standpoint of Protestant Theology. New York: Scribner's Sons, 1937; London: I. Nicholson & Watson, 1937; Naperville, Illinois: Allenson, 1958; London: J. Clarke, 1958.

The Predicament of the Church Today. London: Lutterworth Press, 1940.

Revelation and Reason: The Christian Doctrine of Faith and Knowledge. Philadelphia: Westminster Press, 1946; London: Student Christian Movement Press, 1947.

The Scandal of Christianity. London: Student Christian Movement Press, 1951; Philadelphia: Westminster Press, 1951.

The Theology of Crisis. New York, London: Scribner's Sons, 1929.

The Word and the World. New York: Scribner's Sons, 1931; London: Student Christian Movement Press, 1931.

Books—as Contributing Essayist:

Best Sermons, 1947-1948. Ed. by G. Paul Butler. New York, London: Harper and Bros, 1947.

"The Christian Message to Postwar Youth," in *Preparatory Documents.* World's Committee of Y.M.C.A. Genf. 3. 1947.

"The Christian Understanding of Man," in *The Christian Understanding of Man; Church, Community and State.* Vol. II, London, 1938.

"Continental European Theology," in *The Church Through Half a Century.* Essays in Honor of William Adams Brown. New York, London: Scribner's Sons, 1936.

Last Chance. Eleven Questions on Issues Determining Our Destiny, excerpts. Ed. by Clara Urquhart. Boston: Beacon Press, 1948.

"A Message to the Plenary," in *Forward Together in Faith.* Report of the Plenary Meeting of the World's Committee of the Y.M.C.A., 1950: "The Y.M.C.A.—Success or Failure?"

"Nature and Grace," in *Natural Theology.* London: Geoffrey Bles (Centenary Press), 1946 (with Karl Barth's essay: "No!").

The Theology of Emil Brunner. Ed. by Charles W. Kegley and Robert W. Bretall. Vol. 3 of the Library of Living Theology. New York, London: Macmillan, 1963.

"Some Remarks on Reinhold Niebuhr's Work as a Christian Thinker," in *Reinhold Niebuhr, His Religious, Social, and Political Thought.* Ed. by Charles W. Kegley and Robert W. Bretall. Vol. 2 of the Library of Living Theology. New York, London: Macmillan, 1956.

"A Unique Christian Mission: The Mukyokai (non-church) Movement in Japan," in *Religion and Culture,* Essays in Honor of Paul Tillich. New York: Harper & Brothers, 1959.

Essays: A Chronologically Representative Selection:

1919 "Religious Socialism in Switzerland," *The Social Preparation* nos.14/15.

1920 "New Religious Movement in Switzerland," *American Journal of Theology* 24:422-35 July.

1921 *"Rezension,* unter dem Titel *The Decline of the Occident,* von Spengler, Untergang des Abendlandes. *The World Tomorrow* November.

1926 "Die Absolutheit Jesu," in Vorträge, gehalten auf der 29. Aarauer Studentenkonferenz, 1926. Berlin: *Furche-Verlag,* 1926, S. 39-64. S.A. 2 Aufl., 28 S., "Stimmen aus der deutschen christlichen. Studentenbewegung," Heft 47, Berlin: *Furche-Verlag,* 1932. 3. Aufl. 1934. Trans. in: *The Union Seminary Review,* no. 4, vol. 46, 1935.

1928 "Zachäus der Zöllner. Predigt, gehalten in der Kirche Oberstrap," *Zwischen den Zeiten.* 6, 1928 Heft 4. Trans. in *The Christian Century* no. 13, 1930.

1930 "Secularism as a Problem for the Church," *International Review of Missions* 19:495-511 Oct. 1930.

1934 "Die Unentbehrlickeit des Alten Testaments für die missionierende Kirche," Vortrag am Basler Missionsfest 1934. 24 S. Stuttgart und Basel, *Evang. Missionverlag,* 1934. Trans. in *The Lutheran Church Quarterly,* 1947.

1938 "The Place of Reason in Religion," *International Review of Missions* 27:338-40 July.

1939 "The Present-Day Task of Theology," *Religion in Life* 2:176-186, August.

1940 "A Sermon Preached to Soldiers and Civilians at Zürich, Sept. 17, 1939," *Round Table* 30:469-74 March.

1945 "War as a Problem of the Christian Church," *Christendom* 10 No. 4:472-8.

"Was hat Amerika uns, was haben wir Amerika zu geben?" Vortrag vor der Swiss-American Society for Cultural Relations. IV, 19S., Zürich, Schulthess & Co., 1945. Trans in *USA-Switzerland,* No. 1 & 2, May, July 1946.

1947 "One Holy Catholic Church," *Theology Today* 318-31.

1948 "Kommunismus, Kapitalismus und Christentum," 35 S., *Kirchliche Zeitfragen* Heft 23. Zürich: Zwingli-Verlag, 1948. Also in: *Christ und Welt,* 1, 1948 No. 15 (Excerpt). Trans. London: Lutterworth Press, 1949.
"The Foundations of Personalism," *Manhood,* Y.M.C.A. National Magazine No. 10-2.

1949 "The Church Between East and West," An Address Delivered to the Assembly of the Congregational Union of England and Wales, May 1949, *Congregational Quarterly* No. 3, 27 .

1950 "Christian Sense of Time," *Cross Currents* 1:25-33 Fall.

1951 "The Christian Understanding of Time," *Scottish Journal of Theology* 4, No. 1.

1952 "The Year in Europe," *World Communiqué* World Review Number, 62, No. 1.

1956 "Until Christ Be Formed in You," *Theology Today* 12:434-5 Jan.

1958 "In Search of an International Ethos," *Cross Currents* 8:1-8 Winter.

1960 "Fresh Appraisal: The Cleveland Report on Red China," *Christianity Today* 4:3-6 April 25.

1961 "Easter Certainty" (excerpt from a sermon), *Theology Today* 18:14-15 April.

RUDOLF KARL BULTMANN

Books—as Sole Author:

Essays, Philosophical and Theological. London: Student Christian Movement Press, 1955; New York: Macmillan, 1955.

Existence and Faith. London: Hodder and Stoughton, 1961; New York: World (Meridian), 1960.

Gnosis. London: A. & C. Black, 1952.

History and Eschatology: The Presence of Eternity. New York: Harper & Row (Torchbooks), 1962; Edinburgh: Edinburgh University Press, 1957.

The History of the Synoptic Tradition. New York: Harper & Row, 1963; London: Blackwell, 1960.

Jesus and the Word. London: Nicholson & Watson, 1935; New York: Scribner's Sons, 1934, (paper) 1958; London: Collins (Fontana), 1962.

Primitive Christianity in its Contemporary Setting. London, New

York: Thames & Hudson, 1956; London: Collins (Fontana),
1960; New York: World (Meridian), 1956.

Theology of the New Testament. 2 Vols. New York: Scribner's Sons,
Vol. I, 1951; Vol. II, 1955. London: Student Christian Movement Press, Vol. I, 1952; Vol. II, 1959.

This World and the Beyond. New York: Scribner's Sons, 1960; London: Lutterworth Press, 1960.

Books—as Contributing Essayist:

Faith (with Artur Weiser). London: A. & C. Black, 1961.

Form Criticism, Two Essays on New Testament Research (with Karl
Kundsin). Gloucester, Mass: Peter Smith; New York: Harper
& Row (Torchbook), 1962.

Hope (with K. H. Rengstorf). London: A. & C. Black, 1963.

Kerygma and Myth (with others). Ed. by Hans W. Bartsch. London:
S.P.C.K., Vol. I, 1953, Vol. II, 1962; New York: Harper & Row
(Torchbooks), 1962.

Myth and Christianity (with Karl Jaspers). New York: Farrar, Straus
(Noonday), 1958.

Essays:

"From a Marburg Sermon" (reprint), *Theology Today* 17:10-11
April 1960.

"Humanism and Christianity," *Journal of Religion* 32:77-86 April
1952.

"New Approach to the Synoptic Problem," *Journal of Religion* 6:337-
62 July 1926.

"On Behalf of Christian Freedom" (preprint), *Journal of Religion*
40:95-9 April 1960.

"On the Problem of Demythologizing," *Journal of Religion* 42:96-102
April 1962.

"The Problem of Miracle" (reprint), *Religion in Life* 27:63-75 Winter
1957/58.

YVES (JOSEPH MARIE) CONGAR

Books:

After Nine Hundred Years. New York: Fordham University Press,
1959.

The Catholic Church and the Race Question. Paris: UNESCO, 1953.

Christ, Our Lady, and the Church; A Study in Eirenic Theology.

London: Longmans, Green, 1957; Westminster, Maryland: Newman Press, 1957.

Divided Christendom; A Catholic Study of the Problem of Reunion. London: Geoffrey Bles (Centenary Press), 1939.

Laity, Church and World. Baltimore: Helicon Press, 1960; London: G. Chapman, 1960.

Lay People in the Church; A Study for a Theology of the Laity. Westminster, Maryland: Newman Press, 1957, 1959; London: Bloomsbury Pub. Co., 1957; London: G. Chapman, 1959.

The Mystery of the Church. Baltimore: Helicon Press, 1960; London: G. Chapman, 1960.

The Mystery of the Temple. London: Burns & Oates, 1962; Westminster, Maryland: Newman Press, 1962.

Report from Rome. London: G. Chapman, 1964.

The Wide World, My Parish; Salvation and its Problems. Baltimore: Helicon Press, 1961; London: Darton, Longman, & Todd, 1961.

Essays:

"Attitudes Toward Reform in the Church," *Cross Currents* 1:80-102 Summer 1951.

"Conscientious Objection," *Commonweal* 51:214 Nov. 25, 1949.

"Ecumenism at the Council Session," *Clergyman* 27:70-1 March 1963.

"Getting Beyond the Ecclesiology of the Counter Reformation," *Orate Fratres* 22:502-507 Oct. 3, 1948.

"Holy Write and Holy Church," *Blackfriars* 41:11-19 Feb. 1960.

"The Idea of Conversion," *Thought* 33:5-20 Spring 1958.

"Inspiration and the Apostolicity of the Church," condensed from *Revue des Sciences Philosophiques et Théologiques,* 45 (1961), *Theology Digest* 11:187-91 Fall 1963.

"Integratists" (excerpt), *Commonweal* 54:598-9 Sept. 28, 1951.

"Laymen, the Church, and the World," *Jubilee* 5:16-19 June 1957.

"Laymen in the Church," *Commonweal* 65:378-80 Jan. 11, 1957.

"Moral Dilemmas: Spiritual Maturity," *Blackfriars* 34:528-35 Dec. 1953.

"Note on Conversion," *Life of the Spirit* 14:62-68 Sept. 1959.

"Progress of the Ecumenical Dialogue," *Theology Digest* 11:67-71 Summer 1963.

"The Real Significance of the Incarnation," *Theology Digest* 8:74-75 Spring 1960.

"The Reality of the Church," *Perspectives* 5:17-20 Aug. 1960.

"Reform in the Church," *Perspectives* 5:3-9 Feb. 1960.

"Rome, Oxford and Edinburgh," *Blackfriars* 18:646-59 Sept. 1937.

"Salvation and the non-Catholic," *Blackfriars* 38:290-300 Aug. 1957.

"The State of Israel in Biblical Perspective," *Blackfriars* 38:244-9 June 1957.

"Theology of the Apostolate," *World Mission* 7:283-94 Fall 1956.

"The Theology of Religious Women," *Review of Religion* 19:15-39 Jan. 1960.

"The Three Ages of the Spiritual Life," *Theology Digest* 4:48-51 Winter 1955.

"True and False Reform in the Church," *Orate Fratres* 23:252-9 April 17, 1949.

"The Unity of God's Plan," *Perspectives* 8:151 Sept.-Oct. 1963.

"What is a Layman?" *Theology Digest* 1:8-12 Jan. 1953.

"What to Look for in the Bible" (condensed), *Integrity* 8:9-10 Feb. 1954.

ROMANO GUARDINI

Books:

The Church and the Catholic; and, *The Spirit of the Liturgy.* London: Sheed & Ward, 1935, 1940, 1953 (the latter alone: 1930, 1937).

Conscience. London: Sheed & Ward, 1932.

The Conversion of Augustine. Westminister, Md.: Newman Press, 1960; London: Sands, 1961.

The Death of Socrates: An Interpretation of the Platonic Dialogues: Euthyphro Apology, Crito, & Phaedo. New York, London: Sheed & Ward, 1948; Cleveland, New York: World (Meridian), 1962.

The End of the Modern World; A Search for Orientation. New York: Sheed & Ward, 1956; London: Sheed & Ward, 1957.

The Faith and Modern Man. New York: Pantheon, 1952; London: Burns & Oates, 1953.

Freedom, Grace and Destiny. New York, Pantheon, 1961; London: Harvill Press, 1961.

The Humanity of Christ; Contributions to a Psychology of Jesus. New York: Pantheon, 1964.

Jesus Christus, Meditations. Chicago: Regnery, 1959; London: Burns & Oates, 1960.

The Last Things: Concerning Death, Purification after Death, Resurrection, Judgment, and Eternity. New York: Pantheon, 1954; London: Burns & Oates, 1955.

The Life of Faith. Vols. I & II. Westminster, Maryland: Newman Press, 1961; London: Burns & Oates, 1961; Glen Rock, New Jersey: Paulist Press, 1963.

The Living God. New York: Pantheon, 1957; London, New York: Longmans, Green, 1956.

The Lord. Chicago: Regnery, 1954; London, New York: Longmans, Green, 1956.

The Lord's Prayer. New York: Pantheon, 1958; London: Burns & Oates, 1958.

The Lord; The Rosary of Our Lady. London, New York: Longmans, Green, (both in one volume), 1957.

Meditations Before Mass. Westminster, Maryland: Newman Press, 1955; London: Longmans, Green, 1956.

Power and Responsibility, A Course of Action for the New Age. Chicago: Regnery, 1961; London: Bailey & S., 1961.

Prayer in Practice. New York: Pantheon, 1957; London: Burns & Oates, 1957.

Prayers from Theology. New York: Herder & Herder, 1959; Freiburg: Herder, 1959.

Rilke's Duino Elegies: An Interpretation. Chicago: Regnery, 1961; London: Darwen Finlayson, 1961.

The Rosary of Our Lady. New York: P. J. Kenedy, 1955.

Sacred Signs. London: Sheed & Ward, 1930, 1937; St. Louis: Pio Decimo Press, 1956.

The Way of the Cross of Our Lord and Savior Jesus Christ. London: Sheed & Ward, 1932, 1944; Chicago: Scepter, 1959.

The Word of God on Faith, Hope and Charity. Chicago: Regnery, 1963.

The Word of God: Scriptural Interpretations. Chicago: Regnery, 1962.

Essays:

"The Absolute Absolute and the Christian Religion," *Philosophy Today* 2:211-20 Winter 1958.

"The Blow Is Meant to Shake the Soul Awake," *Catholic Digest* 25:10 Dec. 1960.

"Dostoyevsky's Idiot, a Symbol of Christ," *Cross Currents* 6:359-82 Fall 1956.

"Hand," *The Catholic Worker* 11:8 Jan. 1944.

"The Jewish Problem; Reflections on Responsibility," *Dublin Review* 227:1-14 Spring 1953.

"Kneeling and Standing," *Catholic Digest* 25:12-13 Nov. 1960.

"The Legend of the Grand Inquisitor," *Cross Currents* 3:58-86 Fall 1952.

"Meditations in Lent," see issues of *Tablet* Feb. 19-April 2, 1955.

"Memorial of Blaise Pascal," *Dublin Review* 224:37-52 Spring 1950.

"Myth, and the Truth of Revelation," *Cross Currents* 1:3-12 Winter 1951.

"The Patience of God," *Jubilee* 5:17-19 May 1957.

"The Realm of Prayer," *Jubilee* 5:10-13 Dec. 1957.

"Sacred Images and the Invisible God," *Furrow* 8:350-63 June 1957; *Cross Currents* 10:211-20 Summer 1960.

"Some Reflections on Freudian Psychology," *Philosophy Today* 2:274-82 Winter 1958.

"The Sound of Silence," *Jubilee* 3:22-27 Feb. 1956.

"The Stages of Life and Philosophy," *Philosophy Today* 1:75-79 June 1957.

"Thoughts on the Problem of the Film," *Cross Currents* 6:189-99 Summer 1956.

"Totalitarianism" (excerpt), *Commonweal* 58:323-4 July 3, 1953.

REINHOLD NIEBUHR

Books—as Sole Author:

Beyond Tragedy, Essays on the Christian Interpretation of History. London: Nisbet & Co., 1938; New York: Scribner's Sons, 1937, 1961.

The Children of Light and the Children of Darkness: A Vindication of Democracy and a Critique of Its Traditional Defenders. London: Nisbet & Co., 1945; New York: Scribner's Sons, 1944, 1960.

Christian Realism and Political Problems. New York: Scribner's, 1953; London: Faber & Faber, 1954.

Christianity and Power Politics. New York: Scribner's Sons, 1940, 1952.

The Contribution of Religion to Social Work. New York: Columbia University Press, 1932; Oxford: Oxford University Press, 1932.

Discerning the Signs of the Times: Sermons for Today and Tomorrow. New York: Scribner's Sons, 1932.

Does Civilization Need Religion? New York: Macmillan, 1927.

Essays in Applied Christianity. New York: World (Meridian), 1959.

Faith and History. New York: Scribner's Sons, 1949; London: Nisbet & Co., 1949.

The Godly and the Ungodly: Essays on the Religious and Secular Dimensions of Modern Life. London: Faber & Faber, 1959.

An Interpretation of Christian Ethics. London: Student Christian Movement Press, 1936; New York: Harper & Bros., 1935; New York: World (Meridian), 1956.

The Irony of American History. London: Nisbet & Co., 1952; New York: Scribner's Sons, 1952, 1962.

Leaves From the Notebook of a Tamed Cynic. Chicago: Willett, Clark, & Colby, 1929; Hamden, Conn.: Shoe String Press, 1956; New York: World (Meridian), 1957.

Love and Justice: Selections from the Shorter Writings. Ed. by D. B. Robertson. Philadelphia: Westminster Press, 1957.

The Meaning of Revelation. New York: Collier, 1963.

Moral Man and Immoral Society. New York: Scribner's Sons, 1932, 1960; London: Student Christian Movement Press, 1963.

The Nature and Destiny of Man: A Christian Interpretation. New York: Scribner's Sons, Vol. I, 1941; Vol. II, 1943. London: Nisbet & Co., Vol. I, 1941; Vol. II, 1943. New York: Scribner's Sons: One Volume Edition, 1949.

Pious and Secular America. New York: Scribner's Sons, 1958.

Reflections on the End of an Era. New York: Scribner's Sons, 1932.

Reinhold Niebuhr on Politics. Ed. by Harry R. Davis and Robert C. Good. New York: Scribner's Sons, 1960.

The Self and the Dramas of History. New York: Scribner's Sons, 1955, 1958; London: Faber & Faber, 1956.

The Social Sources of Denominationalism. New York: World (Meridian), 1962.

The Structure of Nations and Empires / Nations and Empires; Recurring Patterns in the Political Order /. New York: Scribner's Sons, 1959; (latter title) London: Faber & Faber, 1960.

The World Crisis and American Responsibility; Nine Essays. New York: Association Press (Reflection Books), 1958.

Pamphlets:

Do the State and Nation Belong to God or the Devil? London: Student Christian Movement Press, 1937.

Doom and Dawn (with Sherwood Eddy). New York: Eddy & Page, 1936.

Europe's Catastrophe and the Christian Faith. London: Nisbet & Co., 1940.

Five Years of the North Atlantic Alliance, "The Moral and Spiritual Content of the Atlantic Community." Contributor with others. New York: American Council on NATO, 1954.

The Illusions of World Government. New York: Whitestone, 1949.

Jews After the War. London: Inter-University Jewish Federation of Great Britain and Ireland, 1943.

A Mike Wallace Interview with Reinhold Niebuhr. New York: Fund for the Republic, n.d.

The Moral Implications of Loyalty to the United Nations. New Haven, Conn.: E. W. Hagen Foundation, 1952.

Our Moral and Spiritual Resources for International Cooperation. Washington, D.C.: U.S. Government Printing Office, 1956.

"The Perils of American-European Relationship," in *The Community Pulpit Series.* Ed. by J. H. Holmes. No. 11, 1928-1929.

The Protestant Opposition Church Movement in Germany, 1934-1937. London: Friends of Europe Publications, No. 55, 1937.

The Role of the Newspapers in America's Function as the Greatest World Power. Minneapolis, Minn.: Newspaper Guild of the Twin Cities, 1950.

The Spirit of Life. New York: N.E.A. of the U.S., Addresses and Proceedings, 1930.

"The Unethical Character of Modern Civilization," in *The Community Pulpit Series.* Ed. by J. H. Holmes. No. 10, 1928-1929.

Why the Christian Church is Not Pacifist. London: Student Christian Movement Press, 1940.

Your Christian Conscience and American Abundance (with Leland Gordon). New York: National Council of Churches of Christ, 1955.

Books—as Contributing Essayist:

"An American Approach to the Christian Message," in *A Traffic in*

Knowledge. Ed. by W. A. Visser 'T Hooft. London: Student Christian Movement Press, 1931.

"Biblical Thought and Ontological Speculation in Tillich's Theology," in *The Theology of Paul Tillich*. Ed. by Charles W. Kegley and Robert W. Bretall. Vol. I. of the Library of Living Theology. New York: Macmillan, 1952.

A Book That Shook the World (with others). Pittsburgh: University of Pittsburgh Press, n.d.

"Christian Faith and the Common Life," in *Christian Faith and the Common Life*. Oxford Conferences Series, Vol. 4. London: George Allen & Unwin, 1938.

"Christian Faith and the Economic Life of Liberal Society," in *Goals of Economic Life*. Ed. by A. Dudley Ward. New York: Harper & Bros., 1953.

"Christian Faith in the Modern World," Introduction to *Ventures in Belief*. Ed. by H. P. Van Dusen. New York: Scribner's Sons, 1930.

"Christian Faith and Social Action," in *Christian Faith and Social Action*. Ed. by John Hutchison. New York: Scribner's Sons, 1953.

"Christian Politics and Communist Religion," in *Christianity and the Social Revolution*. Ed. by John Lewis. New York: Scribner's Sons, 1936.

The City of Man: A Declaration on World Democracy. Committee of Fifteen: Reinhold Niebuhr, H. Agar, F. Ayelelotte, G. A. Borgese, *et al*. New York: Viking Press, 1941.

"Coercion, Self-Interest, and Love," in *The Organizational Revolution*. Ed. by Kenneth E. Boulding. New York: Harper & Bros., 1953.

"The Common Root of Joy and Pain," in *What Can Students Believe?* Ed. by E. M. McKee. New York: R. R. Smith, 1931.

"The Commitment of the Self and the Freedom of the Mind," in *Religion and Freedom of Thought*. Perry Miller, Robert C. Calhoun, Nathan M. Pusey, and Reinhold Niebuhr. New York: Doubleday, 1954.

"The Contribution of Religion to Cultural Unity." Hazen Pamphlets No. 13, 1945.

"The Foolishness of Preaching," in *Best Sermons*. Ed. by J. F. Newton. New York: Harcourt, Brace & Co., 1924.

Germany and the Future of Europe (with others). Ed. by Hans J. Morgenthau. Chicago: University of Chicago Press, 1957.

"God's Design and the Present Disorder of Civilization," Introduction to Vol. III of the Amsterdam Studies, *The Church and the Disorder of Society*. New York: Harper & Bros., 1948.

"The Minister as an Expert," in *Effective Preaching*. Boston: Boston University School of Theology, Conference on Preaching, 1929.

A Nation So Conceived (with Alan Heimert). New York: Scribner's Sons 1963; London: Faber & Faber, 1964.

"Our Relations with Russia," in *Christianity Takes a Stand*. Ed. by Bishop William Scarlett. New York: Penguin Books, 1946.

"Political Action and Social Change," in *A New Economic Order*. Ed. by Kirby Page. New York: Harcourt, Brace, 1930.

"The Practical Unbelief of Modern Civilization," in *Religion on the Campus*. Ed. by F. P. Miller. New York: Association Press, 1927.

Reinhold Niebuhr, A Prophetic Voice in Our Time, Essays in Tribute. Ed. by Harold R. Landon (with others). Greenwich, Conn.: Seabury Press, 1962.

Reinhold Niebuhr: His Religious, Social, and Political Thought. Ed. by Charles W. Kegley and Robert W. Bretall. New York, London: Macmillan, Library of Living Theology, Vol. 2, 1956, 1961.

"The Relevance of Reformation Doctrine in Our Day," in *The Heritage of the Reformation*. Ed. by E. J. F. Arndt. New York: R. R. Smith, 1950.

"Religion and Modern Knowledge," in *Man's Destiny in Eternity*. The Garvin Lectures. Boston: Beacon Press, 1949.

"Religion and Moral Experience," in pamphlet, *What Religion Means to Me*. Reinhold Niebuhr, H. E. Fosdick, A. B. Curry, E. F. Tittle, *et al*. New York: Doubleday, Doran & Co., 1929.

Renewal of Man, by Alexander Miller (edited by Reinhold Niebuhr). New York: Doubleday, 1955.

"The Role of Prophetic Religion in the World Crisis," in *Men of Tomorrow*. Ed. by T. H. Johnson. New York: G. P. Putnam's Son's, 1942.

"Sex and Religion in the Kinsey Report," in *An Analysis of the Kinsey Reports on Sexual Behavior in the Human Male and Female*. New York: E. P. Dutton Co., 1954.

"The Situation in the U.S.A.," in *The Church and the Disorder of*

Society. Vol. III of the Amsterdam Studies. New York: Harper & Bros., 1948.

"The Spirit of Life," in Addresses and Proceedings of the National Educational Association of the U.S., 1930.

"Students and the Religion of Today," in *A Survey of Our Student Life and of the Present Religious Situation as it Affects American Students.* Reinhold Niebuhr, Bruce Curry, and G. A. Studdert-Kennedy. At the National Student Conference, Milwaukee: NSC, Dec. 28, 1926-Jan. 1, 1927.

"Theologian and Church Statesman," in *This Ministry, The Contribution of Henry S. Coffin.* New York: Scribner's Sons, 1945.

Toward a New Economic Society: A Program for Students by a Commission. Introduction by R. N., Student Christian Association Movement, Economics Commission, F. A. Henderson, Chairman. New York: Eddy & Page, 1931.

"The Truth in Myths," in *The Nature of Religious Experience, Essays in Honor of D. C. Macintosh.* New York: Harper & Bros., 1937.

"The Use of Force," in *Pacificism in the Modern World.* Ed. by Devere Allen. New York: Doubleday, 1929.

Essays: A Chronologically Representative Selection:

1916 "The Nation's Crime Against the Individual," *Atlantic Monthly* 118:609-14 Nov.

1920 "Religion's Limitations," *The World Tomorrow* 3:77-79 March.

1921 "Heroes and Hero Worship," *The Nation* 112:293-94 Feb. 23.

1922 "The Church and the Middle Class," *Christian Century* 39:1513-15 Dec. 7.

1923 "Wanted: A Christian Morality," *Christian Century* 40:201-203 Feb. 15.

1924 "What Are the Churches Advertising?" *Christian Century* 41:1532-3 Nov. 27.

1925 "Shall We Proclaim the Truth or Search for It?" *Christian Century* 42:344-6 March 12.

1926 "Does Religion Quiet or Disquiet? *The World Tomorrow* 9:220-1 Nov.

1927 "Why I Am Not a Christian," *Christian Century* 44:1482-3 Dec. 15.

1928 "Confessions of a Tired Radical," *Christian Century* 45:1046-7 Aug. 30.

1929 "The Terrible Beauty of the Cross," *Christian Century* 46:386-8 March 21.

1930 "The Preaching of Repentance," *The Christian Century* 47:1080-81 Sept. 10.

1931 "The Religion of Communism," *Atlantic Monthly* 147:462-70 April.

1932 "Catastrophe or Control: The Alternatives for America," *Harper's* 165:114-18 June.

1933 "Germans: Unhappy Philosophers in Politics," *American Scholar* 2:409-19 Oct.

1934 "Pacificism Against the Wall," *American Scholar* 5:133-261-5 May.

1935 "Christianity in Its Relation to the Perennial and the Contemporary Man," *Religion in Life* 4:551-8 Autumn.

1936 "English Church: An American View," *Spectator* 157:373-4 Sept. 4.

1937 "Pawns for Fascism—Our Lower Middle Class," *The American Scholar* 6:145-52 Spring.

1938 "The Creed of the Modern Christian Socialists," *Radical Religion* 3:13-18 Spring.

1939 "Synthetic Barbarism," *New Statesman and Nation* 18:368-9 Sept. 9.

1940 "Christian Faith and Natural Law," *Theology* 40:86-94 Feb.

1941 "An Ineffectual Sermon on Love," *Christianity and Crisis* 1:1-2 Nov. 3.

1942 The Spirit and the Body in War," *Christianity and Crisis* 2:1-2 Aug. 10.

1943 "Marxism in Eclipse," *Spectator* 170:518-19 June 4.

1944 "Survival and Religion," *Contemporary Jewish Rec.* 7:239-46 June.

1945 "Will Civilization Survive Technics?" *Commentary* 1:2-8 Dec.

1946 "The Myth of World Government," *The Nation* 162:312-14 March 16.

1947 "Democracy as a Religion," *Christianity and Crisis* 7:1-2 Aug. 4.

1948 "Churches and Society," *New Statesman and Nation* 36:232-3 Sept. 18.

1949 "The Spirit and the Mechanism of Partnership," *Christianity and Crisis* 9:121-22 Oct. 3.

1950 "The Pope's Domesticated God," *Christian Century* 67:74-75 Jan. 18.

1951 "Coherence, Incoherence, and Christian Faith," *Journal of Religion* 31:155-68 July.

1952 "Prayer and Politics," *Christianity and Crisis* 12:138-39 Oct. 27.

1953 "Hope Needs Faith and Love," *Ecumenical Review* 5:358-63 July.

1954 "The Catholic Hierarchy's Analysis of the Ills of Our Day," *Christianity and Crisis* 14 No. 22:171-73.

1955 "Liberalism: Illusions and Realities," *New Republic* 133:11-13 July 4.

1957 "Theology and Political Thought in the Western World," *Ecumenical Review* 9:253-62 April.

1959 "Moral and Political Judgments of Christians," *Christianity and Crisis* 19:99-103 July 6.

1960 "Cold Comfort of a 'Mystic Unity' (in South Africa)," *Christianity and Crisis* 20:65-66 May 16.

1961 "Mater et Magistra," *Christianity and Crisis* 21:142-3 Aug. 7.

1962 "Boulder in the Currents," *Spectator* 209:488ff. Oct. 5.

"Katanga and Primitive Anti-Communism," *Christianity and Crisis* 21:245 Jan. 22.

"Logical Consistency and the Nuclear Dilemma," *Christianity and Crisis* 22:48 April 2.

"Internationalism and DeGaulle's Nationalism," *Christianity and Crisis* 27:98-99 June 11.

"Intractability of Race Prejudice," *Christianity and Crisis* 22:181 Oct. 29.

KARL RAHNER

Books:

Christian Commitment; Essays in Pastoral Theology. New York: Sheed & Ward, 1963.

The Church and the Sacraments. New York: Herder & Herder, 1963; London: Nelson, 1963; Freiburg: Herder, 1963.

Dynamics in the Church. New York: Herder & Herder; London: Nelson.

Encounters with Silence. Westminster, Md.: Newman Press, 1960.

Episcopate and the Primacy (with Ratzinger). New York: Herder & Herder, 1962; Freiburg: Herder, 1962; London: Nelson, 1962.

Free Speech in the Church. New York, London: Sheed & Ward, 1959, 1960.

Happiness Through Prayer. Westminster, Md.: Newman Press, 1958; London: Burns & Oates; Dublin: Clonomore & Reynolds.

Inspiration in the Bible. New York: Herder & Herder, 1961; Freiburg: Herder, 1961; London: Nelson, 1961.

Mary, Mother of the Lord: Theological Meditations. New York: Herder & Herder, 1963; London: Nelson, 1963; Freiburg: Herder, 1963; Montreal: Palm Publishers, 1963.

Nature and Grace. New York, London: Sheed & Ward, 1963.

On the Theology of Death. New York: Herder & Herder, 1961; London: Nelson, 1961; Freiburg: Herder, 1961.

Theological Investigations, 2 vols.

    Vol. I—*God, Christ, Mary, and Grace.* London: Darton, Longman, & Todd, 1961; Baltimore: Helicon Press, 1961.

    Vol. II—*Man in the Church.* London: Darton, Longman, & Todd, 1964; Baltimore: Helicon Press, 1964.

Prayers for Meditation (with Hugo Rahner). New York: Herder & Herder, 1962; Freiburg; Herder, 1962; London: Nelson, 1962.

Visions and Prophecies. New York: Herder & Herder, 1963; Freiburg: Herder, 1963; London: Nelson, 1963.

Essays:

"Apostolate of Laymen," *Theology Digest* 5:73-79 Spring 1957.

"Church of Sinners," *Cross Currents* 1:64-74 Spring 1951.

"Fundamental Principle of Mariology," *Theology Digest* 4:72-78 Spring 1956.

"Latin as Church Language," Summary, *Clergyman* 27:95-99 April 1963.

"Lay Apostles," *Cross Currents* 10:363-74 Fall 1960.

"Multiplication of Masses," Summary, *Orate Fratres* 24:553-62 Nov. 1950.

"Personal and Sacramental Sanctity," *Theology Digest* 3:93-98 Spring 1955.

"Prayer in the Name of the Church," *Theology Digest* 11:119-25 Summer 1963.

"The Priesthood," Sermon, *Jubilee* 10:8-11 April 1963.

"Reflections on Obedience," *Cross Currents* 10:363-74 Fall 1960.

"Religious Poverty in a Changing World" (reprint), *Theology Digest* 11:51-56 Spring 1963.

"Sinners in the Church" (excerpt), *Commonweal* 54:311 July 6, 1951.

"Take the Child and His Mother," *Theology Digest* 6:169-73 Fall 1958.

HEINRICH SCHLIER

Book:

Principalities and Powers in the New Testament. New York: Herder & Herder, 1961; Freiburg: Herder, 1961; London: Nelson, 1961.

PAUL TILLICH

Books—as Sole Author:

Biblical Religion and the Search for Ultimate Reality. Chicago: University of Chicago Press, 1956; London: Nisbet & Co., 1956.

The Courage to Be. London: Nisbet & Co., 1952; London: Collins (Fontana), 1962; New Haven, Conn.: Yale University Press, 1952, 1959.

Christianity and the Encounter of the World Religions. New York: Columbia University Press, 1963.

Dynamics of Faith. London: Allen and Unwin, 1957; New York: Harper & Bros., 1957. (Torchbooks) 1958.

The Eternal Now. New York: Scribner's Sons, 1963.

The Interpretation of History. New York, London: Scribner's Sons, 1936.

Love, Power, and Justice; Ontological Analyses and Ethical Applications. Oxford: Oxford University Press, 1954. (Galaxy ed.) 1960.

Morality and Beyond. New York: Harper & Row, 1963.

The New Being. New York: Scribner's Sons, 1955; London: Student Christian Movement Press, 1956, 1963.

The Protestant Era. Chicago: University of Chicago Press, 1948; abridged Phoenix Paperback edition, 1957.

The Religious Situation. New York: Henry Holt, 1932; London: Thames & Hudson, 1932; New York: World (Meridian), 1956.

Religious Sources of Moral Action. New York: Harper & Row, 1963.

The Shaking of the Foundations. New York: Scribner's Sons, 1948; London: Nisbet & Co., 1950; New York: Penguin, 1962.

Systematic Theology. 3 Vols. Vol. I, 1951; Vol. II, 1957; Vol. III, 1963. Chicago: University of Chicago Press; London: Nisbet & Co.

The Theology of Culture. Ed. by Robert C. Kimball. Oxford: Oxford University Press, 1959.

Pamphlets:

Advanced Problems in Systematic Theology (Lectures). New York, 1952.

Art and Ultimate Reality. A Lecture Given at the Museum of Modern Art, New York. New York: Museum of Modern Art, 1959.

The Church and Contemporary Culture. Address of 1955. New York: National Council of Churches, 1956.

Informal Report of a Lecture Trip To Japan—Summer 1960. Cambridge, Mass.: Harvard University Press, 1960.

The Impact of Psychotherapy on Theological Thought ... (in *Pastoral Psychology,* Feb. 1960). New York: New York Academy of Religious and Mental Health, 1960.

The Kingdom of God and History. Oxford Conference Series. New York: Willet & Clark, 1938.

The Recovery of the Prophetic Tradition in the Reformation (Lectures) 1950. Washington, D.C.: Organizing Committee, Christianity and Modern Man, 1955.

The Theology of Missions. New York: The Missionary Research Library, 1954.

Books—as a Contributing Essayist:

"The Disintegration of Society in Christian Countries," in *Man's Disorder and God's Design.* World Council of Churches. New York: Harper & Bros., 1949.

"The Escape From God," in *Best Sermons, 1949-1950.* Ed. by G. Paul Butler. New York: Harper & Bros., 1949.

"Ethics in a Changing World," in *Religion and the Modern World.* Philadelphia: University of Pennsylvania Press, 1941.

"Freedom in the Period of Transformation," in *Freedom: Its Meaning.* Ed. by Anshen. New York: Harcourt, Brace, 1940.

"Meaning of the German Church Struggle for Christian Missions," in *Christian World Missions.* Ed. by Anderson. Nashville, Tenn.: Parthenon, 1946.

Reinhold Niebuhr: A Prophetic Voice in Our Time; Essays in Tribute. Ed. by Harold R. Landon. Greenwich, Conn.: Seabury Press, 1962.

A History of Christian Thought. Ed. by Peter H. John. Providence, R.I.: Union Theological Seminary, 1956.

Religion and Culture. Ed. by Walter Leibrecht. London: Student Christian Movement Press.

Religion and Health, A Symposium. Ed. by Simon Doniger. New York: Association Press, 1958.

The Theology of Paul Tillich. Ed. by Charles W. Kegley and Robert W. Bretall. New York: Macmillan (Library of Living Theology, Vol. 1), 1961.

"Trends in Religious Thought that Affect Social Outlook," in *Institutes of Religious Studies.* New York: Harper, 1944.

Where Do We Go From Here in Theology? (with others). Ed. by Nels Ferré. Nashville, Tenn.: Methodist Publishing House, 1955.

"The World Situation," in *The Christian Answer.* Ed. by H. P. Van Dusen. New York: Scribner's Sons, 1945.

Essays: A Chronologically Representative Selection

1934 "The Religious Situation in Germany Today," *Religion in Life* 3:163-73 Spring.

1935 "What Is Wrong with the Dialectic Theology?" *Journal of Religion* 15:127-45 April.

1936 "The Social Functions of the Churches in Europe and America," *Social Research* 3:90-104 Feb.

1937 "The End of the Protestant Era," *Student World* 30:49-57 Spring.

1938 "Nicholas Berdyaev," *Religion in Life* 7:407-15 Summer.

1939 "Conception of Man in Existential Philosophy," *Journal of Religion* 19:201-15 July.

1940 "The Idea of a Personal God," *Union Seminary Review* 2:8-10 Nov.

1941 "Symbol and Knowledge: A Response," *Journal of Liberal Religion* 2:202-206 Spring.

1942 "Kierkegaard in English," *American Scandinavian Review* 30:254-7 Sept.

1943 "Flight to Atheism," *The Protestant* 4:43-48 March.

1944 "Estrangement and Reconciliation in Modern Thought," *Review of Religion* 9:5-19 Nov.

1945 "Nietzsche and the Bourgeois Spirit," *Journal of the History of Ideas* 6:307-309 June.

1946 "The Relation of Religion and Health: Historical Considerations and Theoretical Questions," *Review of Religion* 10:348-84 May.

1947 "The Problem of Theological Method," *Journal of Religion* 27:16-26 Jan.

1948 "Martin Buber and Christian Thought," *Commentary* 5:515-21 June.

1949 "Psychotherapy and a Christian Interpretation of Human Nature," *Review of Religion* 13:264-8 March.

1950 "Religion and the Intellectuals," *Partisan Review* 17:254-6 March.

1952 "Victory in Defeat: The Meaning of History in the Light of Christian Prophetism," *Interpretation* 6:17-26 Jan.

1956 "Relation of Metaphysics and Theology," *Review of Metaphysics* 10:57-63 Sept.

1957 "Let Us Dare to Have Solitude," *Union Seminary Review* 12: 9-15 May.

1958 "Psychoanalysis, Existentialism, and Theology," *Pastoral Psychology* 9:9-17 Oct.

1959 "The Good I Will. I Do Not," *Religion in Life* 28:539-45 Fall; *Union Seminary Quarterly Review* 14:17-23 March; *Pastoral Psychology* 12:10-16 April 1961.

1960 "The Impact of Pastoral Psychology on Theological Thought," *Pastoral Psychology* 11:17-23 Feb.

1961 "Nuclear Dilemma—A Discussion," *Christianity and Crisis* 21: 203-204 Nov. 13.

1962 "Man, the Earth and the Universe," *Christianity and Crisis* 22: 108-12 June 25.

"The Permanent Significance of the Catholic Church for Protestants," *Dialogue* 1:22-25 Summer.

"Philosophy of Social Work," *Social Service Review* 36:13-16 March.

"Spiritual Presence," a Sermon, *Union Seminary Quarterly Review* 17:121-8 Jan.; *Pastoral Psychology* 13:25-30 Oct.

"Symbols of Eternal Life," the Ingersoll Lecture, 1962. *Harvard Divinity Bulletin* 26:1-10 April.